World English

BILINGUAL EDUCATION AND BILINGUALISM
Series Editors: Professor Colin Baker, *University of Wales, Bangor, Wales, Great Britain*
and Professor Nancy H. Hornberger, University of Pennsylvania, Philadelphia, USA

Other Books in the Series
At War With Diversity: US Language Policy in an Age of Anxiety
  James Crawford
Becoming Bilingual: Language Acquisition in a Bilingual Community
  Jean Lyon
Cross-linguistic Influence in Third Language Acquisition
  J. Cenoz, B. Hufeisen and U. Jessner (eds)
Dual Language Education
  Kathryn J. Lindholm-Leary
English in Europe: The Acquisition of a Third Language
  Jasone Cenoz and Ulrike Jessner (eds)
An Introductory Reader to the Writings of Jim Cummins
  Colin Baker and Nancy Hornberger (eds)
Languages in America: A Pluralist View
  Susan J. Dicker
Learning English at School: Identity, Social Relations and Classroom Practice
  Kelleen Toohey
Language, Power and Pedagogy: Bilingual Children in the Crossfire
  Jim Cummins
Language Revitalization Processes and Prospects
  Kendall A. King
Language Use in Interlingual Families: A Japanese-English Sociolinguistic Study
  Masayo Yamamoto
The Languages of Israel: Policy, Ideology and Practice
  Bernard Spolsky and Elana Shohamy
Reflections on Multiliterate Lives
  Diane Belcher and Ulla Connor (eds)
The Sociopolitics of English Language Teaching
  Joan Kelly Hall and William G. Eggington (eds)
Studies in Japanese Bilingualism
  Mary Goebel Noguchi and Sandra Fotos (eds)

Other Books of Interest
Can Threatened Languages be Saved?
  Joshua Fishman (ed.)
A Dynamic Model of Multilingualism
  Philip Herdina and Ulrike Jessner
Language and Society in a Changing Italy
  Arturo Tosi
Language Planning: From Practice to Theory
  Robert B. Kaplan and Richard B. Baldauf, Jr (eds)
Multilingualism in Spain
  M. Teresa Turell (ed.)
Encyclopedia of Bilingualism and Bilingual Education
  Colin Baker and Sylvia Prys Jones

Please contact us for the latest book information:
Multilingual Matters, Frankfurt Lodge, Clevedon Hall,
Victoria Road, Clevedon, BS21 7HH, England
http://www.multilingual-matters.com

BILINGUAL EDUCATION AND BILINGUALISM 34
Series Editors: Colin Baker and Nancy H. Hornberger

World English

A Study of its Development

Janina Brutt-Griffler

MULTILINGUAL MATTERS LTD
Clevedon • Buffalo • Toronto • Sydney

Library of Congress Cataloging in Publication Data
Brutt-Griffler, Janina
World English: A Study of its Development/Janina Brutt-Griffler
Bilingual Education and Bilingualism: 34
Includes bibliographical references and index
1. English language–Foreign countries. 2. English language–English-speaking countries. 3. Communication, international. 4. Intercultural communication. 5. English-speaking countries. I. Title. II. Series
PE2751.B78 2002
420–dc21   2001047707

British Library Cataloguing in Publication Data
A catalogue entry for this book is available from the British Library.

ISBN 1-85359-578-0 (hbk)
ISBN 1-85359-577-2 (pbk)

Multilingual Matters Ltd
UK: Frankfurt Lodge, Clevedon Hall, Victoria Road, Clevedon BS21 7HH.
USA: UTP, 2250 Military Road, Tonawanda, NY 14150, USA.
Canada: UTP, 5201 Dufferin Street, North York, Ontario M3H 5T8, Canada.
Australia: Footprint Books, PO Box 418, Church Point, NSW 2103, Australia.

Typeset by Florence Production Ltd.
Printed and bound in Great Britain by the Cromwell Press Ltd.

Contents

Glossary

CO   Colonial Office
EFL   English as a Foreign Language
EIL   English as an International Language
ELT   English Language Teaching
ENL   English as a National Language
ESL   English as a Second Language
IL   Interlanguage
SLA   Second Language Acquisition
TL   Target Language
L1   First Language
L2   Second Language

Preface

I am an Indian, very brown, born in
Malabar, I speak three languages, write in
Two dream in one. Don't write in English, they said,
English is not your mother-tongue. Why not leave
Me alone, critics, friends, visiting cousins,
Everyone of you? Why not let me speak in
Any language I like? The language I speak
Becomes mine, its distortions, its queernesses,
All mine, mine alone. It is half English, half
Indian, funny perhaps, but it is honest,
It is as human as I am human, don't
You see? It voices my joys, my longings, my
Hopes, and it is useful to me ...

(Kamala Das, 1997: 10)

Kamala Das captures the paradox of English in the world today. To some, English anywhere outside the mother tongue context is an alien language, perhaps even an imposed language. From this standpoint, English has a fixed identity, both political and linguistic. It represents something peculiarly English, or perhaps Anglo-American, but at all events certainly Western. English has become a world language because – and to the extent that – Anglo-American, Western culture has become hegemonic in the world.

To others English, although not their mother tongue, is nevertheless *their* language, an expression of their own unique identity. It is theirs because they have *made* it so – through their lived experiences in the language that have gained expression in the way they use English. In this view, English has become a world language to the extent that it has been stripped of any simplistic association with Anglo-American and

Western culture. World English has emerged because its users have changed the language as they have spread it. Of the many English writers from Africa and Asia who have addressed this topic, perhaps none has expressed the point so eloquently as Chinua Achebe:

> What I ... see is a new voice coming out of Africa, speaking of African experience in a world-wide language. ... The price a world language must be prepared to pay is submission to many different kinds of use. ... The African writer should aim to use English in a way that brings out his message best without altering the language to the extent that its value as a medium of international exchange will be lost. ... He should aim at fashioning out an English which is at once universal and able to carry his peculiar experience ... I feel that the English language will be able to carry the weight of my African experience. But it will have to be a new English, still in full communion with its ancestral home but altered to suit its new African surroundings. (1994: 433–4)

The first conception described has been well articulated by scholars working within, in particular, the framework of linguistic imperialism (Phillipson, 1992). That conception of language spread makes use of notions such as linguicism, cultural and linguistic hegemony, and language imposition. Agency is invested in various representations of institutionalized power. In contrast, the speech communities acquiring the language figure as passive recipients of language policy (cf. Canagarajah, 1999; Pennycook, 2000). It is assumed that to have *political* control is to have *linguistic* control. The center-driven narrative of English language spread writes people residing outside the West out of their central role in the spread of English and their place in making the language we call English.

As Said (1993) has forcefully argued, in this narrative of the making of modernity, non-Western peoples barely appear at all, except insofar as they are oppressed by the irresistible forces of imperialism. After they free themselves, they remain subject to ideological control through *hegemony*, a vague force by which the former colonial masters continue to impose their will on their former colonies. Even in the present age this worldview chooses to emphasize the "colonial in the postcolonial," as Alastair Pennycook (1998) puts it. On the other hand, such a standpoint almost entirely ignores the *postcolonial in the colonial* – that is, the process by which the peoples colonized by European powers shaped the world in which we live, including their own independence, in profoundly significant ways.

A key contention of the present work is that English owes its existence as a world language in large part to the struggle against imperialism, and not to imperialism alone. Rather than dismissing the significance of evidence that shows the active historical role of non-mother tongue English speakers in the development of a world language, the theoretical framework developed here emphasizes their agency and historicizes their will. In this conception, World English is not simply made *through* speakers of other languages but *by* them.

In this book, I investigate the agency of non-mother tongue English speech communities in the two principal processes by which English has become a world language: language spread and language change. This account stresses that these linguistic processes cannot be studied in isolation from one another. Although the idea of combining the study of language spread with language change might appear overly ambitious, the failure to do so hinders the goal of understanding how a host of post-colonial writers from Asia and Africa, like Kamala Das and Chinua Achebe, can claim the linguistic space of English to express their experience. It offers an alternative to the notion that hundreds of millions of people around the world have set out to learn English because they are the passive victims of Western ideological hegemony, emphasizing instead their agency in (re)making world culture. The conception put forward tying language spread to its change holds that World English is a *phase* in the history of the English language – the phase in which most of its speakers do not belong to a dominant national speech community or even a few mother tongue speech communities. Instead, it is the historical phase in which the vast majority of English speakers belong to bilingual speech communities. I suggest that the proliferation of varieties of English are a necessary result of the development of World English, and not a temporary, unfortunate effect that we can expect to disappear in time. The conception developed in this book provides an historical and linguistic justification for first, second and foreign language users of English to claim their rightful place in the creation of the multicultural identity of English.

Chapter 1 opens with a consideration of the nature of the subject matter: what is the meaning of *World English*? It is argued that the English language spread that has produced it requires primarily linguistic analysis rather than sociopolitical. In these terms, English spread appears not as the territorial expansion of the language but as second language acquisition by speech communities, or what will be called in this work *macroacquisition*.

Toward the development of this new understanding, Chapter 2 undertakes a reexamination of some methodological questions in linguistic analysis. It suggests the necessity of a shift in the unit of analysis employed by linguistics from the individual idealized speaker/listener to the speech community in discussing questions of language spread and change. This paradigmatic refocusing from the linguistic individual to the linguistic social allows for the examination of second language acquisition processes that take place at the speech community level and that have ultimately produced new English varieties. The chapter also justifies the detailed empirical study of language spread in the former British Asian and African colonies in the nineteenth and early twentieth centuries.

Chapter 3 examines the objectives of empire and the role of ideology versus economics in the formation of British colonial policy in the nineteenth and early twentieth centuries. The chapter finds that the formation of British language policy was not necessarily about ideology and ideology was not necessarily about spreading the language. The objectives of the empire involved a complex interplay of ideology and economics. The case of American rule in the Philippines in first third of the twentieth century demonstrates that ideological imperatives might have dictated language policy. In the British empire, however, economics took precedence. An examination of three key architects of British language policy reveals that attitudes toward language in colonial settings involved hitherto largely overlooked complexities.

The agency of speech communities previously viewed as passive recipients of language policy forms the focus of Chapter 4. It undertakes a detailed examination of historical documents spanning more than a century from the mid-nineteenth to mid-twentieth centuries relating to British colonial language policy to complicate the notion of English language imposition in Great Britain's African and Asian colonies. The empirical data suggest that British language policy is perhaps best characterized as *reactive* in its quest to limit access to English. The chapter connects access to English with the creation and preservation of social class stratification. Limiting access to English provided a means of social control over the working classes. Colonial authorities promulgated indigenous language education for the majority of the population and promoted local lingua francas. In the case of Southern Rhodesia (present-day Zimbabwe), the British engineered a new national language where none previously existed.

Chapter 5 details the extent to which English education was reserved for the colonial elite and kept safely out of the reach of the vast majority of the population of British colonies throughout the history of its colonial empire. Descriptive statistics show a heavy emphasis on providing indigenous language rather than English-based education. The chapter also examines empire-wide institutional formulations of language policy to counteract the notion that mother language industrial education was a later development, brought about specifically by the intervention of an American educational commission in the 1920s (Phillipson, 1992; Berman, 1982; Clatworthy, 1971; King, 1971). The chapter includes an account of post-World War I imperial politics, which saw the British and the French clash within the administrative bodies of the League of Nations, the French calling for the teaching and use in the colonies of European languages and the British advocating indigenous.

If the emergence of World English is not a function of the linguistic imperialism of British colonialism, why has English rather than languages such as Chinese, French, Turkish, Spanish, Arabic or Portuguese become the world language? Chapter 6 offers an historical explanation. It demonstrates how the advent of non-settler colonies together with British dominance of the world market combined to inaugurate World English via the macroacquisition of the language in Africa and Asia. This process is distinguished from the mode of spread of English within the British Isles via speaker migration, which resulted not in bilingual speech communities but the adoption of English as a mother tongue. Four differentiating features of a world language are posited: econocultural functions, transcendence of the role of an elite lingua franca, stabilized bilingualism, and language change.

Chapter 7 develops the key new construct of macroacquisition, second language acquisition by speech communities, that links language change to its spread. That process involves the genesis of bilingual speech communities. Two forms of the development of bilingual speech communities are distinguished. In *Type A* macroacquisition, the process coincides with the development of *an entirely new speech community*. Type A macroacquisition takes place in a multilingual setting in which the acquired language serves as a unifying linguistic resource, the speakers otherwise belonging to separate mother tongue speech communities. *Type B* macroacquisition involves the transformation of a monolingual mother tongue speech community (or a section thereof) into a bilingual speech community. It takes place, in general, in a formerly predominantly monolingual setting – one in which one mother tongue dominates.

Chapter 8 uses of the two types of bilingual speech community to explain the degree of stabilization of language change as new varieties. Bilingual speech communities of Type B have available a versatile and flexible mechanism for the communication of culture bound knowledge or meaning in the form of code-switching. In the case of Type A, on the other hand, without a common medium to express culture bound knowledge, language change is far more likely to stabilize. This is particularly true when the new variety becomes tied to expressing a national identity that has no other linguistic expression to fall back on – as might be the case in certain postcolonial settings. To illustrate macroacquisition, the book discusses the development of new varieties of English, with a section devoted to the South African case.

As Chapter 8 discusses the tendencies toward the proliferation of varieties of English within World English, Chapter 9 takes up the question of why the language has maintained its essential unity. The explanation focuses on the emergence of a world language speech community. The resultant centripetal force spawns a process of world language convergence, a center of gravity around which international varieties revolve.

The final chapter suggests that the field of English applied linguistics is inherently tied to the history of the language. The construction of applied linguistics is in large part linked with the spread of the language, including the prominent role of non-mother tongue English-speaking teachers. Chapter 10 suggests the need to *reclaim* the role and contributions of non-mother tongue teachers of English within the international history of English. It argues that an imperialist ideology has not been at work in the spread of the language but in the attempt to ground English applied linguistics in "Center"-driven conceptions of methodology.

Acknowledgements

I owe a great debt to Colin Baker and Nancy Hornberger, who have seen this project through from the early stages to its completion. Their dedication, support, timely feedback, and wise counsel, have made this a better book. From the first time I met Elizabeth Meese, she has given generously of her time, pointed me to sources, and shared her insights. She not only read a full draft of the manuscript and provided detailed and incisive commentary, but she did so in record time, for all of which I am grateful. Harold Weber also gave the manuscript a close reading, to its great advantage; both his detailed comments and his interest in the work were extremely helpful. I would like to thank Sandra McKay for reading the manuscript and for valuable suggestions grounded in her vast knowledge of English and English teaching internationally. Comments from Myron Tuman, who also gave the manuscript a full reading, proved particularly valuable in helping me reconceptualize the organization of certain parts of the book. I am indebted to Jacqueline Toribio for taking the time to read and comment on the chapters on language change and for generously sharing her work with me.

I would like to express my appreciation to all of my colleagues in the English Department at the University of Alabama. Salli Davis and Catherine Davies deserve a special thank you for their ongoing support and arranging for an additional research assistant while I was completing the manuscript. Sharon O'Dair, Celia Daileader, Gary Taylor, Peter Logan, and Robert Young have all contributed to this book in ways of which they are probably not even aware. My linguistics program colleagues Catherine Davies and Lucy Pickering deserve thanks for being wonderfully supportive colleagues and friends.

I want to express my appreciation to everyone at Ohio State University who contributed to this work, most importantly my good friend and collaborator Keiko Samimy. Without her guidance and faith in this project, it never would have materialized. Special thanks go to Diane Belcher as well, who has always been a valued colleague for her support, encouragement, and constructive input.

Elizabeth Bernhardt provided the initial impetus for me to explore this topic and merits gratitude for many other contributions to its progress as well. I not only owe thanks to Terry Wiley for his ongoing interest in my work but also for putting me in touch with Multilingual Matters. Others to whom I want to express my gratitude for a multitude of reasons include: Rakesh Bhatt, Suresh Canagarajah, Russel Durst, Charles Hancock, Alan Hirvela, Susan Jenkins, Braj Kachru, Yamuna Kachru, Alamin Mazrui, Lupenga Mphande,Terrence Odlin, Alastair Pennycook, Barbara Seidlhofer, Carmen Silva-Corvalan, Manka Varghese and Henry Widdowson. Keith Neltner designed the cover illustration and Reata Strickland the appendices; I thank them for their many hours of creative work. Special appreciation is due to my research assistants at the University of Alabama, Kelli Loggins and Jasmine Hodges. I also want to thank Mike Grover and the staff at Multilingual Matters for all of their assistance, efficiency and friendliness. They greatly eased the process of completing the last stages of the manuscript.

One debt I can never hope to adequately acknowledge is also the first I incurred: to my family. The final thank you is reserved for Keith Griffler, to whom this book is dedicated.

Chapter 1

Images of World English: Writing English as an International Language

Defining World English

It might appear that nothing should be easier than to define the subject matter of a book about English. Given that the book is written in the medium of its topic, English, the author might reasonably operate on the tacit assumption that this is one subject, at the least, about which she and her reader have a shared knowledge. It is, after all, the language of their communication.[1] Thus, while this is certainly not the first book to investigate the (international) history of English, it might be the first to begin by questioning the subject of the investigation.

In what does the shared knowledge of English consist? Just what is it that we know about this language? Perhaps, the answer to those questions is suggested by its name: English, a language born in England, the language of England. That notion locates the language in a particular nation, or more accurately, a particular people. It is their language, to spread, to change, to share or withhold from the world. By that view, World English is the means and results of the spread of English from its historical (perhaps even natural) boundaries to its current position as the preeminent global means of communication.

Every language has its history, real or imagined – or, perhaps, real *and* imagined. English was *not* precisely "born" in England. It was transported there from another place, or more exactly, it traveled there together with the Anglo-Saxon migrants to the island. That is why we call it a Germanic language. And there is another consideration. Those Anglo-Saxons who first made the trip across the English Channel would be utterly at a loss to understand the English of the fourteenth century, that of Chaucer's day. For in the intervening centuries, the language was irrevocably altered by the Norman Conquest in 1066, which Latinized the Germanic language of the Angles and Saxons.[2]

Perhaps recognition of those two caveats solidifies the common notion of English. For certainly the final result is an English language suitably distinct from the Germanic languages that gave rise to it. The language was, after all, all the more English for its specifically English history and thereby all the more at home in the British Isles, or more exactly, the non-Celtic portion of them. Then again, does not that history immediately call to mind the other inhabitants of those islands, who spoke various Celtic languages amongst others? Did their languages not inhibit the islands first, and was English not an interloper in their midst, just as were, initially, the Angles and Saxons who migrated there (or invaded)?

What should be made of the fact that the process by which the English language became a distinctively English product involved the subjection of the English people at the hands of a French-speaking people, the admixture of the two languages, a change so dramatic that the language had become incomprehensible to its forbears? In a crowning irony to the attempt to associate the language with a land, a nation, and a people, English became associated with all three precisely because its history was so mobile, its context so transnational, and the people who made it so diverse: Germanic, Celtic, French and Nordic.

Of course, all of that might be said to belong to the prehistory of the language, just as every social phenomenon must have roots in some more remote past. Perhaps the investigator need not trace the language back quite that far. The discussion might be confined to a more recent period, what is often called "the modern world." If so, how is it to be decided what constitutes the proper frame of reference for English between our own day and the aftermath of the Norman invasion some nine centuries ago? Should we split the difference – say, some 450 years or so, or approximately the time of the English Renaissance? Already by that time, however, English was not confined to its earlier "natural" (or is it "historical"?) boundaries: within the British Isles it was, or was on the verge of, spreading to Ireland, Scotland, and Wales. It was, moreover, making trans-Atlantic voyages to the "New World," opening up vast new territories for itself. And it was soon thereafter to begin its world historic *tour de monde* – Asia, Australasia, and Africa. Nevertheless, it continued to belong to the English, who, after all, had the longer claim on it.

At the least, if a consideration is carefully delimited to a brief historical window, some few centuries in the middle of the past millennium, it seems justifiable to claim English as the language of England, and so return to the comfortable notion, the imagined history, with which textbooks on the history of English begin. Or is it? What makes those few centuries so special in the history of English? What sets them apart from the other centuries of English's development? Why should those centuries and those peoples be privileged over others? And just who were those peoples? Were they really Anglo-Saxons? Or were they not also Celts, Norse French, and others? So just what, then, are we so sure about that we do not question what we mean by English?

There is another problem with this familiar, commonsense, interpretation of the history of English. It may suggest a conception of stages in the history of English, a *prehistory* (linguistic origins), a *developmental* stage, and a *finished product* – presumably an unalterable linguistic entity that we stamp with the name *English*. Implicit in this notion is a teleological and normative view of language development in which the language as process gives rise to language as final product, its whole development leading to that point. Prior to some arbitrary point in time (perhaps the English Renaissance), the language was incomplete. Now it is complete. It is *English*.

The same, however, holds true for any language at any stage in its development: insofar as it exists, is spoken, it is a language and not a stage in the development of some future language. To measure it by a fixed standard ("modern English") applies a subjective standpoint, just as surely as when we divide history into the pre-Christian (or pre-Muslim, or pre-Hindu, or pre-Buddhist) epoch as opposed to "ours." Those who spoke the language of Beowulf did not view themselves as speaking "old English." They did not view their language as a developmental stage of some future language, any more than we do so today. And yet the one is no more justified than the other.

That idea suffers from an obviously presentist flaw: that what has gone before is history, but what is now is removed from time, space, and development. This conception privileges the language as we know it – or, rather, as we imagine it.

The usual approach to the history of English consists precisely in privileging this brief portion of the history of English since the English Renaissance and calling it the "true" history, the essential history, the defining history. For the development of any language is a continuous process, and boundaries that we mark in that process are only more or less arbitrary and *convenient* (in both senses of the word) breaks in the continuous flow of the language as process. Taking a non-teleological approach, it is just as possible to divide the history of English as follows (cf. McArthur, 1998):

(1) Germanic roots; development in Northern Europe by Germanic peoples (prior to *c.*500 AD);

(2) Period of development in the British Isles by Jutes, Angles, Saxons, Celts, and others, prior to the Norman Conquest (c.500–1150);

(3) Period of development subsequent to the Norman invasion under the influence of the English, French, Celts (to whom the language continuously has spread), Danes, etc. (c.1150–1450);

(4) Period of development that accompanied the consolidation of a "people" and a nation out of the heterogeneous elements of the earlier phase, often called the "Early Modern" period of English (McArthur, 1998: 87) (c.1450–1700);

(5) The epoch constructed as "Modern English," which featured the continued change of the language within the British Isles, where it continued to spread, joined by other outposts of English speaking communities, in particular in North America and Australia;

(6) Period of development in the world, as English continuously spread around the globe, jointly developed by the English, but also by Asians, Africans, and others.[3]

The identification of the first five periods of the history of English more or less corresponds to the common view, one reproduced in most texts on the history of English. Where this approach differs, following scholars like Graddol *et al.* (1996) and particularly McArthur (1998), is in not regarding Phase 5 as a finished product, but one that, like its predecessors, gives place in turn to a new "stage" in the history of English, that is, the continued development of the language. Following this demarcation of the history of English, this study takes the last period as encompassing the subject matter of the field of World English. The topic of this work is the phase of the development of English that has taken place on the world scale.

This account regards the English language that has spread globally not as a finished product but a continually developing language, conceiving its international spread as part of that further development. Defining World English as a *phase* of the process of development of English necessarily historicizes the question. That is, it grounds the subject matter in the definite sociohistorical conditions or contexts in which English has evolved.[4]

Writing World English

The first five periods of the history of English have long been subjects of scholarly inquiry. Yet, while the English language has been spreading beyond the confines of the British Isles for some three centuries, World

English as a field of study has only recently emerged. Closely identified with the globalization of English Language Teaching (ELT), and arising out of its scholarly tradition, the understanding of World English has pivoted not so much on theoretical linguistic questions but on practical and even ethical issues of English spread.

Conceptions of World English

Smith (1976) provided an early account of World English under the term *English as an International Language* (EIL).[5] Smith operationalized the term *international language* as a language other than one's mother tongue – that is, a *second language* – "which is used by people of different nations to communicate with one another" (p. 38). As such, he distinguished it from the more traditional *auxiliary language*, one used for internal communication in a multilingual society. In these functional terms, English in the Philippines, for example, constitutes an *auxiliary* language, whereas English in Brazil represents an *international* language.

In conceiving this definition by domain of use, Smith (1987) was concerned with raising practical questions, those pertaining to English usage among speaker from mother tongue and non-mother tongue contexts. Smith found through his (and others') long practice a sense of "ownership" of English on the part of its mother tongue speakers. They seemed to feel instinctively that since the language was theirs it fell to them to dictate the terms of use of English when its speakers met in the international realm, a modus operandi that Smith found to hinder international and intercultural communication.

Smith (1987) delineated several essential characteristics of an international language:

(1) It implies no essential relationship between speaking the language and assimilating an associated culture. There is no necessity for second language speakers to internalize the cultural norms of behavior of the mother tongue speakers of a language to use it effectively.
(2) An international language becomes denationalized. It is not the property of its mother tongue speakers.
(3) Since English as an International Language plays a purely functional role, the goal of teaching it is to facilitate communication of learners' ideas and culture in an English medium.

The core of Smith's (1987) argument is that a non-mother tongue user does not need to "become more like Americans, the British, the Australians, the Canadians or any other English speaker in order to lay claim on the language. To take the argument a step further, it isn't even necessary to appreciate the culture of a country whose principal language is English in order for one to use it effectively" (p. 39). For a language to become internationalized, it must lose its identification solely with one culture or nation.

Smith's (1987) work helped to touch off a longstanding controversy over whether the "ownership" of English (and thereby authority and control) is vested in its mother tongue users. The debate has been rather one-sided, as numerous scholars have taken the field to deny the proposition (B. Kachru, 1996; Rampton, 1990; Widdowson, 1994). That they continually feel called upon to do so, however, attests to the resiliency of the opposite, tacitly assumed, standpoint.

Linguistic imperialism

Although Smith's (1987) work in EIL centered on practical issues of English's worldwide use, World English scholarship thereafter turned to questions of the ethics of English spread. The question of the "ownership" of English was itself cast in moral terms, far from the practical realm of Smith's concerns. The attempt to assert something other than "native-speaker custodians" of English – to use Widdowson's (1997) apt phrase – met with Quirk's (1988) characterization as "liberation linguistics" – the encroachment of politics into a linguistic realm ostensibly insulated from such issues. This transition to the ethical and ultimately the political reached full fruition in Phillipson's (1992) influential, albeit controversial, work *Linguistic Imperialism*, in which he transferred to the scholarly realm the characterization of English as an alien influence in postcolonial African and Asian society present for decades within nationalist discourse.

Phillipson's (1992) theory of linguistic imperialism is one of the few to attempt a comprehensive theoretical account of "the contemporary phenomenon of English as a world language" (p. 1). According to Phillipson, English attained its current "dominant" position through its active promotion "as an instrument of the foreign policy of the major English-speaking states" (p. 1). He traces the development of World English to the imperialist domination of the world at the hands of England and the United States, positing a linguistic form of imperialism, or subjugation and oppression of certain peoples by others, taking its place alongside of others (political, economic, cultural).

In basing itself in a central process in modern world history, European colonial rule in Africa and Asia, Phillipson's framework offers a compelling, historically-grounded, thesis. Since colonialism coincides chronologically with the development of World English, it is certainly justifiable to inquire whether causal significance attaches to the role of imperialism in the international spread of English.

It is worth posing this question whether Phillipson himself does so. He remarks rather ambiguously that "English is now entrenched world-wide, as a result of British colonialism, international interdependence, 'revolutions' in technology, transport, communications and commerce, and because English is the language of the USA, a major economic, political and military force in the contemporary world" (pp. 23–4). Of these factors, apparently only the first, however, is intended to refer to the pre-World War II period, a circumstance that might appear to imply that British imperialism lies at the root of the question. Phillipson's lack of specificity notwithstanding, it has seemingly become customary to regard the conceptual framework that linguistic imperialism presents as an explanation for the development of World English (Alatis & Straehle, 1997; Canagarajah, 1999; Davies, 1996b; Pennycook, 1994; Widdowson, 1997, Willinsky, 1998). And it is, perhaps more importantly, implicit in the widespread characterization of English as a colonial language in Africa and Asia. Taken as a coherent explanatory framework for World English, the central premise of linguistic imperialism is that the spread of English represents a culturally imperialistic project, which necessarily imparts English language culture to its second language learners.

Linguistic questions in World English

While this debate over the praxis and ethics of World English helped inaugurate a new scholarly discipline, linguistic issues have subsequently come increasingly to the fore. One question emerged above all: taking not a functional but a linguistic standpoint, just what sort of system, if any, does World English represent? Given that the study of World English grew out of concerns of the field of applied linguistics, it was perhaps not surprising that the attempts to represent that system should be drawn first from theories of second language acquisition (SLA).

Almost a decade after his seminal paper on English as an International Language, Smith (1987) addressed what he considered to be a possible misinterpretation of the notion of EIL: Referring to professionally and technologically based limited domains of English usage, he insisted "EIL is not English for special purposes with a restricted linguistic corpus for use in international settings" (p. xi).[6] In direct contrast, in Widdowson's (1997) understanding of World English, the international language comprises varieties of English for specific purposes, "autonomous registers which guarantee specialist communication within global expert communities" (p. 144).[7]

Davies (1989), relating the question of World English to current theories of SLA, posits the question: "Is International English an Interlanguage?" – alluding to a dominant paradigm for explaining the second language learner's progress.[8] He rejects the notion of defining World English as an interlanguage (IL) on the grounds that the latter properly accounts for individual language development and variation, whereas World English "deals with societal varieties" (p. 447). He argues that an IL cannot be "an international language because it is not a full language, nor is it a reduced or treated one. [An interlanguage] is a point on the way to a full natural language" (p. 461). World English, on the other hand, is used for all international purposes and is a "continuum that permits at one end treated reduced codes (e.g. Airspeak) and at the other end standard educated written English" (p. 460). Davies does not rule out the possibility that speakers might use their interlanguages for international purposes. Yet, unlike the changing nature of IL, Davies (1989) sees World English as "quite stable and not very open to change" (p. 450).

Even if World English itself is not an interlanguage, at least one scholar has asserted that many international varieties of English, termed the "New Englishes"[9] (Platt et al., 1984; Pride, 1982) of Asia and Africa, may be (Selinker, 1992).[10] Widdowson (1997) takes exception to this view. For Widdowson, the emergent varieties of English in Africa and Asia are not fossilized interlanguages. They are "regional varieties [that] do not have the dependent status of dialects" (p. 142). And yet, Widdowson perceives an inherent problem in constructing World English on such a basis. He comments, "[I]f English is to be an international means of communication, the evolution of different and autonomous Englishes would seem to be self-defeating." There is the "paradox" of "independence without autonomy" (p. 142). That is, "New Englishes" spoken in Africa and Asia are not subordinated to the mother tongue varieties of which, it would appear, they can only logically be the offshoots. How can they be independent of the language that gave rise to them? Widdowson's solution is to make them languages in their own right, the linguistic offspring of English, but "something else" in themselves. Thus, we need not speak, for example, of "Ghanian or Nigerian English, but Ghanian, Nigerian *tout court*" (pp. 141–2). The result is that the "New Englishes" appear to find no place in World English: their "Englishness" is denied (For a more detailed critique, see Brutt-Griffler, 1998).[11]

With these types of questions, the study of World English has taken off in a perhaps unexpected direction. From the fundamental question that inaugurated the field – the relation of the acquisition of English language and "English" culture – scholars have increasingly turned to questions of standard and variety (C.-J.N. Bailey, 1986; Pennycook, 2001; Quirk 1988, 1990, 1996). This focus appears all the more interesting since, with perhaps one notable exception (C.-J.N. Bailey, 1986), no one has actually claimed the existence of one international standard. The intro-duction of issues of standard and variety highlight the complexities of the development of an increasingly global language. The field has also had to grapple with an inherited discourse that has tended to dichotomize English speakers and English-speaking contexts (B. Kachru, 1996; B. Kachru & Nelson, 1996). There are, for example, distinctions made between the "native" and "non-native" contexts (Davies, 1991; Medgyes, 1994; Phillipson, 1992). Within the "non-native" there is a further differ-entiation of the English as a second language (ESL) and English as a foreign language (EFL) environments (Görlach, 1991), the former refer-ring to contexts in which English serves internal functions as a societal lingua franca in a multilingual nation, the latter to countries with an established national language where English is considered to play a role only in external communication. Again, among the varieties of English, there is a division into the "Old Englishes" (usually British, American, Australian, Canadian and a few others; cf. Fishman, 1977) and the "New Englishes" that have emerged in such nations as India, Nigeria, Singapore, and the Philippines (B. Kachru, 1985, 1986; Platt *et al.*, 1984). All of these dichotomies take root within the unprecedented historical spread of English.

Language Spread

Since any particular language develops in relatively localized condi-tions, a *world* language posits a process of language spread. Indeed, the study of World English has traditionally focused on this very question. For the most part, scholars have taken a political standpoint, framing their accounts in terms of such purported political structures as imper-ialism and concentrating their discussions on such constructs as language imposition, ideology, and language rights (e.g. B. Kachru, 1986; Kontra *et al.*, 1999; Mühlhäusler, 1996; Phillipson, 1992, 1999; Pennycook, 1998; Skutnabb-Kangas & Phillipson, 1994). The most familiar form of this type of treatment is the theory of English linguistic imperialism (Phillipson, 1992), discussed above.

Quirk's (1988) analysis is considerably more complex, dividing the spread of English into three separate varieties – *imperial*, *demographic* and *econocultural*. His imperial model, in which language is spread via the asserting of political control over colonized peoples, essentially anticipates Phillipson's (1992), albeit as a somewhat more limited conception, confined apparently to the spread of English to Asia and Africa in the nineteenth and early twentieth centuries. At the same time, Quirk finds the basis of the spread of English to America and Australasia in the migrations of English-speaking peoples from the British Isles. This basis has led Quirk (1988) to refer to this type of language spread under the "demographic" model. Finally, he makes econocultural features of language, its combination of economic or commercial centrality and its cultural/intellectual role in the world community, the basis for his third model of language spread. Econocultural reasons, in this conception, underlie English's current spread to such varied destinations as continental Europe and Latin America. Quirk (1988), however, provides no basis for connecting the different models into a comprehensive theoretical account, while Phillipson, in positing such a model, folds the other components into the imperial.

Brosnahan (1973) has also placed the spread of English under the rubric of language imposition. Unlike Phillipson, however, he does not distinguish it from the spread of languages such as Greek, Latin, Arabic and Turkish under quite different historical conditions. Strevens (1978), in contrast, finds the basis for the rapid spread of English at least in partly in characteristics of the language itself that have made it an adequate, if not ideal, candidate for filling purposes of international communication.

Language spread via second language acquisition

It is a central contention of this book that these models of language spread, however, are insufficient for the consideration of the development of World English because they abstract from the linguistic processes by which that spread takes place. In place of a concrete investigation of the language spread, a political terminology has been employed: *imposition, dominance, subordination, hegemony*. The metaphors chosen are not particularly apt from the linguistic standpoint. A language is not imposed in the manner of a curfew, military rule or a set of laws.

Within this body of work, the term *language spread* has remained curiously unanalyzed.[12] In fact, it is used in the literature is two distinct senses. It has been used to refer to a territorial movement brought about by the migrations of groups of language speakers (e.g. Quirk, 1988). For example, if English-speaking peoples relocated from England to Australia, this has been classed under the term *language spread*. There is, however, something imprecise about this usage. Language is by its nature a social phenomenon; the locus of language is the speech community rather than a geographical territory. The migration of speakers of a particular language involves a geopolitical rather than a linguistic process. For that reason, I will call this form of "language spread" *speaker migration*. Used in this sense, language spread only falls within the purview of the present study insofar as it implies the second meaning of language spread, *the spread of a language to other speech communities*.

It is this latter usage of *language spread* that corresponds to a specifically linguistic process. The migration of English speakers to the American continents was not a case of language spread in this sense; the acquisition of English by Native Americans, Africans and European settlers of other speech communities was. From a linguistic standpoint, the process takes the form of the *acquisition* of the language. Contrary to the assumptions associated with the political contextualization of language spread, the ends of such *linguistic* processes, as this study will attempt to demonstrate, are not so easily forecast, or for that matter, externally controlled.

The second form of language spread involves language acquisition of a specific type. That the acquiring speakers come from different language groups specifies the condition that they do not acquire English as their first language. The linguistic process concomitant with language spread of this type is necessarily *second language acquisition* (SLA). Furthermore, this SLA process pertains to not simply the individual learner but the *speech community* to which English is spreading. The kind of language spread that forms the essential process of the development of World English, therefore, is *the process of second language acquisition by speech communities*, which I term *macroacquisition*.

English spread and language change: The "New Englishes"

Theories addressing the political side of global English spread (particularly when conceived as language imposition or linguistic imperialism) tend to conceive linguistic outcomes of the process in terms of such phenomena as language shift, or the abandonment of the first language in favor of English (Phillipson, 1992; Skuttnab-Kangas & Phillipson, 1994; Tsuda, 1997). It is important that the study of English not be driven by such extra-linguistic a priori assumptions. On the contrary, current statistics on English use show that the vast majority of its speakers worldwide are bilingual. According to recent estimates, 80% of the approximately one-and-a-half to two billion English users in the world today belong to that category (Crystal, 1997; Romaine, 1995; World Englishes, 1998: 419).[13]

On the other hand, theories of global English spread all but ignore what is by far the best documented linguistic outcome of English spread: the language change that has resulted in the development of varieties of English in such African and Asian nations as Nigeria, India and Singapore known collectively as the "New Englishes."[14] The emergence of the "New Englishes," also referred to as the "Indigenized Varieties of English" has been documented in great detail over the last two decades (e.g. Bokamba, 1992; Görlach, 1991; B. Kachru, 1985; Platt *et al.*, 1984; Pride, 1982; Trudgill & Hannah, 1985).

Most work on the "New Englishes," in contrast to that by scholars concerned with the mechanisms and politics of English spread, concentrates on how the spread of English has resulted in the development of separate English varieties through a process variously termed "indigenization" or "nativization" (B. Kachru, 1990). This process, as yet largely lacking a fully-articulated theoretical explanation, involves the establishment of the separate linguistic and sociolinguistic identity of, in particular, postcolonial African and Asian varieties of English through their "decolonization" or "deanglicization" (B. Kachru, 1985). Scholars concentrate on attempting to substantiate how the New Englishes reflect the uniqueness of the national conditions in which they arise and how they express the national culture (Gonzalez, 1987; B. Kachru, 1990; Y. Kachru, 1987; K.K. Sridhar & S.N. Sridhar, 1992).

Mufwene (1997) has taken the debate out of the sociolinguistic realm of prestige and back into the linguistic realm of explanation in insisting that the New Englishes should be placed alongside other categories of English varieties, the "old" mother tongue American and British varieties, the "new native" varieties such as Irish, and the English creoles. The distinctions, he has noted, have referred not to their structure, but to their pedigree (a fact he also argues pertains to creoles). Quirk (1990) and others *continue* to debate whether New Englishes should be permitted to exist as target standards for English learners in Africa and Asia. In contrast, Mufwene has refocused attention back to the specifically linguistic question of how these varieties came into being, a key point in the explanation of World English. Although English language change through its emergence as a world language has been much more thoroughly studied than its spread, there exists as yet no comprehensive theoretical framework that adequately fits the New Englishes into our understanding of larger linguistic processes and so explains their development as language varieties.

The most convincing and useful accounts have considered the socio-cultural conditions in which New Englishes have arisen. Pennycook (1994) situates their existence within the "cultural politics" of English globally, emphasizing that language has meaning only within definite contexts. The "worldliness of English," a concept which in keeping with his theoretical premises he does not attempt to define, has permitted its settlement in "alien" contexts. Most notably, he investigates the role of various social groups in the colonies that facilitated English spread, attributing it to a more complex process than that posited by linguistic imperialism (Phillipson, 1992). Pennycook's valuable work, then, establishes much of the backdrop of which a linguistic model of development of the New Englishes must take account.

Platt *et al.* (1984) call attention to another crucial component of the sociolinguistic context of the New Englishes. They delimit the boundaries of the New Englishes as separate language varieties on the basis of their being learned in educational settings, differentiating them from pidgins and basilects of English. An irony of this finding, however, comes in the circumstance that the New Englishes are thereby defined as languages only insofar as they more closely approximate standard British or American English, a seemingly paradoxical basis upon which to substantiate the existence of a separate variety. Such a construction creates the necessity of erasing the impression that there are sociopolitical as opposed to linguistic reasons for designating these as distinct varieties of English.

A few investigators have attempted to apply established linguistic theories. Lester (1978) bases his explanation on language contact theory in calling the varieties of International English, among which he includes "Greek English" and "Japanese English," "creolized forms of English" or *contact languages.* In this way, he says, "International English is a contact language made up of contact languages" (p. 11). Lester's theoretical framework, which he admits lacks "solid empirical evidence," is driven by an underlying assumption that it is "unrealistic" to expect non-native speakers to learn "native-speaker" English. As such, in his view the New Englishes represent an inchoate mass of simplified Englishes that serve the same purpose as Quirk's (1981) one simplified international, or "nonnative," version. In so conceiving the matter, Lester tends to lose sight of the condition that the New Englishes do not represent such reduced languages, as Platt *et al.* (1984) have shown.

Selinker (1992) also bases his understanding on a conception of the inherent limitations of the ability of second language learners to acquire a "complete" grammar of a language. He applies his interlanguage (IL) theory, which holds that second language learners progress in predictable ways along a continuum between the learner's first language and the target language, to the emergence of the New Englishes.[15] In this way, a New English simply reflects the range of interlanguages of its speakers. This framework, however, has been convincingly refuted as an attempt to explain the existence of New Englishes (cf. B. Kachru, 1996; Y. Kachru, 1993; Lowenberg, 1986; K.K. Sridhar & S. N. Sridhar, 1994). Y. Kachru (1993) points out, among other things, that IL theory is not applicable to the understanding of the New Englishes as the ideal target language proposed by IL theory is not the goal of learners and speakers of New Englishes. Moreover, she argues that to label the language of second language English speakers in Asia and Africa "fossilized" speech ignores their sociohistorical development and the sociocultural context. It may be added that the inadequacy of the IL standpoint for the explanation of the New Englishes is particularly evident in the fact that New Englishes have developed their own standard varieties (B. Kachru, 1990), while the idea of a standard interlanguage contradicts the notion of the IL continuum.

Macroacquisition as language spread and change

As the work on the "New Englishes" establishes, an essential result of the spread of English is its language change. The history of World English has been one of language change. Distinct varieties arose not accidentally or occasionally but systematically. There is, therefore, an historical and empirically verifiable relationship between language spread and language change within the development of World English. This condition establishes the scope of a theoretical model for the development of World English. It must account for language change within the second language acquisition of English by speech communities, conceiving them as mutually interacting processes rather than separate and only incidentally related.

Language spread as macroacquisition makes such explanatory breadth possible. Since the historical results of English spread are both *language spread* and *language change*, macroacquisition as a linguistic process is language spread and change. This book is intended to bring English spread and change under a unified theoretical framework. In focusing on questions of language policy, it relates the means of spread to the linguistic outcome, language change, and conceives this as the process of *macroacquisition*. Its result is the further development of that language we call English.

Notes

1. Honey (1997: 70), for example, remarks, "By standard English I mean the language in which this book is written, which is essentially the same form of English used in books and newspapers all over the world."
2. Baugh and Cable, noted contemporary scholars of the English language, write: "What the language would have been like if William the Conqueror had not succeeded in making good his claim to the English throne can only be a matter of conjecture. It would have pursued much the same course as the other Germanic languages, retaining perhaps more of its inflections and preserving a predominantly Germanic vocabulary, adding to its word-stock by the characteristic methods of word formation . . . and incorporating words from other languages much less freely" (1993: 105).
3. Others have dated the commencement of this last period as *c.*1945 (cf. McArthur, 1998: 86–7). I purposely leave the last two periods undated. If pressed, I would place its commencement at no later than 1900. The transition from one to the other probably commenced in the nineteenth century and lasted until well into the twentieth.
4. What makes the six phases of English as identified by Graddol *et al.* (1996) something more than the purely arbitrary mode of classification that it might otherwise appear to represent (cf. McArthur, 1998) is that each represents the period of development of the language by a particular combination of speech communities, from the original Germanic peoples, to their descendants in contact with Celts, Normans, and others. In this respect, Mufwene (1997) has cogently argued that the importance of language contact to the history of English has not been given sufficiently recognition.
5. English as an International Language, together with related names including English as a Global Language (Crystal, 1997) and English as a World Language, is based on and appropriate to a functional definition. I have therefore decided to break with this traditional nomenclature in favor of the simpler and more direct *World English*, an approach McArthur (1998) also appears to favor.
6. Hardin (1979: 2) has made the same point: "The simple fact is that international communication cannot be reduced to the limited range and patterns of communication which are, I think, characteristic of ESP. Neither can it be seen as the sum of all kinds of ESP, since it is a language, not a corpus."
7. Interestingly, Widdowson conceives the question that way in part to accomplish one of Smith's objectives: to liberate English from the control of its mother tongue native speakers. There is, he writes, thereby "no need of native-speaker custodians" (p. 144).
8. Ellis (1994: 710) writes, "Selinker (1972) coined the term 'interlanguage' to refer to the systematic knowledge of an L2 which is independent of both the learner's L1 and the target language."
9. Mufwene (1994: 21) defines New Englishes as "a cover term for varieties other than that spoken originally by the people called the English and living in the part of the world called England before this territory expanded its political and economic hegemony to Scotland, Ireland, and then outside Europe through colonization." He remarks that the term is preferable to the other names these varieties have been given, including "non-native," "nativized," or "indigenized" varieties.

10. Selinker seems to suggest that New Englishes speech communities consist of individuals with "an entirely fossilized IL competence" (p. 232).

11. In a subsequent commentary, Widdowson (1998: 400) clarifies his intention with regard to the place of various varieties, saying that World English represents a "composite lingua franca," which brings it substantially closer to the view adopted in this work.

12. Cooper (1982) has undertaken the most extensive analysis to date. Cooper, however, ties the question into the function of language in a way that limits the usefulness of his definition. While Cooper's work raises some of the same questions as the present study, the approaches rest on fundamentally different conceptions of language and language change. Cooper, insofar as he connects language spread and language change, does so in an additive sense, insofar as one builds off the other. The conception developed here seeks to understand this as an integrated process.

13. In contradistinction to the presuppositions of many investigators, it is crucial that this fact be kept in mind in studying the macroacquisition processes, as will be discussed in Chapter 7, since SLA in a stable bilingual situation cannot be assumed to be identical to SLA in a language shift and language attrition context.

14. Phillipson (1992) notes their existence only in passing, and has subsequently admitted that even some of his supporters view this as a crucial oversight. Quirk has given this phenomenon greater attention, but has come to the position that they should not be accorded any sort of formal linguistic acceptance, even dismissively labeling the attempt to do so "liberation linguistics."

15. This view has at least to some degree influenced the characterization of particular New Englishes. Gough (1996: 57) writes, "In what appears to be the most extensive study of black [South African] English, Wissing (1987: 18–32) describes it as a fossilised interlanguage with the primarily cause of such fossilisation being mother-tongue interference and the general lack of exposure to English."

Chapter 2

The Representation of the Social in a Social Science: Methodology in Linguistics

It has become something of an article of faith that the study of linguistics centers on the monolingual individual – the native speaker (cf. Romaine, 1996). World English, however, owes its existence to the fact that some 80% of its approximately one-and-a-half to two billion users are bilingual (or multilingual) (Crystal, 1997; World Englishes, 1998: 419). Since the existence of World English results from the process of language spread as macroacquisition – second language acquisition (SLA) by speech communities – bilingualism necessarily occupies a central role in the study of World English. In refocusing its study from the global, often geographic, spread of the language to its acquisition by speech communities, the prevalence of bilingualism as a historical phenomenon emerges as being of theoretical as well as practical importance (cf. Romaine, 1995). That shift of emphasis, in turn, carries with it significant implications for the choice of methodology.

The unit of analysis in linguistics

As approached in this work, the study of World English centers on the English *bilingual speech community*, here defined as any speech community that begins and carries out to some extent the process of macroacquisition. This bilingual speech community may be a subset of a larger speech community. (The definitions of *community*, *speech community*, and *bilingual speech community* are considered in greater depth in Chapter 7.)

Conceiving the speech community as the unit of analysis of a linguistic investigation differs from the methodology that has become standard in the field. Chomsky (1965) has given the classic statement of that conception:

Linguistic theory is concerned primarily with an ideal speaker-listener, in a completely homogenous speech-community, who knows its language perfectly ... This seems to me to have been the position of the founders of modern general linguistics, and no cogent reason for modifying it has been offered. To study actual linguistic performance, we must consider the interaction of a variety of factors, of which the underlying competence of the speaker-hearer is only one. In this respect, study of language is no different from empirical investigation of other complex phenomena. (p. 3)

The standpoint Chomsky describes, however, assumes a narrow construction of "linguistic theory." Hymes (1996) has remarked,

The phrase "Linguistic Theory" ought to refer to a general theory of language, or at least a general theory of the aspects of language dealt with by linguists, but it has been appropriated for just those aspects of language dealt with in transformational generative grammar – or by competing forms of formal grammar – [a] consequence of Chomsky's skill as a polemicist. (p. 60)

Hymes (1996) and Labov (1997) among others have argued that however important the method characteristic of the transformational generative grammar approach has been to the study of a certain limited range of linguistic questions, it cannot be said to constitute an absolute method for linguistics – one suited to the investigation of the full range of questions that theoretical linguistics must examine.

The method employed in transformational grammar is inadequate to the investigation of language change by macroacquisition for two reasons. First, the study of language change requires that language not be viewed as a fixed code. Second, it is a contradictory method to undertake the study of social processes through the unit of analysis of the individual speaker. Each of these points will be considered in turn.

Chomsky's assumptions and language change

With respect to the first point, Chomsky's assumption of an "ideal speaker-listener, in a completely homogenous speech-community, who knows its language perfectly" (Chomsky, 1965: 3) suits the attempt to describe systematically the grammar of a particular language at a particular fixed or isolated point in time. If the scope of the problem to be solved is such that the language can be held to be complete and unchanging, then the investigator can assume, with Chomsky, that the highly idealized speaker "knows the language perfectly."

If, on the other hand, the object of inquiry is either to derive how a language has developed into its present state or how language changes in general, then such an assumption becomes logically impossible. For a language in the process of its development cannot be taken as fixed and complete. On the contrary, any given state is necessarily partial and subject to constant change. It therefore becomes untenable to suppose that, even in principle, an individual speaker, no matter how idealized, could "know the language perfectly." The speaker would have to know both the present state of the language (L) and its future, as yet undetermined, state (ΔL).

To assume such a possibility is necessarily to make two teleological claims. First, it would have to be postulated that languages can evolve only within definitely predetermined bounds – with respect to all of the aspects of the language that are to be known "perfectly," including semantic range, lexis, syntax, and morphology. Such a claim would not conceive merely universal grammar, but universal language. Second, such a claim would require a speaker to have perfect facility in understanding and speaking a changed state of a language (ΔL) before it had come about. As an example, it would require a speaker of Anglo-Saxon to be *in nuce* perfectly competent in Middle English, or at least two more nearly related successive states of those developmental phases of English.

In short, for a language to be known "perfectly," it must be taken as a fixed code, which on the theoretical level amounts to abstraction from change. It is for this reason that sociolinguists such as Halliday (1997), Hymes (1996) and D. Cameron (1990), have noted that Chomsky's approach to linguistics takes an idealized, abstracted, and perhaps even mythical starting point. However useful the method has been to transformational grammar, it is far from adequate for sociolinguistics, a field centrally concerned with language variation and change. A chief shortcoming of transformational generative linguistics has been that it lacks a coherent theory of language change and linguistic development.

Linguistic theory and the social

The second fundamental shortcoming of the usual method employed in linguistic inquiry is its assumption that all linguistic phenomena can be explained by taking the individual speaker as the unit of analysis. Positing the individual speaker as the only fit subject for linguistic inquiry assumes that no social processes exist that cannot be found in their entirety within the explanatory realm of ideal speaker-listener. The limits of this conception have been exposed by scholars of language change, who have called attention to the different processes that take place in group acquisition as opposed to individual (Romaine, 1995; Thomason & Kaufman, 1988; Weinreich, 1974). To account for problems of language spread and change, linguistics has need of a theory of the social.

The social is not absent from Chomskyan linguistics, despite its conceiving its subject as the individual speaker-listener. It is the need for a conception of the social that induces Chomsky to imagine the *"ideal* speaker-listener."* The pitfalls of attributing perfect knowledge of a language to a particular member of that speech community are only too apparent. As Martinet (1974) pointedly remarks, "Who knows all of his language?" (p. vii). In having recourse to an *ideal* speaker, Chomsky implicitly recognizes that it is not adequate to generalize in any simple fashion conclusions garnered in the study of a *given* individual speaker, to whom many accidental, inessential phenomena may and do attach. In place of the concrete individual, an idealized individual speaker is assumed, a speaker who is made to represent a *composite picture* of all speakers in a particular speech community. In the average, it is held, the individual peculiarities mutually cancel one another and disappear, yielding the typical, the essential. So we are left with a kind of atomic speaker, as it were: the fundamental building block for linguistic theory.

On closer examination, however, this fundamental unit of linguistic theory reveals itself to be not the actual *individual* but an abstract representation of the *social*. In fact, the resort to the social to justify the individual as a possible conceptual starting point is present in the very conception of the "ideal speaker-listener" with which Chomsky begins. For that ideal speaker to know her language "perfectly" presupposes the existence of the language to be known. Such a presumption is not problematical in itself, but it is from the standpoint of the ideal speaker whose competence is to be defined. Against what standard is the knowledge of the ideal speaker to be measured and designated "perfect"? The only possible answer is against the standard of the other members of the *speech community* to which the ideal speaker belongs.[1] In other words, while it is perfectly possible to assume the existence of an ideal speaker in the abstract, such a presupposition only becomes *meaningful* if perfect competence of a particular language is ascribed to that speaker. That sort of linguistic knowledge requires postulating the existence of a speech community. Hence, even in Chomsky's presentation of the case, the ideal speaker is *affiliated to* a "completely homogenous speech-community" and said to know *"its* language perfectly" – i.e. the particular language that *can only be defined – or demarcated from other particular languages – in relation to the speech community that speaks it, never against the individual speaker in isolation.* That is to say, the very definition of a particular language (L_a as opposed to L_b) is constructed on the basis of the _speech community_. Consequently, any attempt to conceive the linguistic individual relies on – is derived through or constructed on the basis of – a _previous_ conception of the linguistic social, the speech community. The speech community is as much present in and as much forms the basis of the Chomskyan construction of linguistic theory as the "ideal speaker-hearer," which, Chomsky maintains, it is "primarily concerned."

Insofar as there is something identifiable as a language, it is because of the social group. Language finds its locus in the explanatory realm of the social rather than the individual. For the social is nothing other than the total – the whole into which the peculiarities of the individual disappear. The very fact that a particular speaker cannot be held to know the entirety of her language shows that language is a social phenomenon. The speech of the _idealized_ individual speaker–listener represents that of the speech community, embodied in the notion of _perfect knowledge_. Taking not the individual, but the speech community, it becomes a logical condition rather than an idealized one that in total the speakers of a language know all of that language, and can even be said to know it "perfectly," at least within the limits of ascertainable knowledge. For the whole cannot but coincide with itself. The speech of the _idealized individual speaker–listener_ stands in for, replaces for certain definite purposes, that of the speech community, embodied in the notion of _competence_.

In that sense, it might appear that the two approaches being contrasted here – the _ideal speaker–listener_ as opposed to the _speech community_ as the fundamental unit of linguistic analysis – are rather identical. From the standpoint of linguistic theory, nevertheless, that is far from true. As the foregoing analysis suggests, a subset of linguistic theoretical problems have been approached by employing the ideal speaker–listener as a theoretical stand in for the speech community as the essential unit of analysis in linguistics. Within a certain circumscribed range of linguistic questions, this method does not appear to introduce a substantial problem and even facilitates inquiry in the way Chomsky maintains. In particular, it allows the linguist to take the data generated from a concrete individual speaker. Otherwise, linguists would face the formidable task of taking empirical data from whole speech communities, or at least they would need to pay much closer attention to questions of reliability of data collection as a function of statistical sampling techniques.[2] Whatever its justification for methods of data collection, the approach Chomsky seeks to substantiate as the method of linguistics nevertheless yields claims that pertain not to the social but the individual level.

However productive this method has been within a limited sphere, therefore, it does not come without its own set of problems in examining other types of questions. In such cases, the social nature of language must be made theoretically explicit rather than tacit. For example, in the case of macroacquisition, or SLA by speech communities, taking the standpoint of the individual L2 learner ignores a fundamental condition: *where the SLA does not take place as an isolated case, but collectively, individuals mutually influence one another*. In his classic work on language contact, for example, Weinreich (1974) recognizes the distinction between language contact in the case of the *individual* bilingual speaker and that of *groups* of bilinguals (p. 3). In the latter case, processes are at work that do not appear in the case of individual learners. In attempting to understand macroacquisition such a recognition is crucial.

Language change as a social process

From the general standpoint, there are two levels of language change: variation across speech communities and the variation within the same speech community over time – or variation across linguistic time and space. Although often viewed as two separate forms of change falling in the domain of different subdisciplines, historical linguistics and socio-linguistics (McMahon, 1994), language change across time and space both involve phenomena on the societal level that cannot be reduced to the terms in which transformational generative linguistics has approached the study of language.[3] On the contrary, each has reference to what appear from such a standpoint as "extralinguistic" processes. The study of language spread and change, then, must adopt a view of language that does not abstract it from its social context (cf. Halliday, 1997). Approaching language spread and change through the process of SLA by speech communities answers a fundamental explanatory requirement.

Speech community as unit of analysis

It is a contention of the present work that in studying language spread and change linguistics should take as its subject not the individual speaker but the speech community. It has been argued that the speech community constitutes the starting point for the investigation of language spread and change because it is the social unit that corresponds to a particular language, and it is also the subject of the process of macroacquisition.[4]

That is not to say that any conception of speech community suffices. For the idea of the speech community can be taken in two ways – as the abstract, idealized speech community in general, or as a historical product. Saussure (1922), for example, puts forward the conception of langue as the social, but the social as abstract and idealized, in other words as the ahistorical social. The categorical distinction between langue and parole serves precisely the same purpose in Saussure as the distinction between competence and performance in Chomsky's theory: to explain, in Platonic fashion, language in the concrete via invoking an idea of language in the abstract.

The present conception, on the contrary, takes the social as consisting in the concrete and historical conditions in which language develops: language in its process of spread and change and the speech community that lies behind it. What distinguishes the speech community is generally approached through the conceptual lens of *culture*, but in this account it will be considered under the category of *shared subjective knowledge* (see Chapter 7). Since a speech community is defined in this study on the basis of shared subjective knowledge, it follows that it may be subnational, national, or supranational. Whether it has the status of a nation is a political and historical question, requiring investigation of its concrete context. At the same time, speech community affiliation is not exclusive by its nature; an individual may belong to two or more, as Saville-Troike (1996) has argued. In Chapter 8, the dimensions of the speech community will be explored in greater detail.

Language spread and change cannot be conceived through conceptual frameworks that involve historically active agents imposing their language on passive recipients (as with linguistic imperialism, discussed in Chapter 1 and again below). It is, rather, a process in which the essential actor is the acquiring speech community. In developing an understanding of World English, macroacquisition conceives the speech community as bringing about language spread and change. The language change, because it takes root in speech communities, manifests itself in variety, or as varieties of the language.

Precisely because the speech community belongs to the realm of shared subjective knowledge, it is grounded in a historical context. When approached from this standpoint, the speech community as a historical product becomes a concrete, material starting point suitable for empirical investigation. In this study, therefore, the spread and change of English is placed within the context of definite sociohistorical processes, such as colonialism and the struggle against it.[5] And so the understanding of macroacquisition as a process of English language change entails a study of the *context of its spread.*

Methodological Questions in Language Spread and World English

Platt *et al.* (1984: 1) have pointed out that the spread of English "has been the most striking example of 'language expansion' this century if not in all recorded history. It has far exceeded that other famous case, the spread of Latin during the Roman Empire." Given both this immense spread and the circumstances in which it has taken place, explanations of World English have necessarily had to tackle the historical processes of the modern world by which peoples have collided and interacted, including colonialism, political and economic subjugation, and regional and world markets. Some scholars have tended to portray the realm of language as another battle-field in which these epochal struggles have been fought out, expressed as a range of linguistic outcomes, principally language dominance, language shift, language death, and language maintenance[6] (Brosnahan, 1973; Fishman, 1977; Mülhäusler, 1996; Phillipson, 1992; Skutnabb-Kangas & Phillipson, 1994). Given such an approach, it appears that these linguistic processes are determined by extra-linguistic factors.

The present account also grounds the linguistic within the larger historical processes that accompanied English spread, therein providing the "extra-linguistic" context without which language change cannot be understood (Thomason & Kaufman, 1988; Romaine, 1995; Weinreich, 1974). It does not, however, conceive these processes quite so dichotomously as "extra-linguistic" but instead as essentially linguistic, since they embody the history of the speech community embedded in the development of language. The history of a speech community takes account of all of the historical processes that go into its making, maintenance, and transformation, necessarily focusing on how these factors influence its language usage.

As such, language policy and planning (LPP) analysis serves as a methodological tool to explicate and concretely study the phase of the development of World English. For despite the name, language policy and planning is a phenomenon that is carried out with respect to speech communities and not languages (cf. Wiley, 2000).

Chapters 3, 4 and 5 investigate the history of English-learning communities throughout the former British Asian and African colonies. Without this concrete investigation of the history of these communities, it is impossible to approach either the development of English varieties or the transformation that English has undergone as a result of its globalization. A number of approaches within the field have contributed to the mode of analysis employed in this work. Tollefson's (1991) historical-structural approach aims "to locate individual actions within the larger political–economic system" (p. 35). Drawing partly on the sociolinguistic work of Fishman (1972), the historical-structural work in language policy and planning seeks to connect language policy with sociopolitical development. As the name indicates, the unit of analysis is the *historical process* (Tollefson, 1991: 33). The historical-structural study aims at "a social-scientific critique of the goals and aims of plans and policies in such areas as language rights or the distribution of economic wealth and political power" (p. 34). Toward this end, the historical-structural approach focuses on social *class* as "the central macrostructural unit of analysis" (p. 35). "The major goal of policy research is to examine the historical basis of policies and to make explicit the mechanisms by which policy decisions serve or undermine particular political and economic interests " (p. 32). Tollefson (1991) has studied, for example, the role of English in such newly independent nations as Namibia, pointing out the important socioeconomic questions involved in the use of that language as a national medium.

B. Kachru (1981) has cogently argued that the neo-classical focus on planning and planners must be broadened into language *policy*. A narrow focus on individual planners and planning decisions does not hold up in a larger sociohistorical context, nor does it account for comparative analysis of language planning. Phillipson and Skutnabb-Kangas (1996) argue for the need for "comparative language policy analysis . . . that goes beyond consideration of language in a few domains and permits valid comparison of fundamentally different sociopolitical units" (p. 434). Toward that end, taking the emphasis off planning as such and putting it onto policy fulfills the aim of the historical process as the "proper unit of analysis" (Tollefson, 1991: 33). This means, essentially, that the development of the macroeconomic structures of society must be studied: colonialism, imperialism, neocolonialism as well as the liberation movements aimed against them. This project explicitly connects LPP to other sciences, as called for by Ricento and Hornberger (1996), giving interdisciplinary content to the field.

Grounding the study of language planning and policy in a larger theoretical framework is necessary for another reason. Ricento and Hornberger (1996) note that "[T]he field of LPP research still lacks sufficient explanatory and predictive analytical tools that can be applied to diverse settings" (p. 411). For that reason, the explanatory framework of the development of World English put forward here combines the conception of macroacquisition with an explanatory model of the development of world language, the "linguistic" and the "extra-linguistic" that must be taken in conjunction to form a theory of World English.

Conceptual Questions in the Global Spread of English

Macroacquisition versus speaker migration in the history of English spread

Chapter 1 posits that language spread in its linguistically meaningful sense refers not to speaker migration but to macroacquisition. Thus the language spread of English as such is not coincident with its international history. This is important for two reasons. First, the initial period of the expansion of the area in which English was spoken did not take it outside of the British Isles, and so was not so much international as regional. When combined with the fact that this was tied to processes of the internal political and socioeconomic development of the British Isles, and that it was carried out by a large speaker migration over the territory of those islands (O'Riagain, 1997), this period does not take us into the formation of World English as a separate phase of the history of English.

The second phase of the expansion of the area in which English was spoken commenced in the seventeenth century with the establishment of permanent English colonies in first America and later Australia. Again, however, this result was obtained primarily through speaker migration. Where there is extensive speaker migration, the likelihood of language shift and language attrition among those peoples who are subjected to sociopolitical domination is much higher. English became the mother tongue of these countries, spoken by a predominantly monolingual population, for reasons that will be discussed in Chapter 6.

English began to spread to other speech communities on a world scale with the development of European non-migratory colonization in Asia and Africa during the eighteenth century. Here in contrast to the experience in the Americas and Australia, there was no speaker migration on a significant scale (with few exceptions) and so English did not develop into a mother tongue. It was, therefore, in this phase of the expansion of the territory over which English was spoken that the roots of World English lie, in the macroacquisition of English within Asia and Africa. It is with this process that the study must begin.

Explaining the development of World English: Linguistic imperialism revisited

Although the origins of this phenomenon began in the eighteenth century, it has been usual to date the development of World English as a post-World War II phenomenon (Crystal, 1997; McArthur, 1998; Phillipson, 1992). World English, however, cannot be explained by events that took place after its establishment – after World War II. Instead, World English can only be explained by processes that took place during the *whole* of its development. It is not necessary to show that World English existed at any particular point, but *that its process of formation was under way*. It is not customary to attribute causality in history to processes that postdate the phenomenon to be explained. For the development of World English, that stricture clearly includes in the scope of the question the period of the extension of the British Empire into Asia and Africa. Otherwise, cause postdates effect. Since the development of World English extends back at least until the early nineteenth century, it is hardly possible to attribute World English to the conscious policies concerning English teaching that took place after World War II. The attempt to do so has been a hallmark of the theory of linguistic imperialism (Phillipson, 1992), an account of World English that has become so widely disseminated as to require separate treatment.

The thesis that English in much or most of the world represents the result or at least a legacy of linguistic imperialism involves a few important assumptions:

(1) Linguistic imperialism is a separate type of imperialism that amounts to a conscious language policy on the part of the imperial power to impose its language and is, in the case of the UK and the US, responsible for the spread of English (cf. Davies, 1996b).
(2) This policy emanates from the Center (imperialist nations like the US and UK).
(3) The spread of English is ideologically-driven; language is spread entirely or mainly for its own sake.

Just as important, one crucial implication follows from this view:

(4) English is an imposed language in those parts of the world where it is not spoken as a mother tongue.

It might well be that Phillipson or other proponents of the theory of linguistic imperialism would not explicitly claim adherence to all of these presuppositions. The question, however, is not simply what Phillipson might or might not assert so much as what the theory of linguistic imperialism as a coherent explanatory framework postulates or implies about the development of World English. If linguistic imperialism is said not to represent an explanatory framework for the *development* of World English, then the theory's explanatory power is greatly weakened. It reverts to a rather unenlightening set of observations about language policy makers in "Center" nations. If the impetus and agency for English language spread lies outside Center nations, wherein lies the analogy to imperialism? If nothing else, the name is badly chosen. In that case, too, the concept loses its connection to cultural imperialism, of which Phillipson (1992: 53) says it is "a primary component."

To be sure, linguistic imperialism is generally taken as language imposition, as the alienness of English to "un-English" contexts; by linking it to both cultural imperialism and neo-colonialism as a phase of imperialism, Phillipson also at least tacitly makes such claims. As he comments about his *Linguistic Imperialism* elsewhere, "the work is avowedly historical" (1993: 366).[7]

Implicit in the construct of linguistic imperialism is its determination as a separate aspect of the politico-economic system known as imperialism. Phillipson (1992) accepts this requisite in commenting, "it is necessary to establish linguistic imperialism as a distinct type of imperialism, in order to be able to assess its role within an imperialist structure as a whole" (p. 53). It is a conditio sine qua non of the theory of linguistic imperialism that a tangible, traceable policy of linguistic imperialism lie at the root of the international spread of English. "[I]t is linguistic imperialism if the English language is imposed (by sticks, carrots, or ideas) on the Welsh or the Ugandans, and linguicism[8] is in operation. In the neo-colonial phase of imperialism inter-state actors from the Centre and representatives of the elite in the Periphery (their counterparts and collaborators) are the key agents of this linguistic imperialism" (p. 55). Since this language imposition represents a joint effort of the Center and the elite from the periphery, the obvious implication is the historical process of the imposition of English on the non-elite is contemplated under this theory as it pertains to English language spread. In other words, it is not sufficient to the hypothesis that English spread as a function of English linguistic imperialism that English should have spread historically during the epoch of imperialism. It must be shown that it did so as a result of a linguistic-based imperialism, a distinctive language policy. Indeed, Phillipson argues that linguistic imperialism has existed as an aspect of British (and American) imperial policy (p. 53). Critics of this framework have widely noted that this thesis so far lacks strict empirical verification in primary source materials (Davies, 1996b; Fishman, 1993; Kibbee, 1993). Phillipson (1993) has also endorsed calls "for further empirical verification" and acknowledged that "the utility and validity of the essential elements of the conceptual framework need to be put to the test" (p. 369).

Testing Phillipson's theoretical framework empirically means asking the question of whether there was a relatively *uniform* colonial policy, and whether it was ideological and imperial. In other words, for linguistic imperialism to be a consistent explanatory framework, World English must have developed as the product of a conscious policy developed and put into effect during the colonial epoch. Hence, by Phillipson's own admission, the evidence he presents pertaining to the British Council and other post-colonial agencies, while *necessary* to the substantiation of his thesis, does not provide *sufficient* demonstration of the role of linguistic imperialism in the *development* of World English.

The fact that, as the subsequent chapters demonstrate, no uniform British empire-wide language policy developed tends to disconfirm the hypothesis of linguistic imperialism as responsible for the spread of English. At the same time, it already suggests that no distinctive ideology existed concerned with spreading English in the colonial dependencies for cultural or linguistic reasons. There is evidence of the existence of advocacy of something like a linguistic imperialist policy here and there. Sentiments were occasionally expressed by English citizens who had no direct connection to colonial policy. For example, an imperialistically-minded English schoolmaster declared: "The future has few certainties or none; but if there be any, one is that, if ever there is a universal language – *a language spoken or understood among all members of the human family* – it will be English" (Welldon, 1895: 889, emphasis added). For such isolated sentiments to have explanatory significance for the global spread of English, it must be shown that they formed the basis of imperial policy.

Such a linguistic imperialist policy should display to at least some extent the following features:

(1) universal and exclusive education in English;
(2) replacement of the indigenous languages with English, as was the case in Ireland (O'Riagain, 1997).

Given the demands of a linguistic imperialist policy, it should not be a difficult one to locate in the historical record. We might, therefore, expect that Phillipson's (1992) account would adduce the clear trail that such a policy would necessarily leave. Instead, Phillipson provides what Davies (1996b) has characterized as a "conspiracy theory" that centers on the role of the British Council since its post-World War II inception. In contrast, the historical substantiation of linguistic imperialism consists of a very brief chapter on "colonial inheritance," 24 pages in length, of which only eight pages are devoted to the period before World War II vis-à-vis English – one page on India and Macaulay, four on the post-

World War I period, with only broad generalizations to cover the period in between. While 12 pages are devoted to the post-World War II period, four pages are devoted, paradoxically, to French colonial policy, and one page is given to a discussion of the fictional character Robinson Crusoe. The reader searches in vain for any specific discussion of language policy or descriptive statistics on the number of English-learning students in the British colonies. The only statistics presented are for French colonies, with a passing reference to Tanganyika, a British colony inherited from Germany only in 1920. What actually pertains to British policy for the period in question appears to contain factual inaccuracies, as will be discussed later in the book.

Rather than a detailed empirical study of the question, Phillipson tries to substantiate the requisites of a linguistic imperialist policy through repeated assertion of their presence. He quotes as proof of England's linguistic imperialist policy in India the statement that "English became the sole medium of education" and comments subsequently that "The job of education was to produce people with a mastery of English" (p. 111). Given not only that the vast majority of education consisted of "vernacular education," by design, and that, in addition, the British colonial administrations came to fear the results of English education (discussed in Chapters 3 and 4), what are we to make of Phillipson's (1992) statement that "instruction through a local language was invariably seen as a transition phase prior to instruction in English" (p. 112)? As will be shown, not only was this not "invariably" the case, it was only so in a very small minority of cases.

In addition, seemingly echoing the sort of fervor for the spread of English that Phillipson leads the reader to suppose the British entertained, he proclaims, "English was the master language of the empire" (p. 111). Since we do not have in question merely the parameters of language policy in general but the testing of a hypothesis which asserts that the goal of the British was systematically to promote English language spread, it is clear that such a policy must be manifested above all in the educational setting in which by far the greater number of English users in the colonial context acquired English (Platt *et al.*, 1984). "Linguistic imperialism" implies that the mother language is replaced and not supplemented by the imperial language (English). The teaching of English by itself, therefore, even where it did take place, is not sufficient grounds to identify the policy of the British empire with linguistic imperialism. If English did not merely traverse a part of the globe in company with British rule and British and American commercial dominance, then we should find more than a trend toward a certain spread of the language among the elite of the country, a tendency that was also evident in parts of the world over which neither Great Britain nor the United States exerted imperial control.

An example of something resembling an official linguistic imperialist policy in the British empire can be found in British Papua New Guinea. During its very brief tenure as a British colony (1890 to the turn of the century when the colony became the property of Australia), the colonial government made known its intention to establish English as a common language in the dependency. In the view of the government, the large number of indigenous languages made any other policy than the implementation of English as a common language impossible: "It is tolerably clear that the trading and working language of the west end, of the east end, and of the islands, will be English" (CO, Papua New Guinea, 1896: 189–191). To this end, the local government supported the use of English by instructing all government officers to use English when interacting with indigenous persons, employees, prisoners, and so on. It was the administration's belief that such close contact in conjunction with the spread of English among miners and traders "would probably eventually make English the common language" (CO, Papua New Guinea, 1896: 189). The local colonial government also appealed to missionaries, e.g. the Wesleyans, to provide assistance in teaching English. All indigenous teachers were instructed to teach the English language and in the future use it as a medium of instruction (p. 33). Colonial officials believed that English education was necessary if the people of New Guinea were to be fit to work for European employers. Hence, they regarded education without the imparting of English to be of little value (p. 33). The projected policy to spread English and establish it as a common language involved teaching it to all inhabitants in the colony. It is important to realize, however, that it was the local government's policy and not one developed in London.

As will be detailed in the pages that follow, the rest of the empire did not mirror the experience of Papua New Guinea. Thus, although Phillipson (1992) puts forward a compelling thesis that seemingly resonates with important currents in postcolonial studies, the close historical examination of English spread during the colonial period reveals a complexity that cannot be captured by notions of language imposition. Rather than a unidirectional process carried out from an imperial center, the spread of English involved a contested terrain in which English was not unilaterally *imposed on* passive subjects, but *wrested from* an unwilling imperial authority as part of the struggle by them against colonialism. The story of this surprisingly two-sided process forms the subject of Chapters 3, 4 and 5.

Notes

1. Thus, the speech community is said to be homogenous. In other words, the speech of the given "ideal speaker-listener" matches that of all others. There cannot be said to be anything special or peculiar about it.
2. Such a method is not impossible, of course. It would, however, require a fundamental shift in the way linguists work. Methodologically, the construct of the "ideal speaker-hearer," transubstantiated theoretically in to the construction of the *native speaker*, saves the investigator the trouble of using the sampling techniques that characterize much of social science research. Theoretical linguists often work from data that is given no other justification than that it represents the utterance of a native speaker. They justify this practice on the dubious contention that every speaker of a language is a complete reflection of the whole, which, as Chomsky makes clear in the quote above, is justified by *assumption*.
3. Indeed, Lass (1997), Romaine (1995), Thomason and Kaufman (1988) all note that attempts to explain language change over time by means of inherent features of language (or of universal grammar) contain weaknesses.
4. A further disadvantage of the choice of the individual speaker as the unit of analysis of linguistics is that it results in a static, abstract conception of language as something apart from communication as social interaction. For the language each individual speaker speaks must have been learned, and what is learned is always necessarily external to the individual, which is held to be the real subject of study of linguistics. This contains an inherent contradiction that is only resolved in the whole. For it is external to every individual, and thereby appears as something external to the social aggregate (society) as well.
5. They are not, however, held to represent the essential content of language spread and change.
6. Language dominance, as defined by Baker and Prys Jones (1998), refers to "One language being the stronger or preferred language of an individual, or the more prestigious language within a particular region" (p. 702). Language shift describes the process of a speaker or speech community discontinuing the use of one language in favor of another, as in immigrant communities that lose their mother tongue and adopt that of the nation to which they have migrated. Language death occurs when a language disappears through the loss of its last remaining speakers. Baker and Prys Jones (1998) define language maintenance as "The continued use of a language, particularly amongst language minorities (for example through bilingual education). The term is often used with reference to policies that protect and promote minority rights" (p. 703).
7. Phillipson is evidently not unaware that the historical record does not bear out his presuppositions, and seems to have taken lately to backtracking from his claim that England proclaimed English "the master language of the empire" (1992: 111). More recently he has stated that "my understanding of linguistic imperialism was developed primarily in relation to the experience of the post-colonial world" (2000: 92). Ironically, some commentators have more readily accepted his unsubstantiated account of the distant historical past in preference to the post-World War II period he treats in detail. Thus,

Davies (1996: 486–7) accepts that "English became so dominant" as a result of its "spread by bible, trade, and flag, like all those more distant empires," yet dismisses the postcolonial portion as an unconvincing conspiracy theory. Kibbee's (1993) reaction is similar.

8. Phillipson (1992) writes, "Linguicism involves representation of the dominant language, to which desirable characteristics are attributed, for purposes of inclusion, and the opposite for dominated language, for purposes of exclusion" (p. 55).

Chapter 3

Ideological and Economic Crosscurrents of Empire

American Rule in the Philippines: Ideology and Language Planning

When the United States had finished pacifying the newly acquired colony of the Philippines at the turn of the twentieth century, it did something few imperial powers ever had: it mapped out a detailed plan of colonial policy. An extensive commission – significantly under the auspices of the Department of War – studied the economy, geography and people of the group of islands in Southeast Asia. In the multivolume report running into the thousands of pages it issued (*Report of the Philippine Commission*, 1900), it extensively documented the linguistic situation of the nation, noting the presence of some 87 indigenous languages and the limited impact that Spanish had made under the last colonial regime over a period of three centuries (*Annual Report of Governor General of Philippine Islands*, 1926: 5). The commission latched onto a simple, solution – English.

Perhaps unsurprisingly, Filipinos were to have the language of the colonizing nation forced on them – all of them. English was envisioned as not only the official language of government, but as the common language of the inhabitants of the colony and the nation that American officials envisioned growing out of it after some suitable lapse of time. According to the American colonial government, this language policy would above all "build up national solidarity" (*Annual Report of Governor General of Philippine Islands*, 1926: 5). It also certainly occurred to them that supplanting Spanish with English would, as they hoped, help to build loyalty to the new regime.

Serving as justification of this policy was the sort of arrogance to be expected of a conquering power. American culture was judged superior to the Filipino, as English to the languages of the islands. The English language was regarded as the "language of a civilized nation" while the local

34

languages were judged as lacking the means to facilitate the student in "increasing his knowledge" (p. 881). Even if the educational system cultivated literacy in the native language of the Philippines' children, such students "would have found only a barren waste before them" (*Third Annual Report of the Philippine Commission*, 1903: 880). The report asserted, "The few newspapers that are printed in the native language do not furnish all the intellectual guidance or stimulus needed by the inhabitants of the islands in their aspirations to be counted among civilized peoples" (p. 880).

Under Spain's rule, although Spanish was designated as the language of instruction, in reality education, such as it was, was carried out in the local languages (*Report of the Philippine Commission*, 1900: 31). In fact, the Spanish left the impression that they were more concerned with limiting access to knowledge of Spanish than spreading it (Gonzalez, 1987). The American Bureau of Education proclaimed that the majority of the population was "ignorant" of Spanish, and that the Filipino people welcomed with enthusiasm the American effort to teach English (*Third Annual Report of the Philippine Commission*, 1903: 881).

Educational language policy on the part of the United States differed considerably. At the very outset, the goal was clearly specified: "Common schools must be established everywhere, and as a minimum standard every child must be taught arithmetic and to read and write the English language" (*Reports of the Taft Philippine Commission*, 1901: 108). The state was to monitor carefully the centralized public school system, assuring that its two goals were met: (1) the provision of education to every child with (2) the teaching of English as its centerpiece. The colonial government willingly provided financial support toward to permit primary instruction to be made compulsory for children up to the age twelve (p. 110).

At the root of the American plan was to use the English language as the sole means of instruction in the public school system from the moment of its establishment. Moreover, to further promote the teaching and the spread of English in the Philippines, pressure was put on private schools to give instruction in English, with the recommendation of imparting all instruction in private schools in the English medium as well. The Bureau of Education justified this decision on the grounds that it would be impracticable to translate textbooks, even into the principal indigenous languages, and that none of these languages could serve as the common medium of communication. But there was a more fundamental reason: "universal free education for all the children of the islands" would make "this country . . . one of the several nations of the world scattered in every portion of the globe where the English language will be spoken" (*Report of Governor General of Philippine Islands*, 1919: 110).

The official reports of the Bureau of Education consistently emphasized the success of the inauguration of the teaching of English. After some two decades of American rule, the colonial government could already boast that half of all Filipinos under 35 "are daily communicating with each other in business and social intercourse through the medium of the English language" (*Report of the Governor General of the Philippine Islands*, 1919: 110). The optimistic prediction was that in 15 years, English would not only constitute the common unifying language in the islands but also would substitute for the use of Spanish in the government and legislature. The encroachment of English portended a bleak future for other languages spoken in the colony: the opinion among experts was that they would be confined to use at home, possibly for one or two generations, before disappearing altogether (*Report of the Governor General of the Philippine Islands*, 1919).

The reality remained quite a bit different, to be sure. The length of primary education in English was fixed at three years only (*Report of the Philippine Commission*, 1905). In practice, the great majority of the population continued using local languages, despite the reported 97% of Filipino children who passed through the colonial educational system by late 1920s (*Report of the Governor General of the Philippine Islands*, 1927: 206). Official proclamations aside, therefore, it was admitted that "the mass of Filipinos do not now stay in school long enough to develop for permanent use even the rudiments of an education" (p. 206). The majority of the students enrolled in the public system only began learning English. In fact, the emphasis on English had come to be considerably curtailed once it was discovered that English proficiency led to the expectation of "white collar" employment. Indeed, students' brief stay in school was much more devoted to practical industrial training, to the virtual exclusion of the "classical" (*Report of the Philippine Commission*, 1905: 823). Thus, long after official American policy might have had the indigenous languages of the nation eradicated, they remain firmly entrenched.

It would be tempting to believe, on studying the history of American rule in the Philippines, that therein lies the story of the spread of English throughout Asia and Africa. Such an assumption would be wrong. The US was a minor player in world colonialism. Its only other significant Asian/Pacific colony was Hawaii, where it instituted precisely the same policy (cf. Niedzielski, 1992), and it possessed no African territories. By far, the dominant English-language imperialist nation was Great Britain. Indeed, the British empire was larger than that of all of its European rivals combined. The story of English spread lies with British language policy and not American.

The Purposes and Pitfalls of Imperial Language Policy

Details of the implementation aside, the underlying vision of American language policy in the Philippines very much accords with what much of the work on colonial language policy would lead us to expect. As Mazrui and Mazrui (1998) observe on the African context, "Colonial authorities tend to be regarded as having pursued a monolithic language policy aimed at destroying African languages and establishing the supremacy of European languages for the explicit purpose of controlling the world view of the colonized" (p. 55).

Such a result might easily be held crucial to purposes of empire. Proponents of a linguistic imperialist policy would necessarily have argued that the goal of an empire was to ensure its utmost influence in its dependencies. In this view, the interests of the mother country would be paramount. Linguistic imperialism – making the mother tongue of the conquerors that of the subjugated people – might be made to serve those ends. A pure linguistic imperialist standpoint might assume that the people in the colonies would, in replacing their local languages with English, also change their customs, thinking, and values, to those of the English or American mode, thus becoming "denationalized." To the degree that English education robbed the youth of the colonies of their indigenous identities, it left those to be replaced with an English-language imparted identity as loyal subjects of the mother nation, Greater America or Greater England. As the inspector of schools in British Hong Kong observed, "[A]n imperial policy ... may regard the Chinese boys and girls who leave the Hong Kong schools every year as so many pro-English missionaries" (Irving, 1905: 80–1).

Linguistic unity would thus promote the interests of the empire, not only vis-à-vis the colonies, but also as against the other imperial powers, which at the end of the nineteenth century were competing in the division of Africa and Asia. The imposition of English on the colonies already acquired would cement the stability of the empire assuring that British or American imperialism would be more than a fleeting moment in history.

However logical such assumptions might appear, they overlook the fact that the American and British colonial experiences diverged in crucial respects. There was, after all, a significant difference between the American experience as a large nation with an exceedingly small colonial territory and a small nation with a vast empire. The US could afford to put money into its colonies. Britain was determined to do no such thing.

All ideology aside, these purely practical considerations had far-reaching ramifications for language policy. In practical terms, the imperial language policy described above would have necessitated universal and exclusive teaching of English to every speaker in all of the empire's dependencies. And therein, the aforementioned British inspector in Hong Kong indicated, lay the problem: the universal English education it envisioned would require substantial government funding to supply well qualified teachers or provide for the training of local teachers, production of materials, and the construction and maintenance of facilities. Among other requisites, this would necessitate a financial burden that went beyond what British colonial administrations could – or, rather, were willing to – pay. And since as a general matter little tax revenue could be gotten out of the indigenous population, especially in the early period of colonial rule – certainly not enough to fund such an ambitious educational project, even if all tax revenue were diverted to this purpose – the burden of such a project would fall upon the taxation of British commercial enterprise in the colonies. Since, as the inspector pointed out, the commercial class did not find such schemes in its interest and vigorously resisted paying for them, it meant a contest in which the empire would be forced to defend its imperial interests above the local interests on the ground in the colonies. In short, an imperial policy required strict centralization of the kind American colonial rule in the Philippines depended on but British would neither achieve nor strive for.

Once British colonial policy is removed from the restricted scope in which it has been viewed, a closer consideration reveals a quite different picture than emerges out of the study of the American (or the French). It is not that British colonial language policy was not designed to serve imperial ends. It is simply that its goals were of quite a different order than those envisioned by linguistic imperialism and articulated by American policymakers in the Philippines. Rather than a *separate* policy designed to serve cultural and linguistic purposes, language and educational policy in British Asia and Africa during the two centuries of its colonial rule there was intrinsically intertwined with the essentially socioeconomic concerns of empire. It served as a basis for the determined effort to preserve class stratification the British believed to be indispensable to the economic exploitation of its colonies. The next three chapters tell that story.

The British in Asia and Africa: Politics, Economics and Language Planning and Policy

The Macaulay Doctrine in nineteenth century India

Those who have argued for the existence of an unambiguous policy of linguistic imperialism on the part of the British have invariably cited the first attempt to articulate any consistent language policy in the British empire – the controversy over medium of instruction in 1830s India that produced the now famous Macaulay Doctrine.

Macaulay, chairman of the Governor-General's Committee on Public Instruction, became embroiled in a controversy between the "Orientalist" British administrators in India and the "Anglicists." The Orientalists believed that the British should encourage the study of traditional Indian languages among those Indians in higher education. The "Anglicists," as the name implies, favored the use of English. The victory went to Macaulay and the "Anglicists," a fact that has created the impression that with that triumph the English linguistic imperialist impulse simultaneously gained the ascendancy.

The Macaulay Doctrine has become synonymous with the notion of a strident effort to impose English on the people of India (Phillipson, 1992). The scholars who point to the seminal nature of the series of policy decisions in the 1830s and 1840s with respect to the language of education in India are quite correct about the important precedent it set. But they are mistaken in their interpretation. Far from the uncompromising attempt to impose English on India, the Macaulay Doctrine aimed at something quite different. Not only was the replacement of the mother languages of the Indian people with English never contemplated; on the contrary, the lasting impact of this episode was the insistence that the vast majority of the Indian people who received education did so in their mother language at the behest of the British Indian Government. As would be the case throughout the empire, not ideological proclivities but fiscal realities combined with economic objectives dictated the bounds of legislation. Although this policy has been much discussed in the literature (Khubchandani, 1983; Pattanayak, 1981; Pennycook, 1998; Phillipson, 1992), it is necessary to take a fresh look at this episode to dispel lingering misperceptions.

To better understand the context and purposes of British colonial language policy in the British empire, it is useful to examine the textual basis of the policy developed, the Macaulay Minute of 1835. In this document, Macaulay argues for the implementation of English education as a means for the "intellectual improvement of those classes of people who have the means of pursuing higher studies" (quoted in C.H. Cameron, 1853: 68). His philosophy for English education stemmed from his belief that "the dialects commonly spoken among the natives of this part of India contain neither literary nor scientific information" (p. 68). For Macaulay, that conviction constituted a compelling reason to advocate English education in India.

Nevertheless, Macaulay had no intention of "Anglicizing" all of India, as is generally supposed. In his Minute, Macaulay states, "It is impossible for us, with our limited means, to attempt to educate the body of the people" (quoted in C.H. Cameron, 1853: 78). Rather, the "Anglicist" policy would be aimed at "forming a class who may be interpreters between us and the millions whom we govern" (p. 78). In short, Macaulay advocated the intention of creating "a class of persons Indian in blood and colour, but English in taste, in opinions, and in intellect. To that class we may leave it to refine the vernacular dialects of the country, to enrich those dialects with terms of science borrowed from the Western nomenclature, and to render them by degrees fit vehicles for conveying knowledge to the great mass of the population" (p. 78). However harshly we may judge the opinions and intentions of Macaulay, he was far from envisioning an Indian future devoid of indigenous languages, nor did he ever express the view that English should dominate the linguistic landscape of the nation. On the contrary, he placed local languages at the center of Indian life for the "great mass of the population," assigning to English a role that he may have modeled on that of Latin in a Europe of a then still recent vintage.

Commentators on the Macaulay doctrine have seen in his ideas a grand ideological conception. However much that may or may not be true, there nevertheless exists an underlying political motivation closely tied to developments in England that outweighs the purported cultural agenda. Without this context that has hitherto been largely missed, Macaulay, a minor functionary in the British colonial administration in India, would never have gained the upper hand in the policy struggle then raging between "Orientalists" and "Anglicists."

Most important to the adoption of Macaulay's policy, the British Parliament in 1833 issued a directive to the government of India that Indians were to be employed in ever growing numbers in the administration of the colony, a policy actuated not by ideological motives but for reasons of economy in the cost of governance (Mayhew, 1926: 19). Prior to this desire to lower the costs of empire, an outgrowth of the general political tenor of the times, Parliament had shown little interest in matters of policy in India that touched even indirectly on language policy. In fact, Parliament never took any direct interest in language policy in India. It confined itself to vague pronouncements and left it to the colonial administration in India to decide how such directives were to be implemented.

Parliament first decreed in 1813 that the colonial administration of India was to allocate money for "reviving literature in India" and "for the introduction and promotion of a knowledge of the sciences among the inhabitants of the British territories" (quoted in C.H. Cameron, 1853: 65). This ambiguous wording was met by the colonial administrators in India by funding of the study of Arabic and Sanskrit. The 1833 Parliamentary act said no more about the question of language, and did not even consider it. That element came to the fore in India itself, as British administrators pondered the means of putting Parliament's edict into effect. They soon latched onto English education as a solution to the dilemma. As a British administrator in India remarked, "to give the natives a complete English education was the surest way of putting them in real and practical possession of the privilege of eligibility to all offices in their own country" (C.H. Cameron, 1853: 63), so long as that country was to fall under British rule.

Politics and colonial language policy

Because of the central role that this use of indigenous peoples for the tasks of imperial administration would play in British colonial history, a closer consideration of this point is needed. As the British empire developed, the colonial service became more and more dominated, at least at the lower levels, by nationals of the colonial countries rather than Europeans. There was one overriding motivation for such a substitution: finances. It was quite expensive to maintain a European colonial service. In addition to the higher wages Europeans commanded in the colonial system, there was the question of transport, including dependents. Further, in tropical areas British administrators would often spend one half of a year in England recuperating for every year of service in the colony. In these areas, effective service was thus reduced by one third (Orr, 1905). Finally, England was too small a country to spare enough of its civil servants in an empire that numbered hundreds of millions and reached far-flung lands. Employing local civil servants thus became a matter of practical economics for the colonial government.

The decision to employ Indian people dated back to at least the 1833 Parliamentary decision discussed above. It grew greatly with time. In some colonies, e.g. Gold Coast by 1920, persons indigenous to the country held all the posts in the subordinate clerical services and in numerous technical departments. By the same year in Nigeria 4500 posts in administration and 2500 posts in the technical departments were held by Nigerians (Lugard, 1923: 87). As one of the foremost British colonial administrators of the first decades of the twentieth century wrote: "The progress made in the development of Africa would have been impossible were it not for the enormous number of Africans who fill posts in which a knowledge of English, of reading, writing, and arithmetic, and, to a lesser degree, of book-keeping and accountancy, is required" (Lugard, 1923: 443).

The efficiency and the economy of the British administration in its empire necessitated the training of a well-qualified group of civil servants from among the colonized nations, and that education had to include the English language. Civil servants needed to be conversant with English, whether any goal existed to make English the language of the nation. It constituted a natural decision for the convenience of those British subjects in colonial service, who brought with them their language into that employment. In the multilingual contexts necessitated by the arbitrary boundaries into which Asia and Africa were carved up under European colonialism, English as the language of government could hardly have been avoided. On the contrary, the need for a small proportion of English-speaking subjects necessarily arose without any separate language policy goals, and, indeed, even if the British should come to fear the widespread dissemination of English. What is actually most striking, perhaps surprising, about British colonial rule throughout its history is the virtually universal requirement for employment in the colonial service of a knowledge of at least one and often several local languages of the colonies (e.g. Lugard, 1923).

Tailoring education to the needs of training civil servants

Britain's task of administering an empire many times its own size and population, therefore, dictated English education for a selected class of functionaries. The experience of British rule in Egypt exemplified this circumstance. In the eyes of long-time governor Lord Cromer, good government in Egypt, like in other parts of the empire, meant inexpensive government. Hence, he favored a plan designed to save money by having Egyptians take up the bulk of the civil service jobs, particularly at the lower levels, but including also the higher ranks (Cromer, 1909; Loyd, 1933). His administration, therefore, had in its employ by 1906

12,027 Egyptians and 1252 Europeans. Cromer devoted the resources at his disposal for education virtually entirely to fulfilling this goal (Montgomery, 1919).

Since, as Cromer pointed out, "a large section of the upper and middle classes of [Egyptian] society depends on Government employment" (1909: 531), education of the elite naturally turned on the practical ends of government. This consisted of primary and secondary schools in which English and French were taught, although Arabic was the medium of instruction, due in large part to Egyptian preferences. Only in the "higher colleges" did Arabic give way to English as the medium of instruction (Montgomery, 1919). It should be noted that Lord Cromer not only wanted Arabic to be made the medium of instruction at these higher colleges, but also advocated restricting the number of "foreign languages" taught (Cromer, 1909).

Although government-controlled, these schools charged substantial fees, ensuring that they catered to the target population only. The rest of the population was to receive a completely different sort of education. As an educational expert familiar with the Egyptian system commented, "Education in Egypt is now clearly crystallizing into two systems: The Europeanized, which aims at providing education chiefly for the wealthier circles of society, and the vernacular, which aims at a practical education for the rest of the population" (Montgomery, 1919: 94).

The same system of tracking was noted by commentators on educational systems in other parts of the British empire. In colonial Ceylon, for example, the administration commented: "[T]he distinction between primary and secondary education is replaced by the distinction between vernacular and English schools" (CO, Ceylon, 1904: 40). The curricula for "English Schools" and "Vernacular Schools" differed primarily in point of language (CO, Ceylon, 1929). On this foundation, a two-tiered educational system was set up, in which "really good English" was taught to the few in "English Schools," while "Vernacular Schools," which taught in local languages, were established for the majority (CO, Ceylon, 1892: 17).[1]

The ramifications of the use of the indigenous power structure in indirect rule

It was not solely a question of economics that prompted the training of the colonial population for the purpose of British colonial administration. The British understood that in their colonies there already existed a well-established social structure within the community and that indigenous leaders enjoyed social prestige among their people and an understanding of the local culture that the British could use to their advantage in prosecuting colonial control. The existence of this indigenous power structure of the subjugated peoples was perhaps an equally important factor in the use of colonial subjects in building the administration of the empire. The result was the policy of *indirect rule*: the incorporation of the existing indigenous power structures in British rule (Lugard, 1923). In colonies such as Nigeria, for example, this form of administration was to make imperial rule both more effective and cheaper.

Administering the colony through members of the indigenous power structure became a significant part of the system of British colonial administration. For this reason, special attention was given to the education of the sons of the prominent indigenous leaders. For instance, in 1908 a British official in Southern Africa recommended that the governments in all of the larger areas should "establish a boarding-school, primarily for the sons of chiefs, but also open to a limited number of the sons of the wealthier natives who are commoners . . . A Government school, largely on an aristocratic basis, for the Bechuana natives, would much diminish in the future the difficulties of the British administration, and lead to greater harmony between those tribes" (Sargant, 1908: 52).

Thus both economic and the sociopolitical factors in the colonies had a bearing upon the spread of English. Taken together, they dictated the need for training of an indigenous group of civil servants who would be able to maintain communication between the subjugated population and the imperial officials. This dual aim of "indirect rule," both economic and political, led to a modification of the drive for English education. Given these goals, English education was necessary for the relatively small group of civil servants, albeit not to the exclusion of the teaching of their native language. In fact, a knowledge of both was expected: the policy of indirect rule stipulated the teaching of indigenous languages alongside English. An educational official in Hong Kong, for example, insisted that for "tomorrow's officials" the "ability to read and write a plain letter in his own language, whether he is in a lawyer's office, or is a compradore, or court interpreter, needs no showing" (Irving, 1905: 82). Colonial administrators were aware of the dependence of the colonial administration upon the civil servants drawn from the local community and consistently in the early period of empire building reported the shortage of well-qualified civil servants with a sufficient knowledge of English *and* their native language.

The Educational Language Policy of Indirect Rule:
English Education as *Bilingual* Education

For these reasons, the contention that "The British policy of 'indirect rule' was to be effectuated by educating the elite exclusively through the medium of English" (Phillipson, 1992: 111) is inaccurate.[2] Instead, English education for the elite was in its substance *bilingual* education. For both political and educational reasons, bilingualism and multilingualism developed. On the political side, it represented an attempt to ensure that the ruling elite was "kept in touch with the masses," in pursuance of the policy of indirect rule. It was not desirable, as the Under-Secretary of State for the Colonies expressed it, that "in the education of the 10% there should be an absolute divergence from or break with the education of the 90%." (Ormsby Gore, 1928: 99). Toward this end, a sound knowledge of what British officials called the "vernacular" – indigenous languages – was considered essential. Imperial administrators were decidedly against the replacement of the "vernacular" wholly with English even for the English-educated elite.

This political agenda accorded with the view of education officials in British colonies charged with designing and executing the education systems. These officials frequently complained that students could not learn adequately in English, especially in the lower standards. Their solution was to insist upon a "sound education" in the "vernacular" even for those destined to go on to English education at the top levels.

At the Imperial Education Conference of 1911, an inspector of Normal Schools in Burma, reported that even oral instruction of English, given because of the parents' insistence, was found "exceedingly difficult" to implement because of the lack of bilingual teachers, and it was therefore abandoned entirely in the lower levels. Only in Standard V was the pupil allowed to begin any study of English. Furthermore, the transition from Burmese to English as the medium of instruction took at least two years during which the content courses were still often taught in Burmese in order not to "retard the progress of children" (*Report of the Imperial Education Conference*, 1911: 262). In Bombay, pupils had to pass satisfactorily through five standards in the "vernacular" before they could study English or continue their education in the local medium (p. 263). In Malta, where three languages (Maltese, Italian and English) were in use, the Government introduced a system called "the principle of choice" in 1898, which specified that until the third Standard the child was to be instructed in Maltese. Subsequently, the parent chose either Italian or English as the language of instruction for the child; still the child learned the other language in the upper classes, which in practice meant that the pupil left school a multilingual (p. 265).

Even in India, the oldest British colony, in which early provision for the spread of English was made, Lord Curzon's Government issued a resolution in 1904 which insisted on education in the mother language: "As a general rule a child should not be allowed to learn English as a language until he has received a thorough grounding in his mother tongue" (quoted in *Report of the Imperial Education Conference*, 1911: 260). The resolution added, "No scholar in a secondary school should even then be allowed to abandon the study of his vernacular which should be kept up until the end of the school course. If the educated classes neglect the cultivation of their own languages, these will assuredly sink to the level of mere colloquial dialects, possessing no literature worthy of the name" (p. 260). In Bombay, secondary students were given the opportunity to decide between the use of English and the "vernacular" in their studies (*Report of the Imperial Education Conference*, 1911). In the same way, "English education" in Ceylon was of two kinds: (1) "a full course of instruction in the vernacular languages plus a working knowledge of English"; and (2) schools in which the language of instruction was English, but in "the majority" of which the local languages continued to be taught even in the upper classes (CO, Ceylon, 1938: 101–2).

It is equally important to note that colonial administrations tended to perceive something of a danger in introducing English instruction too soon. The early introduction of English in education was deprecated because it was believed to raise the expectation of English education for all, which was not a British goal (*Report of the Imperial Education Conference*, 1911: 262).

British advocacy of bilingualism for the English-speaking colonial elite

Educational officials were satisfied that the result of their policy was the development of bilingualism among the elite in the colonies. As an official from India remarked, "there is an increasing number of those who employ a vernacular and English simultaneously. Of course, these are confined to the great towns, and particularly to the town of Bombay. I once asked a Chief Justice in Bombay what language he spoke as an infant, and he told me that he practically spoke the vernacular and English from the beginning. He began to speak in those simultaneously" (*Report of the Imperial Education Conference*, 1911: 263).

Nor were these purely twentieth century notions. A Select Committee on Education in the Straits Settlements declared in 1870 that the

"Committee is of the opinion that a boy, whether he be Chinese or Malay, can make no real progress in education until well grounded in his own language" (Eleum, 1905: 139).

At the same time, the administering of an English education was far from implying mastery of the language. In cases in which some English was taught in the colonies to a wider segment of elementary school aged children, there was no attempt to ensure that English was learned. Despite the continual insistence by experts that only years of concerted effort would result in a child proficient in English, only a rudimentary education was given at most.

British officials' views of indigenous languages

As the patronizing concern of the Curzon government over the fate of the "vernaculars" in India suggests, the attitude of British imperial administrators toward local languages is more complex than proponents of linguistic imperialism usually describe it. According to Phillipson (1992: 112), "Local languages were never accorded high status." Indeed, it has already been shown that a principal goal of Macaulay's policy was the "enrichment of the vernaculars," to use his words. However we are to take such statements, there can be no doubt that British administrators emphasized the important place of the local languages. For example, the Calcutta University Commission of 1917 commented as follows:

> The mother tongue is of primary importance. The mother tongue is the true vehicle of mother wit. ... It is through the vernacular (refined, though not weakened, by scholarship and taste) that the new conceptions of the mind should press their way to birth in speech. ... A man's native speech is almost like his shadow, insep- arable from his personality. In our way of speech we must each, as the old saying runs, drink water out of our own cistern, for each one of us is a member of a community. We share its energy and its instincts; its memories, however dim, of old and far-off things. And it is through our vernacular, through our folk-speech, whether actu- ally uttered or harboured in our unspoken thoughts, that most of us attain to the characteristic expression of our nature and what our nature allows us to be or to discern. ... Hence in all education, the primary place should be given to training in the exact and free use of the mother tongue. (Calcutta University Commission, 1917: 197–8)

The same commission, it might be noted, recommended that the "vernac- ular" be substituted for English as the language of instruction and examination at Calcutta University. Similarly, in 1919 Sinhala and Tamil were added to the London Matriculation and Cambridge examinations (CO, Ceylon, 1920). As Mazrui and Mazrui (1998) have pointed out, British colonial "policies of indirect rule allowed for considerable cultural and linguistic relativism" (p. 8).

British policy in India in the wake of the Macaulay Minute

Those, therefore, who, as Phillipson (1992), evince the Indian government's Resolution of 7 March, 1835 referred to above, as proof that the intention existed to impose English as the language of all education in India are fundamentally mistaken. The latter act was the expression of the policy of providing English education to create a civil service staffed by Indians. Hence, as Mayhew (1926) observes, Indian governor "Bentinck found in the claims of the Anglicists [advocates of the use of English for higher education] the solution of the problem immediately confronting him, the supply of competent and trustworthy native servants of the Company" (p. 18).

This fact has not been lost on scholars of British educational policy in India. Shelvankar (1940) notes, "The neglect of mass education merely showed that the new rulers of India had not come to the country to indulge in 'Social Uplift,' and the excessive importance attached to English was the natural consequence of their desire to economize in administration by creating on the spot a class of minor officials instead of importing every clerk and civil servant from England" (p. 103). R.P. Singh (1979) concurs: "There is no disputing the fact that Indian education grew to meet the requirements of local bureaucracy" (p. 111). Lord Chirol (1910), himself an important figure in the history of British educational policy in India, concluded the same thing: "The main original object of the introduction of Western education into India was the training of a sufficient number of young Indians to fill the subordinate posts in the public offices with English-speaking natives" (p. 34).

The World Market and the Question of Language

The economics of imperial rule impinged on the decision to institute a measure of English education in another respect as well. At the same time that the British conceived the benefits to the Exchequer of "Indianization" of the civil service, they were resolved to prosecute vigorously what Parliament called the "economic development" of the colony, another factor dictating English education for the elite (C.H. Cameron, 1853). With the development of industrial capitalism in the late eighteenth century, with England, and later also the United States, as its center, English more and more became the language of the world market. As commerce became a more intensive world phenomenon, and linked all parts of the world market (Wallerstein, 1980), the need for a central language of commerce exerted itself, and that language was, by dint of England's commercial supremacy, naturally English. This circumstance is not attributable to any cultural aspirations of the English, but to the economic conditions that created their commercial supremacy. Moreover, the very internal logic of economic imperialism dictated that production in the colonies – whether those of England, the United States, France, Germany, Holland, Denmark, Italy or Japan – was geared toward the world market, as was production in parts of the world not under colonial rule, such as Latin America, Central and Eastern Europe, and parts of Asia (Wallerstein, 1980).

While colonial rule fell to one imperialist nation or another, the commercial exploitation of the colonies was an international effort, with merchants and commercial ventures representing all or most of the major economic powers. In such a situation, one language had to develop as the commercial lingua franca. That language was English. So much had English become the language of the world market that many of the other colonial powers instituted English education in their colonies for the provision of a commercial class suited to carry out the work entailed by the world market (League of Nations, 1923, 1925b). England could hardly have been expected to be an exception to this general trend.

Commercial practice by its nature requires a tremendous amount of clerical work. Correspondence must be conducted, orders placed, schedules ironed out, transport arranged. All of this was no less true in the past than today. The need for a commercial lingua franca arises, not out of any desire to spread the language of a particular nation, but out of the economic basis of society. A principal language of commerce represents a function of the development of the world market. It implies a commercial class conversant with the language of the world market to carry out these commercial functions.

Commercial Needs and its Impact on Varied Colonial Settings

British imperial officials were well aware of this pressing necessity of commerce. The inspector of education for Hong Kong described the practical consequences for language policy at the turn of the twentieth century:

[A] merchant who is solely alive to his own profits ... would ...
require intelligent clerks, and would therefore pay willingly for
schools which turned out a good stock of these ... with a thorough
mercantile education. The Chinese clerks should also have a working
knowledge of their own written language. He would probably be
wise in his generation in objecting to pay for teaching a mere smattering of English, as the necessary minimum of pidgin English can
be easily picked up by shop-boys and domestic servants out of school.
In other words he would prefer to an even but low standard, an
education which aimed at advancing the more promising pupils.
(Irving, 1905: 80)

The need for commercial clerks implies a significant variation in the
number of English educated youths from colony to colony. The need
would be heaviest in commercial colonies like Hong Kong and Singapore,
through which much of the exported produce of an entire region would
pass; on the other hand, demand would be light in colonies whose
economy was based almost entirely on the production of raw materials
transshipped through an external commercial center.

Hence for reasons of expediency, an English speaking elite would
necessarily have come into existence without any special ideologically-
driven goal of spreading the language as such. What proves this all the
more is that such an English speaking elite sprang up in non-English
colonies just as a French speaking elite existed in Europe in the nineteenth century (in Germany, Poland, Russia). The impetus behind
spreading English was not to make a pupil, as one of the colonial inspec-
tors put it, "a potential missionary of the empire" (Irving, 1905: 81), but
rather to produce "to-morrow's officials" and clerks for the mercantile
class (Irving, 1905: 82).

"Indianization" of the Colonial Administration, "Economic Development of the Country" and Their Effect on Language Policy

A consideration of the motives behind the Macaulay doctrine portrays
the decision to convert higher education to English in a different light
than that of an ideological policy. Even if the latter category of considerations weighed heavily in Macaulay's thinking, they played a far less
significant role, if any, in the forces motivating his superiors in the colonial administration and in London. When the context of this policy is
ignored, the introduction of English appears to be ideologically motivated.

"Orientalist"-inspired policy after Macaulay

Phillipson (1992: 110) writes, "This decision on funding firmly slammed the door on indigenous traditions of learning" as part of a drive to make English "the sole language of education." On the contrary, given the actual motivation, this language policy is perfectly consonant with support for indigenous traditions of learning, even if perhaps in somewhat modified form. The Indian government's Resolution of 7 March, 1835 on language policy further declares: "[I]t is not the intention of his Lordship in council to abolish any college or school of native learning, while the native population shall appear to be inclined to avail themselves of the advantages which it affords; and his Lordship in council directs that all existing professors and students at all the institutions under the superintendence of the committee shall continue to receive their stipends" (C.H. Cameron, 1853: 81). The question only related to what the British government intended to promote on its own, and not at all what was to be permitted to exist. Not only was the door not slammed on indigenous traditions, it was purposely left open. So much so that, as Mayhew records, "By 1839 Lord Auckland [governor of India] was allowing grants for oriental publications and refusing to starve existing oriental institutions" (1926: 25). More explicitly "Orientalist" policy measures followed. As Mayhew (1926) records, "In 1853 the Government of the N.W. Provinces, in noting with regret how few Anglo-vernacular students had secured public employment, expressed a determination to give preference to men 'proficient in a sound and enlarged education added to a knowledge of the Sanskrit language and familiarity with the Hindi language'" (p. 26). By the 1880s, the Colonial and Indian Exhibition conspicuously displayed books published by the Indian colonial administration in both local languages – Marathi, Gujerati, Bengali, Kanarese, Tamil, Hindi, Urdu and others – and the classical languages of India – Sanskrit, Arabic and Persian (J. Russell, 1887: 207).

Even if that document had been the colonial government's last word on the subject, the import is quite different from that given by Phillipson. Yet the contrary is the case. The policy continued to evolve, and far from the last word, the Macaulay Doctrine represented only a phase in the development of British language policy in India.

Local language education in India before and after Macaulay

The Committee of Public Instruction soon issued a clarification to offset what a prominent colonial official later called in a speech to Parliament

on education in India the "erroneous interpretation" of the Resolution
of 7 March, 1835 that "government had intended that education in
English should be given in its colleges to the exclusion of education in
the vernacular languages of the country" (C.H. Cameron, 1853: 88).

The statement of the Committee of Public Instruction, because it clears
up so many misconceptions, is worth quoting at length:

> We are deeply sensible of the importance of encouraging the culti-
> vation of the vernacular languages. We do not conceive that the
> order of the 7th of March precludes us from doing this, and we have
> constantly acted on this construction. In the discussions which
> preceded that order, the claims of the vernacular languages were
> broadly and prominently admitted by all parties, and the question
> submitted for the decision of Government only concerned the rela-
> tive advantage of teaching English on the one side, and the learned
> Eastern languages on the other. We therefore conceive that the
> phrases "European literature and science," "English education
> alone," and "imparting to the native population a knowledge of
> English literature and science through the medium of the English
> language," are intended merely to secure the preference to European
> learning taught through the medium of the English language, over
> Oriental learning taught through the medium of the Sanskrit and
> Arabic languages, as regards the instruction of those natives who
> receive a learned education at our seminaries. These expressions
> have, as we understand them, no reference to the question through
> what ulterior medium such instruction as the mass of the people is
> capable of receiving, is to be conveyed. *If English had been rejected,*
> *and the learned Eastern tongues adopted, the people would equally have*
> *received their knowledge through the vernacular dialects.* It was therefore
> quite unnecessary for the Government, in deciding the question
> between the rival languages, to take any notice of the vernacular
> tongues, and consequently we have thought that nothing could
> reasonably be inferred from its omission to take such notice.
>
> *We conceive the formation of a vernacular literature to be the ultimate*
> *object to which all our efforts must be directed.* ... We trust that the
> number of such translations will now multiply every year. ... A
> teacher of the vernacular language of the province is already attached
> to several of our institutions, and we look to this plan soon becoming
> general. (quoted in Cameron, 1853: 89, emphasis added)

In fact, what has generally been lost sight of is that the Resolution of
7 March, 1835 did not touch "vernacular" elementary education at all,

and that the Indian government continued to pursue that objective. The village school that was the mainstay of education in a country in which approximately 90% of the population lived in rural areas (*Indian Statutory Commission*, 1930, Part VI) was left as it was – an institution of wholly indigenous language education – by the policy that became synonymous with Macaulay's name. By 1859 the colonial administration was declaring that promoting elementary "vernacular" education for the "masses" was an educational priority of the colonial administration.

Far from education in British India being entirely in English, it was rather overwhelmingly dominated by indigenous languages. The policy of instituting local language education for the lower socioeconomic classes is evident from the very beginning of British colonial rule in Asia. The decision implementing the Macaulay policy in India in 1835 noted that it was not to have any affect on "vernacular education" for the "mass of the people," as is often wrongly thought (C.H. Cameron, 1853; *Indian Statutory Commission*, 1930, Part VI). In the 1850s, decisions were taken by the colonial administration of India to begin the expansion of indigenous language education. These resolutions were strengthened by the educational commission of the early 1880s, which, as noted above, staunchly supported "instruction of the masses through the vernacular" (J. Russell, 1887: 194). Such was the level of acceptance of this policy that by World War I, a commentator was able to write: "The question of the medium of instruction has never been a troublesome one, primary education being almost always synonymous with vernacular education even in the primary standards attached to the secondary schools" (Montgomery, 1919: 74).

Throughout the history of British rule in India, "vernacular education" constituted the foundation of all education. Virtually all primary education for children from age 5 to 11 was given in local languages. At the level of middle schools, the division between "Anglo-vernacular" (local language based but including English as a subject) and English-medium schools commenced (Montgomery, 1919).

The growing emphasis placed upon "vernacular education" in the 1870s is evident in the five-fold growth of the number of primary "vernacular schools," from 16,473 to 82,916 (J. Russell, 1887). The rate of growth dramatically declined over the next three decades, but the number of vernacular schools continued to dwarf that of English schools. Exact figures on English schools are not available, but it is interesting to consider the number of schools operated by England's Church Missionary Society in India. At the turn of the twentieth century, that body operated 21 High Schools and Colleges in English, 89 "Anglo-vernacular Schools," and 1137 "vernacular schools" (Maconachie, 1905).

"Vernacular education" in other imperial outposts in the nineteenth century

The situation was similar in the other major British colonial Asian possessions established during the nineteenth century, although, as will be shown in Chapter 5, their educational policies developed independently. In the case of Ceylon, local language schools had already been established under its former Dutch colonial rulers (Cull, 1901). When Great Britain inherited the colony, these were left in place, and, with time, greatly extended. By the last decades of the nineteenth century, the policy of drawing a clear line between local language education for the majority and English education for the few was already in place.

The same process was very much in evidence in British Malaya (cf. Pennycook, 1994). Upon becoming a Crown Colony, the Straits Settlements appointed a Select Committee of the Legislative Council in 1870, which recommended "a large extension of Vernacular Schools, by which it means, not such schools as are now established, where Malay children are taught a few verses of the Koran, but schools where children will be educated in their mother tongue" (Eleum, 1905: 139). Upon the appointment in 1872 of an Inspector of Schools, he "devoted his energies chiefly at first to establishing and bringing into order a system of vernacular education in Malay. The policy of the Government from then up to the present time has, roughly stated, been to afford under direct Government control a free education to Malays in their own language, while the provision of English education is left chiefly to the enterprise of various educational committees and missionary and religious bodies, Government assisting by the payment of grants-in aid . . ." (p. 140). In the Federated Malay States, English and vernacular schools were established as early as the 1880s in the main towns of Perak and Selangor (Federal Education Office, Federated Malay States, 1905: 5).

Architects of Language Policy for the British Empire: Cromer and Lugard

The Macaulay Doctrine, however, was far from representing the last word on British colonial language policy, as some have stated or implied. Indeed, it was but the beginning of a long and tortuous road that was to lead Great Britain to a suspicion of the uncontrolled spread of English. And, contrary to what is generally believed today, Macaulay was a minor figure in the evolution of policy, ranking in importance behind such figures as Lord Cromer, Lord Lugard, and Sir Valentine Chirol (the last of whom will be discussed in Chapter 4).

It is simply wrong to assume that Macaulay's philosophy of converting the indigenous people to imbibe English taste, opinions, and intellect was shared by other imperial administrators in British dependencies. Not only did Macaulay's standpoint not become the policy throughout the empire, but most prominent colonial officials actually came to opposite conclusions.

Lord Cromer and the Evolution of British Policy in Egypt

When Egypt came under British control in 1883, a much greater measure of power fell to Lord Cromer, its longtime governor, than Macaulay – a minor official most of his career – had ever wielded. Indeed, Cromer emerged as not only the most influential figure in the history of British Egypt, but also a prominent and much-cited figure throughout the British empire. Cromer's rule was complicated by the long-standing French interest and influence in the area. The British had to consider the French in the establishment of policy in this formerly French colony. Thus, as a later imperial official, Lord Lloyd, noted, "The general policy of His Majesty's Government precluded any attempt to establish the influence of British culture" (1933: 159). Circumscribed by these political constraints in addition to those of a budgetary nature, Cromer concentrated educational efforts to his goal of promoting the employment of Egyptians within the civil service.

Doing so certainly required a measure of English education, as discussed above. Yet Cromer believed that particular advantages to British rule would accrue from that circumstance. He did not concur with Macaulay that pro-British imperial sentiments necessarily followed the spread of English within the British empire. Instead, he criticized "the superficial, and in my opinion, generally erroneous view, that the study of French or English necessarily connotes the creation of French or English political proclivities" (Irving, 1905: 96). There was, in his experience, no such easy relation between language and ideology.

Cromer perceived more potential problems than benefits in the spread of English, and he steered a course designed to introduce English to as few Egyptians as possible. For the vast majority of the population, local (Arabic) language education alone was possible. It consisted of the traditional village schools attached to mosques, called *Kuttabs*, which were left in place by the British, although in 1897 a uniform curriculum was given, consisting of rudimentary "vernacular" literacy alongside religious (Muslim) training. Among the significant provisions of the curriculum mentioned by

Cromer was that "The teaching of any foreign language was rigorously excluded" (1909: 533). Far inferior to the primary schools also offering a four-year course, the "vernacular schools," according to the colonial administration, were "designed merely to equip the pupil with sufficient knowledge to take care of his own interests in his own station of life" (quoted in Lloyd, 1933: 14). There were, in addition, "higher elementary schools," also entirely "vernacular," and stressing mainly manual training. Only one in every 292 students proceeded to this higher course (p. 14).

If Cromer's goal, as he says, was thus to confine any knowledge of English to those for whom he viewed it as strictly necessary, available statistical evidence suggests he succeeded. The first comprehensive statistics on education collected in 1918 show that there were 134 primary schools (in which English was taught) versus 4265 "vernacular elementary schools." Of primary school aged children, fully 92.5% attended the "vernacular schools." However, no more than one in five Egyptian children attended school at all. As of the 1907 census, 96% of the people were returned as illiterate (Montgomery, 1919: 93).

Sir Frederick Lugard, British Nigeria, and the origins of indirect rule

Cromer's prominence paled in comparison to another British colonial administrator in Africa, Sir Frederick (later Lord) Lugard. Born in India, he spent his entire career in the colonial service. After decades devoted to securing Britain's military hold over Africa, Lugard became High Commissioner in Northern Nigeria from 1900 to 1907, his first high-ranking civilian post. Lugard already distinguished himself at this stage of his career by developing the colonial governmental policy that would provide the model for the twentieth century British colonial administration, known as "indirect rule." Lugard's policy of *indirect rule*, as noted above, involved the incorporation of the existing indigenous power structures in British rule in colonies such as Nigeria in order to make imperial rule more feasible in tropical areas – where large importations of English officials was deemed out of the question – as well as to make it more economical elsewhere. Lugard's idea was to take advantage of the established social structure within the community and the social prestige of the local elite among their people. Administering the colony through members of the indigenous power structure became a significant part of the British colonial administration throughout Africa (Lugard, 1923) and the rest of the empire. The impact of the policy of *indirect rule* on language policy would be significant. It meant that the efficiency of the British rule in the colonies was in large part dependent upon the close collab-oration and mutual communication with the colonial population, both in social and linguistic terms.

After establishing the basis of British rule in Nigeria, Lugard was appointed governor of Hong Kong, a post he held through 1913. It was during these years that educational policy first came to his attention, for reasons to be discussed in the next chapter. Lugard formed the view that proper educational policy had to avoid any "concentration on higher education to the neglect of the schools which will train for the University" and in particular the danger of the "sole use of English as the medium of instruction" in education (Lugard, 1911: 241). When he returned to Nigeria in 1913 to take the post of governor of the newly united colony, he formulated a new educational policy for Nigeria, which he recorded in his influential book, *Dual Mandate*.

Assumptions of cultural superiority as a justification for local language education

Racist assumptions, as well as practical considerations, underlay Lugard's outlook. It is sometimes tacitly assumed that the belief in the superior culture of the colonizing nation leads automatically to a desire to want to impose its language, together with its culture, on the subju-gated nation, as is alleged to be the case with Macaulay. Those who take that view have also concluded that the progression from Macaulay to the later policy initiatives can be characterized as the movement toward a language policy actuated by more enlightened views (Phillipson, 1992). Such a view, however, seems to ignore the racist views that actuated "vernacular education" policies, including the *fear* of the spread of British culture. As Mazrui and Mazrui (1998) have concluded, "The English . . . were less preoccupied [than the French] with the imperative of spreading their language as such. On the contrary there were sometimes arrogantly possessive about it, particularly in their colonies" (p. 21).

The thinking of Lugard, the major architect of language policy in British Africa, is especially revealing in this respect. He was at pains to explain how British policy differed from that of most other colonial powers, par-ticularly the French.[3] He quoted "a high official" in the French colonial administration as telling him that "We bring French culture to the Africans and they must learn French, and will become Frenchmen. We believe in French Evolution, and not in the Evolution of the African" (Lugard, 1933: 6). Lugard reported that a Governor-General declared that the mission of French education in the colonies was to impart a "French soul" (p. 6). Of course, such "privileges of complete assimilation are necessarily confined to a few. For the bulk of the population the ideal is universal instruction in the language of the European Suzerein, which must be taught in every village to the exclusion of the vernacular" (p. 6).

It is significant not only that Lugard rejected such notions, but also his reasons for doing so. He criticized the French policy not only on practical grounds. His objection also stemmed from the propensity of such a policy to lead to "complete social equality"; he declared flatly, "where this policy is carried out to the fullest extent, miscegenation may not only be tolerated, but encouraged" (Lugard, 1933: 6). Similarly, what is often lost in the consideration of the debate between the "Orientalists" and the "Anglicists" under Macaulay's leadership is that one of the pillars of the "Orientalist" case consisted in the belief that Indians were incapable of learning English well, a charge that Macaulay refuted. In fact, Macaulay criticized the "Orientalists" in the British administration for their racist assumption of intellectual inferiority of non-Europeans, a prejudice he claimed not to share (C.H. Cameron, 1853). In that sense, Lugard constituted something of a "neo-Orientalist" in his outlook, based not in philanthropy but Realpolitik.

Such thinking became rather commonplace in the British colonial empire. For example, in a document charting the direction for educational language policy for all of British southern Africa, a colonial educational official argued that English and the materials used to teach it were *inherently* out of the reach of an African child and that, therefore, the teaching of English had no value (Sargant, 1908).

The same theme emerges in the critique by a founder of modern Pan Africanism, W.E.B. Du Bois, of Thomas Jesse Jones, the main author of an American philanthropic society's report condemning "literary education" for Africans (see Chapter 5):

> It is . . . absolutely clear that [Jones] means that Africans should not be trained as white Europeans are trained; that on the contrary – and this is the meat of Jones' thesis – Africans should be trained to be content with their present condition, to be submissive, peaceful, and industrious; and work in such ways and under such circumstances that their labor will be most profitable for the countries that are exploiting Africa. (quoted in Schilling, 1972: 376)

Thus, as Mazrui and Mazrui (1998) conclude, "Sometimes for purely racist reasons . . . Germanic Europeans insisted on the greater use of indigenous languages in education and a greater recognition of African cultures" (p. 14).

Lugard reflected all of these attitudes. He noted that indirect rule was designed to ensure that "instead of seeking a fancied equality with the white man by participation in debates in the Legislative Council, [the African] will prefer to exert a genuine influence in his own Native Councils and Native Courts, and in the development of his own people" (Lugard, 1933: 7). Nothing is more illustrative of this point than the opposition to purely "literary" education, which formed the basis of Lugard's thinking and his policy in Africa. Just as Du Bois pointed out, that type of education was something men of Lugard's stamp believed should be reserved for Europeans alone.

Lugard's Vision of Education for the Colonies

Thus, for both practical *and* ideological reasons, Lugard charted recommendations for educational policy that in effect sought to prevent the vast majority of Africans from learning English. Like Cromer, Lugard harbored deep-seated distrust of the ramifications of English spread in colonial Africa. Lugard's notion of education in Africa centered on the importance of circumventing the creation of a class of educated but "unemployable" English-educated youths, who lacked "self-control, discipline," and respect for British authority and exhibited "contempt for manual work" (Lugard, 1923: 428). After all, there were only so many posts in the British administration to go around. English education for more than the civil service could absorb would only raise expectations of lucrative employment that could not be met. Lugard saw dire political ramifications (to be discussed in Chapter 4) if such a trend were allowed to exist. Lugard wrote, "Education has brought to such men only discontent, suspicion of others, and bitterness, which masquerades as racial patriotism, and the vindication of rights unjustly withheld" (Lugard, 1923: 429). In this, he claimed, "They have lost touch with their own people" (p. 429). Lugard attributed such a result to a failure on the part of the colonial governments to supervise education. In his view, it could best be remedied by greater government control over education.

To avoid what he saw as the problems of uncontrolled education, Lugard proposed a dual system of schools in Africa: "literary" schools modeled after the public schools in England that would produce a well-disciplined and qualified clerical service for government and commercial purposes; and the "village" (rural) schools that would produce the industrial class. In the former, a minority would be trained, in the latter the great majority. Lugard's notion of this structure of education in African dependencies was linked to indirect rule. The pupil from the "literary" school would share governmental and municipal responsibilities in the colony (Lugard, 1923).

A completely different education was to be offered to the majority. Lugard emphasized that rural education was crucial, but that it must not consist of a "mere kindergarten, where a half-educated mission-school boy teaches pidgin English to children in a classroom" (Lugard, 1933: 9). The real point was to train workers who would remain in their allotted sphere of manual labor; as a matter of course, language would be confined to the "vernacular" (p. 9).

Lugard's system of education also specified the role and the scope of the spread of the English language. In the "literary" schools, English was to be the medium of instruction in the upper standards; local languages constituted the mediums of instruction in lower standards where "promising" pupils from villages were taught as teachers for village schools or clerks for local courts. In the "village" school that trained the craftsmen and agriculturists, the local language was to be the medium of instruction, although colloquial English might be introduced (1923: 444–5). The "village" school "would not be intended to qualify a boy for Government employment, or to develop into literary schools" (p. 445). In the higher standards in the "village" school available to a small proportion of the rural population, English or a local lingua franca (Arabic, Swahili, or Hausa) was to be used. Lugard suggested that in the dependencies where languages such as Hausa or Swahili were widely used they should be promoted as lingua francas; elsewhere the usage of English for intercommunication should be encouraged (p. 454).

The advocacy of this policy in Lugard's *Dual Mandate*, which an official of the British African service noted "became almost a textbook for British administrators in Africa" (Mason, 1959: 38), ensured its acceptance throughout Africa. Chapter 5 will show that Lugard himself would become the key figure in the creation of an empire-wide commission on educational matters.

One of the weaknesses underlying the theory of linguistic imperialism (Phillipson, 1992) is its facile assumptions about the connection of the attitude of imperialist nations and the type of language policy that necessarily follows from that. In particular, it is tacitly assumed that the belief in the superior culture of the "center" leads of itself to a desire to want to impose its language, together with its culture, on the subjugated nation. An imperialism in which economic interests are paramount, however, need not adhere to such strictures. The wish to spread the language and culture need not follow from the quest to exploit. Rather, imperial agents might be animated by an entirely different set of beliefs about the place of culture and language within empire. As the case of Lugard shows, for many British colonial administrators, there was often a convenient harmonizing of the ideological and the practical. This characteristic would show itself above all when the British faced what they perceived to be a growing threat to the existence of their empire at the beginning of the twentieth century.

Notes

1. In addition to "English Schools" and "Vernacular Schools", there were a very small number of "Anglo-Vernacular Schools" or bilingual establishments, in which the local language gave way to English in the upper standards (CO, Ceylon, 1892).
2. The context seems to imply that Phillipson (1992) is referring to India, though the reference to the policy of "indirect rule" is therefore misplaced.
3. It will be shown in the discussion of the League of Nations Mandate Commission in Chapter 5 that Phillipson's assertion that French and British policies were identical finds little support in their mutual dealings as colonial powers.

Chapter 4

The Contested Terrain of Colonial Language Policy

Agency in Language Policy

In examining the thinking of colonial administrators like Macaulay, Cromer and Lugard in Chapter 3, this treatment has so far considered only half of the story. To understand how a significant shift in British goals and objectives – already evident in the policies advocated by Lord Lugard – came about, it is first necessary to consider in whom language policy and planning agency inheres.

Cooper (1989: 45) has defined language planning as "deliberate efforts to influence the behavior *of others* with respect to the acquisition, structure, or functional allocation of their language codes" (emphasis added). In accordance with this definition, much of the literature in language policy and planning has concentrated on the formulation of policies by authorities (governments, commissions, and the like) and their imposition on speech communities (cf. Wiley, 1996; Ricento & Hornberger, 1996). In this top-down model of language policy, agency is invested in various representations of institutionalized power. In contrast, the speech communities whose language use is in question figure as the *others* to be influenced, the passive recipients of policy. While the authorities constitute the *planners*, the speech community using the language (or prevented from acquiring it) occupy the position of the *planned*.

In employing such an approach, language policy has tended to be conceived as a unidirectional process. The focus has been placed on "language policies as instruments of social control" (Wiley, 1996: 111) and those aimed at the achievement of ideological objectives. The former tend to be tied to theories of state power and hegemony (cf. Wiley, 1996). The latter are most prominently represented by the theory of linguistic imperialism as a means of the transmission of language and culture (Phillipson, 1992), discussed in Chapter 2. Both rely on conceptions of a largely one-sided relationship characterized by imposition and domination. For example, the theory of linguistic imperialism takes for granted that the colonizing nation possesses the power to impose its will on a "subject" population. In this model the state, or imperialism, imposes in accordance with its interests. It is tacitly overlooked that the oppressed might themselves determine or influence the bounds of policy.

Such a conceptualization of the historical process of policy-making does not actually follow from the definition Cooper employs.[1] For institutional planners are not the only social agents with a linguistic agenda. Speech communities are not the passive recipients of language policy that they are often implicitly assumed to be. They should not be conceived as victims on whom language policy-making authorities codify prefabricated plans. Rather, they are active shapers of the language policy environment who at the least codetermine the context and at the most seize the initiative from the institutional planners, thereby forcing the latter into a reactive mode. There is room for the recognition of bottom-up language planning as well (cf. Hornberger, 1997), a mutual shaping of the language policy context. This corresponds to a larger trend noted by Hornberger (1997: 11): "In sociolinguistics more generally, and indeed the social sciences as a whole, scholarly attention has steadily shifted toward the individual and the local community as active agents in dialogue and interaction with their social environment, and away from a governmental, institutional, or societal level focus."

Such a reconceptualization of language policy as a two-sided process recognizes it as contested terrain in which policy is made not unilaterally but as the result of the interplay of conflicting historical wills. The resultant language policy might be just as much what speech communities impose on authorities as the obverse. This conception reexamines the question of what constitutes language policy and planning and who figures as the language planner or policymaker.

The absence of such a critical perspective on received notions leads to a conception of language policy and planning that when applied to the question of the global spread of English becomes charged with value-laden ideological implications. Lost in the discussion of linguistic imperialism, for example, is how this seemingly objective analytical tool asserts a worldview in which the Western, via the imperial, has been the dominant factor in the development of World English. It conceives Western agency alone. This potentially Eurocentric construction of history makes imperialism the central process in shaping world history. If *English spread*, it was because Westerners (the British in the first place) *spread* it. If non-Westerners played a role, they did so as the pawns of

Western policy.[2] The world language remains the sole product of Western historical action and will.

In this narrative, the "colonized peoples" barely appear at all, except insofar as they are oppressed by the irresistible forces of imperialism. Even after they free themselves (or are freed?), they remain subject to ideological control through "hegemony," a nebulous force by which the former "masters" continue to impose their will on their former "subjects." Such an account bestows agency exclusively, or nearly exclusively, on those exercising imperial (or neocolonial) power (cf. Davies, 1996b). At most, while the colonizers act, the "colonized" react. Even in the present age this worldview chooses to emphasize the "colonial in the postcolonial."

On the other hand, it almost entirely ignores the *postcolonial in the colonial* – that is, the process by which the "colonized peoples" have shaped the world in which we live, including their own independence, in profoundly significant ways. This paradigm shifts the focus from an oppression mode to one of the active historical self-determination of peoples. At the same time, it provides empirical evidence that the "richness and potential" inherent in "grassroots initiatives" in language planning to which Hornberger's (1997: 11) work calls attention and that has increasingly been studied in the contemporary world can also be found at work at an earlier period, indeed, during the height of modern colonialism. This historical agency of the subjects of European imperialism, so crucial in the development of World English, has been lost by the emphasis placed on top-down models of language policy that exclude the counternarrative of indigenous self-determination.

A close examination of the history of British language policy, with Eurocentric assumptions of agency removed, reveals a quite different picture than that painted by the conception of linguistic imperialism: one in which its major thrust was the result of the British *reacting* to the historical actions of Africans and Asians. Imperial language policy was not unidirectional, but had to respond to the active agency of the colonized, who constantly forced adjustments from the colonial administrations. Indeed, the central thrust of British colonial language policy in Africa and Asia – what I term the *containment policy* – was not such an ideologically-driven imposition of imperial will, but a makeshift response to the co-opting of English as part of the anticolonial struggle. This fact has been ignored or underplayed by proponents of the theory of linguistic imperialism. And yet it is a crucial point in the understanding of World English, since it shows that it is just as much the result of the struggle against imperialism as of imperialism itself. This has profound implications for the conceptualization of World English, as will be discussed in Chapter 9.

Opposition to British Rule and its Effect on the Development of Educational Language Policy

The British colonial authorities throughout Asia and Africa struggled during the nineteenth and twentieth centuries to design an educational language policy that would meet the demands of empire, both maintaining British rule and fulfilling the economic purpose of the colonies. They discovered that this required a flexible approach, rather than an ideologically-driven policy. First and foremost imperial administrators adopted an attitude of practical caution. What concerned them most was avoiding any disruption to their colonial empire.

Accomplishing such a goal would prove no easy matter. The British found themselves in possession of an empire increasingly under siege. By the turn of the twentieth century, the anticolonial movements in both Egypt and India had become so prominent and so effective that they began to occupy the attention of the British authorities to an ever-increasing extent. Large-scale national movements emerged in each nation, well-organized, popularly-based and increasingly taking the offensive. As British rule rested on an ever more tenuous basis, the British colonial authorities searched for ways and means to quell the opposition. Educational language policy entered their purview. In the minds of colonial administrators, language policy and the maintenance of empire became inextricably linked.

Asians and Africans under British rule deliberately took advantage of the imperial role of English – detailed in the previous chapter – to undertake a language policy of their own. They transformed English from a means of exploitation into a means of resistance. Through *appropriating* the language, they empowered themselves to resist colonialism at the most essential level. In so doing, they used the arena of language policy to begin to erode the basis of British power.

Language thereby played a role in the anticolonial struggle that British colonial officials had never envisioned. It became integrally connected to resistance. English in both Asia and Africa began to develop into the common language of the anticolonial struggle, in effect turning the guns of colonial rule against it (Mazrui, 1975). The appropriation of English transformed it into what Frantz Fanon (1967) called an "instrument of liberation." Through learning the language of the colonizer, Africans and Asians empowered themselves to oppose the aims of empire, which were centered on the existence of a docile work force ripe for economic exploitation. More than individual acts of resistance, in total this anticolonial language policy constituted a concerted drive for the societal acquisition of English.

In seizing the initiative in the language planning arena, Asians and Africans in British-occupied territory forced a reaction on the part of the British. The British found themselves constrained to implement a language policy designed to safeguard their political and economic agenda. This position amounted to a rearguard action to prevent nascent liberation movements from seizing the language as a powerful weapon in the anti-colonial struggle. It reflected not a British initiative at all but the result of British cognizance of the appropriation of English shaping the construction of language policy in the empire. The essence of British imperial language policy embodied in the containment policy that developed is found in its reactive nature.

Imperial Political Economy and Industrial Education: Labor Reserves for the Mines of Southern Africa

The battleground over language that was to help shape the development of World English was inextricably tied to the economic and class structure of the British empire. A principal goal of colonial administration was to promote the socioeconomic stratification of the population, in particular the confining of the vast majority of Africans and Asians to the place designated to them in the world economy by colonialism. Educational language policy was directed toward this end.[3]

The history of British policy in southern Africa demonstrates how language policy served the economic ends of empire. British colonization of Africa commenced with the cession of the Cape Colony on the southern tip of Africa from Holland to Britain in 1803. From there, British control extended over nearly the whole of Southern Africa over the next century. By that time, colonial production was centered on the South African mines that provided the economic mainstay of British Southern Africa and determined colonial policy throughout the region. The circumstances of the other colonies can only be fully understood within the context of their relation to the South African economy dominated by the labor-intensive extractive industries (Crush *et al.*, 1991).

The mining industry concentrated around Johannesburg necessarily needed not only the European managers to run it but more importantly those who would perform the manual labor. The latter task fell to Africans from all over southern Africa. The principal means of recruiting workers for the mines was to limit the already existing economic support of the local population by taking away the land. The various southern African peoples were then crowded onto what were called by the colonial administrators "native reserves," conditions which in no way allowed of even the most meager subsistence (Buell, 1928; Crush *et al.*, 1991; Harries, 1994). Since the peoples inhabiting these lands were forced to search for work to support themselves and pay the taxes levied by the colonial administration, these territories constituted in reality "labor reserves," and they were administered accordingly. The colonial government of one of these, Basutoland, pointedly declared that "the vast majority . . . will remain laborers on the soil or in the lower ranks of industry" (Sloley, 1905: 132).

For all but administrative purposes, all of colonial Southern Africa was a part of the larger South African context. In 1921, it was estimated for Basutoland, for example, that 40% of the adult male population and at least 10% of the adult female population were away at "labor centers" in South Africa (Buell, 1928: 170). A report by the International Labor Office (1936: 484) in 1935 found the proportion for the same colony to be above 50%.[4] Since, however, these migrant laborers returned home periodically, the proportion of the total population that migrated to South Africa annually was in reality much higher. Given this de facto integration into the South African economy, the people of Southern Africa, wherever they lived, found themselves forced to reside in the multilingual environment constituted by South Africa. This situation did not change when South Africa became an independent country in 1913, as the statistics cited above demonstrate.

These economic concerns guided the educational philosophy of the colonial administrators of Southern Africa. As the goal of the imperial functionaries was to secure labor for South Africa's industry, an effort was made to keep education within highly restricted bounds. It was felt that education interfered with the goal of maintaining a subordinate class of workers. As one expressed the general feeling, "book learning . . . lowered [Africans'] usefulness for work," and made them "uppish" and "conceited" – by which was meant that they became "disinclined" to work for the European (Clarke, 1905: 333; see also on this point, Casartelli, 1905; Muir, 1901; R. Russell, 1901; Sargant, 1908; Sloley, 1905; Stewart, 1905;). There was a fear of educated Africans among colonial employers, as colonial officials unanimously reported. The most prominent figure in the history of British imperialism in southern Africa, Cecil Rhodes, even saw fit to weigh in on the importance of this phenomenon. Rhodes declared in 1892, when Premier of the Cape Colony:

> I have, in my tours through the Transkeian districts, found some excellent institutions, where natives are being taught Latin and Greek. These schools are turning out native parsons by the score; but the thing is, in my opinion, being overdone. I do not hesitate to

say that native parsons are becoming more plentiful than congre-
gations. Thus a dangerous class is being evolved. The native
preachers are excellent so long as their number is limited, but the
supply is out of all proportion to the demand. These preachers and
other native Latin and Greek scholars, after the education they have
received, feel it undignified to return to manual labor, consequently
the country is becoming gradually infested with unemployed men,
who will in the end develop into agitators of the most pernicious
type. (quoted in Casartelli, 1905: 290)

Another colonial administrator succinctly summed up the widespread
conviction: the education of all Africans in South Africa "would mean
ruin to South Africa" (quoted in Muir, 1905: 85).

In this context, the formation of educational policy had above all to
address the fear that education would unfit the populations of the
reserves for manual labor. As a missionary in South Africa put it, education was above all charged with combating "the erroneous idea that
manual work is servile toil, and mental work is supposed to elevate a
man to a higher class" (Stewart, 1905: 338). According to this missionary,
"This is the old native idea of social rank" (p. 338). If so, it did not differ
from the idea of social rank of the colonial government, which in 1889
had decreed that the education of European colonists must "fit them to
maintain their unquestioned superiority and supremacy in this land"
(quoted in Muir, 1901: 71). On the other hand, wrote the Education
Adviser to the High Commissioner of South Africa, education for the
people of Basutoland was intended to make them "far more useful to
their white employers than they have ever been before" (Sargant, 1908:
30). Education, then, had to be different for the European settler and the
African worker. The education of each was, in the language of the colonial authorities, to suit each for his or her "environment."

The concern not to alter the conditions of the African worker motivated educational philosophy in South Africa. If the purpose of education
for the peoples of Southern Africa was to limit their chances of leaving
their "environment" – their role as manual laborers – then it followed
that they should "receive and profit by [the education] of the hands
rather than that of the mind" (quoted in Casartelli, 1905: 289). The education suited to this purpose was elementary industrial education, taken
in its broadest sense as education designed for the afterlife of a manual
worker in either industry or agriculture (Casartelli 1905; Muir, 1901;
Sargant, 1908; Sloley, 1905; Stewart, 1905). According to the inspector of
education for southern African colonies, industrial training in the primary

schools established for Africans would "predispose" the young to "serious manual activities, and to see nothing in an industrial livelihood incompatible with the worthy exercise of all of his faculties" (Sargant, 1908: 23–4).

In fact, this movement toward industrial education extended back as far as the mid-nineteenth century in South Africa. The governor of the Cape Colony, the early center of British South Africa, expressed his desire to avoid "bookish" education and confine Africans to practical training (in Muir, 1901: 29). An 1879 commission in that colony recommended that "manual training" should form an "essential part" of the education of Africans (in Muir 1901: 86). In the educational code of Southern Rhodesia of the year 1899, it was specified of the four-hour period of instruction, at least two of those hours "shall be devoted to *industrial training*" (Hammond, 1905: 172). The Resident Commissioner of colonial Basutoland weighed in the 1890s with his opinion that the people of Basutoland were to be manual laborers in industry or agriculture, in which "spheres they are happy, contented, and useful, and for them their best friends can desire nothing better than the most elementary education, sound moral training and encouragement in the habits of steady industry" (Sloley, 1905: 132). Given that most Sotho men and women would leave Basutoland in the course of their lives in the search for work, industrial education would provide a powerful means of ensuring that they had no alternative but to head for the mines of South Africa.

Given the prevalent attitude toward education among colonial authorities, it is not surprising that educational officials should admit, "the bulk of the young people are growing up without education as we understand it" (CO, Basutoland, 1905: 7). Even the largely industrial education mixed in with mother language literacy reached only a small proportion of children. Relatively few children attended school. The statistics kept as to the number of children in school suggest that at the turn of the century the number of children between 6 and 15 years of age attending school may have been as few as one in ten (CO, Basutoland, 1905). This number increased dramatically over the succeeding decades, reaching two in three by the mid-1930s, which Basutoland administrators called "a very remarkable phenomenon for Africa" (CO, Basutoland, 1936: 16). The emphasis of the education, however, had not changed.

Education for the Agricultural Economy of British Asia

Precisely the same set of concerns that ruled the mining-driven economy of southern Africa guided the establishment of education for the agricultural populations of British Asia. Throughout the British Asian possessions, agriculture constituted the dominant factor in the economy, engaging the majority of the population during the colonial period. In Ceylon, for example, the proportion was 88% (Ormsby Gore, 1928; Cull, 1901). Production for this segment of the population rested on the same labor-intensive basis as the mining economy of Southern Africa. Alongside the rural-based production, there was significant urban development in a few colonies, such as the Straits Settlements, India, and Ceylon (C.R. De Silva, 1987). In parts of British Asia, then, economic development depended upon a bifurcated labor force. Nevertheless, the British conceived their primary mission as keeping the rural population "on the land," in both those colonies that were exclusively agricultural, such as the Unfederated Malay States, and those in which some urbanization had taken place by the early twentieth century. This socio-economic structure of British Asia served as the fundamental basis for the development and implementation of educational policy in that portion of the British empire.

One principal goal dominated the design of education in British Asia: maintaining the agricultural basis of production. This economic concern was reflected in the design of education for the future generation of laborers. As an educational commission for India put it in 1882: "[P]rimary education [should] be regarded as the instruction of the masses through the vernacular in such subjects as will best fit them for their position in life, and be not necessarily regarded as a portion of instruction leading up to the university" (J. Russell, 1887: 200). Similarly, elementary education for rural children in Ceylon was intended to keep the child in his proper "environment" (Ormsby Gore, 1928: 99). A Brunei colonial administrator expressed the common sentiment: "Nothing is taught which will tend to drive Malays from their agricultural pursuits" (CO, Brunei, 1929: 22).

In Ceylon, a turn of the twentieth century colonial education commission for Ceylon asserted that general education, while appropriate in a European country, would in rural Ceylon "unfit the population for a life of labour . . . if it is imparted on unsuitable lines and by unsuitable methods" (Ceylon, Commission on Elementary Education, 1906: 8). More specifically, the commission warned that to prepare the children of Ceylon for the occupation of a clerk in rural schools would be "bad for the community" (p. 8).

The economic basis of education was reflected in the curriculum, which a Federated Malay States official called "very elementary, but . . . sufficient for the ordinary requirements of Malay boys, who will become bullock-waggon drivers, padi-growers, fishermen, etc. . . ." (Federal

Education Office, Federated Malay States, 1905: 9). Rural education aimed "to inculcate the dignity of manual labour" (CO, Straits Settlements, 1921: 49) and to combat "the erroneous idea that it is better and more dignified to do clerical than manual work, that generally obtains with native boys" (Federal Education Office, Federated Malay States, 1905: 17). As time passed, the purpose became more specific: to boost "the raayat's agricultural and industrial productivity" (CO, Unfederated Malay States, Kedah, 1937: 40), and so the well-being of the colony that was always viewed as paramount – and synonymous with the continuation of British imperial rule.

Education for manual labor and language policy

The socioeconomic purposes assigned to education dictated educational language policy. If, as shown in Chapter 3, the colonial service and commercial enterprise required officials and clerks well-versed in English, the demands of industry and agriculture for a manual laboring force did not. The economic language of South Africa – particularly of the mines to which most migrants from other parts of Southern Africa headed – was not English, but a variety of Zulu "mixed with a little Dutch and English" in which the African miners communicated with one another and with their European employers (Johnston, 1904). The plantation in British Asia had no more need for English-speaking workers. All the less did the scattered agriculturalists need it. The colonial government of the Unfederated Malay State of Kelantan summed up the point succinctly: "The majority of the people will remain workers on the land and will not therefore require a knowledge of the English language" (CO, Unfederated Malay States, Kelantan, 1932: 30–1). As such, as a Federated Malay States official put it, "The aim of [industrial education] is to give a general education to those boys who have no need for an education in English, and who will find employment either in agriculture or in appointments in which a knowledge of the vernacular is all that is required . . ." (CO, Federated Malay States, 1934: 52).

English education not only served entirely different ends (Lugard, 1923; Schilling, 1972) but entailed a vastly different cost to the colonial administration. Education in English meant that the student would go beyond the rudiments of education, the second or third standard. From the imperial standpoint, such an education constituted so much money and effort wasted on a class that would never be allowed to make use of it.

There was, however, something beyond these purely practical considerations at work. It was not simply the case that manual workers in mining and agriculture did not need to know English, as opposed to their clerical and commercial fellow-countrymen. British policymakers believed that Africans and Asians looked upon English education primarily as a means to relatively well-paying government employment. This ubiquitous notion had its basis in fact. In British colonies, knowledge of English brought with it the possibility of working in the colonial administration or other clerical employment; it constituted a means of obtaining more lucrative work not limited to manual labor. Throughout much of the British empire, knowledge of English constituted "practically the only avenue to remunerative employment of any kind" (Cull, 1901). The Director of Public Instruction in Ceylon noted in 1899, "No Sinhalese lad can now do anything for himself out the agricultural walk of life without some knowledge of English" (quoted in Cull, p. 800). In the Straits Settlements, it was reported that "English education . . . is necessary if [a student] is to aspire to well-paid business or Government" (CO, Straits Settlements, 1922: 49).

It is not surprising, therefore, that a strong demand for English existed and that Asians and Africans knew the economic value of learning the language. In his report for 1866, an inspector of the Government Schools and a headmaster at the Central School in Hong Kong linked the success of the Central School in which English was taught with the condition of "English being convertible into dollars" (quoted in Irving, 1905: 118); more regular attendance at the schools where English was taught revealed that "the education given is a special one having a distinct money value" (quoted in Irving, 1905: 118).

English educated youth, according to the colonial administrators, recognized the economic value of the knowledge of English and expected other means of employment than manual labor.[5] British officials found to their dismay that, in the words of an American missionary report of 1901, there existed "the tendency among all classes to consider any kind of manual labor as beneath the man who has received an education equal to matriculation for college. Those who pass beyond this point feel themselves farther and farther removed from every calling in life except the so-called learned professions or a position under the Government of India" ("Report of the Deputation sent by the American Board of Commissioners for Foreign Missions to India and Ceylon in 1901," 1905: 328).

The Acquisition of English and the Anticolonial Struggle: The Transformation of English into a "Language of Liberation"

The use of education and language policy to create and maintain a socioeconomic structure of the colonies conducive to imperial exploitation contextualizes the struggle of peoples throughout Africa and Asia to resist colonial rule through the attempt to obtain access to non-industrial education and the language of the colonizer. Read in this context, the desire for English is not some form of Western ideological hegemony playing itself out in the actions of the colonial oppressed of Africa and Asia. Rather, it was a rational response and a conscious strategy to resist colonial rule built on the exploitation of labor.

Africans and Asians under British rule were acting as anything other than passive recipients of colonial language policy. They contested colonial rule and the subordinate place it designated for them. Their contestation of the role imperialism assigned to them not only represented a potent challenge to European colonial hegemony but also actively shaped the language policy environment. This struggle already embedded the postcolonial in the colonial, not only politically and economically but linguistically. English would emerge from the process of its spread as no longer merely or essentially the language of colonialism: it was just as much the transformed language of the anticolonial struggle (cf. Canagarajah, 2000).

The near universality of the complaints of British colonial administrators of the results of English education shows how widespread resistance to colonialism was from its inception, and how central a role language played within it. Africans and Asians were challenging the system of colonialism at its weakest point: its dependence on their labor servitude. Colonial authorities consistently report that many Africans and Asians refused to be converted into manual laborers serving purely imperial economic interests. Just as a slave refusing to work undermines the system of slavery, so did this resistance to prescribed socioeconomic roles threaten the foundations of colonial rule. The more it broke out of the narrow circles within which the British attempted to confine it, the more revolutionary a threat it posed to their empire. There was, as the British correctly perceived, an integral connection between the demand for and spread of English and the emergent liberation movements in Africa and Asia. However much the British attempted to frame the desire of Asians and Africans to learn English in terms of individual self-interest, they perpetually encountered its essentially societal implications – political organization, nationalist feeling and, eventually, revolt.

The British colonial authorities found it particularly vexing that the English-educated segment of the population of India and Egypt should have taken such a prominent role in the anticolonial movement (Chirol, 1910). If Macaulay had supposed that English education would facilitate cultural and political domination, that idea certainly did not appear to be upheld by imperial practice. English-educated Indians and Egyptians had not become "pro-English missionaries." To the contrary, they were anti-British militants. From this circumstance colonial officials concluded that one of the important contributing factors to the opposition to British rule was English education.

British colonial administrators considered that this inconvenient result of the system of indirect rule – making English available to the colonized – posed a substantial threat to British power. On the basis of their experience, British administrators came to believe that the teaching of English had what they called an "unsettling" influence upon the people of the colonies under their control. Some worried that it might promote ideas of the development of a Western state and democracy – and as colonial rulers they feared this result. They considered that the spread of English had a negative influence upon the development of the respect for their authority. Unchecked, they claimed, English education was a recipe for revolt.

These fears were realized in India, in the view of the British colonial authorities, by the early years of the twentieth century. The Montagu–Chelmsford Report to the House of Commons of 1918, as summarized by Montgomery (1919), stated:

> Results which have been economically disastrous have been manifest in the fact that the exclusively literary system of higher education has produced a growing native *intelligentsia*, which can not find employment and becomes humiliated and soured, affording the best possible soil for discontented and anarchistic teachings. Education is directly responsible for this political and governmental ulcer on the body of the country. Only of late years has any complaint arisen against the real element which is wrong in the situation, namely, the inadequacy of facilities for training in manufactures, commerce, and the application of science to active industrial life. (pp. 65–6)

British authorities did not hesitate to point the finger at educational language policy. They warned of the "dangerous problem of the educated proletariat" (*Indian Statutory Commission, 1930*, vol. VIII, p. 38) created when the "factories of government officials" (Lloyd, 1933: 166) turned out a supply of the English-educated that outstripped the "market" for government employees. In that case, many of those making up the residual supply became "discontented" and more likely to take part in the opposition movement (Chirol, 1910). Half-a-century later and half-a-world away, administrators in the Gold Coast reached the same conclusion about "unrest" there (CO, Gold Coast, 1948).

Sir Valentine Chirol: Prophet of the Dangers of the Unchecked Spread of English

The most internationally prominent of these critics of the effects of English education was Sir Valentine Chirol (later Lord Chirol), an important architect of British policy in both India and Egypt. Chirol gave wide publicity to his concerns in an influential series of articles in *The Times*, later published as a book, that caught the attention of such key imperial administrators as Richard Lugard. Chirol deprecated what he called the creation of a "a semi-educated proletariat which is not only unemployed, but in many cases almost unemployable" and proclaimed that the "bitterness engendered" by this circumstance can only "vent itself . . . on the alien rulers who have imported the alien system of education by which many of those who fail believe themselves to have been cruelly duped" (Chirol, 1910: 225–6). An educational adviser in Egypt expressed the same sentiment in decrying those students who received English education seeking government jobs that were not available. "Large numbers of youths were thus diverted from their natural career in agriculture or industry . . . without any prospect of obtaining the kind of employment they hoped for, and estranged from their surroundings and parental influences" (quoted in Chirol, 1921: 227). "Large numbers" must be taken here in a relative sense. In India, for example, the number of English speakers at the turn of the century, or after 65 years of the Macaulay policy, was, at 0.68% of males and 0.07% of the females (*Census of the British Empire*, 1906: lvi), a much smaller proportion of the total population than at present, and a figure that did not even encompass all of what could be termed the elite of any society.[6]

It is interesting that Chirol and other British statesmen and colonial officials should have connected the speaking of English to political unrest. Were they really Macauleyists through and through, the thought would not have occurred to them. Even if it had, if the British had wanted only to spread English, they might reasonably have been expected to press ahead with a policy of imposing English on the entire populations of their colonies no matter what the cost. Above all, however, the British wanted to retain their empire. In this as in most features of imperial policy they were pragmatists. Language policy was only one aspect of running an empire, not the means of fulfillment of a purely linguistic or cultural agenda. Thus British policy was directed toward an end that Macaulay would never have imagined. In the words of a prominent British missionary in India: the question that British rule faced there was "how to prevent the production of this disappointed man who is a student only in name" (Chirol, 1910: 217).

With Chirol sounding the alarm across the four corners of the empire – catching the ears of the influential Lugard among others – in both colonies the decision was made to give greater weight to primary "vernacular" education rather than higher English education. British perceptions of the role of English education in the anticolonial movements came to play a significant factor in the formulation of educational language policy by the colonial governments of both Egypt and India. Hence, when even the small extent of English education showed signs of awakening political opposition to British rule (or at least when the British interpreted the matter this way), the British colonial administration's response was to curtail English education in both India and Egypt. British colonial officials tended to translate the connection they perceived between English education and anti-colonial movements into an opposition to English and often "literary" education in general.

British authorities chastised themselves for having "sacrificed popular to higher education ... for the production ... of Government officials" (Chirol, 1921: 223). The emphasis, however, was placed on cutting back on the higher rather than extending the "popular." Colonial authorities opted for a policy of higher education "carefully limited in quantity, and directed chiefly to supplying the technical and professional needs of the country" (Lloyd, 1933: 160).

In practice, little was done to promote mass education, despite repeated declarations by the governments of India and Egypt of the desirability of such a policy. Under Lord Curzon's administration in India in the early years of the twentieth century, an attempt was made to deal with the perceived "evils" of the educational system in the form of a policy decision to emphasize the "vernacular" as the "proper medium of instruction" for primary education, with English tied to higher education. In addition, it deemphasized "literary education" in high schools and limited the number of students in universities. This policy met with "a violent outburst of indignation" among educated Indians, who considered it an attempt to "throttle higher education in India" (Chirol, 1910:

229–30). In Egypt, where previously the primary (English) school certificate had served as a qualification for employment in government service, this certificate was abolished and primary education subordinated to the position of feeder into the secondary schools in the hope of limiting the number of students.

These purportedly new policy initiatives actually represented nothing fundamentally new in either British Asia or in Egypt. They were, moreover, consonant with the developing position in Southern Africa at this time (*c*.1905–14). The most important effect would be that it served to shift policy in newer colonial outposts in the empire, as discussed in Chapter 5.

The Containment Policy and the Purpose of British Colonial Educational Policy

Buffeted by the notion that the spread of English brought civil unrest, a wave of fear of English education swept across the British empire. Colonial administrators and education officials in Ceylon were particularly vocal in their opposition to the widespread teaching of English. In a report to the Colonial Office, the governor of Ceylon in 1889 castigated the "evil effects upon the country of a generation of half-educated idlers who deem that a little pidgin-English places them above honest work" (CO, Ceylon, 1892: 17). Missionaries and colonial administrators shared one view, put succinctly by the Roman Catholic Archbishop of Colombo: "In small towns . . . the teaching of English has the effect of unsettling the population. Boys who are able to converse in English have a repugnance for their paternal trade" (quoted in Casterelli, 1905: 308). Colonial administrators complained that English education led youth in the countryside in Ceylon to regard "industrial work as a social disgrace" and "beneath their dignity" (quoted in Burrows, 1905: 345; see also, Ceylon, Commission on Elementary Education, 1906; Cull, 1901; CO, Ceylon, 1904). In the minds of these officials, even rudimentary English education given to the rural youth of Ceylon had undesirable results. Similar concerns were voiced throughout the empire.

If imparted to the working classes, English education, in the minds of the authorities, would mean the loss of the subjugated labor in the colony (cf. Pennycook, 1994). Far from the notion allegedly held by British administrators like Macaulay that imposing English was the best way to assure British rule, the prevalent view became just the opposite: the greatest threat to the British empire was the uncontrolled spread of English. In the words of the Educational Commission of 1901 in Ceylon:

"a knowledge of English should be looked on in this country much in the same light as that in which a University education is regarded at home" (quoted in Ceylon, Commission on Elementary Education, 1906: 45). That is, as the privilege of the few, or "an important hallmark of elite status" (K.M. De Silva, 1981: 332). Thus while British colonial governments placed various limits on English education, they emphasized "vernacular education."

A close examination of the history of educational policy in the British empire does not show any concerted, consistent attempt to spread English on a wide basis. On the contrary, it indicates a concern to *limit* the spread of English as much as was consonant with the purposes of a colonial empire as part of the *reactive policy of containment*, the effort to counteract the transformation of the colonizer's language into a "language of liberation."

Educational language policy formed the basis of language policy because it provided a means for the British colonial administrations to *control access* to English. This control was meant in a double sense: who received English, and how it was taught. Administrators were concerned not only with the numbers of students taught English. They also believed that certain methods were necessary in carrying out the teaching. Above all, as shown in Chapter 3, English was to be taught in a bilingual curriculum that emphasized local language literacy. Some were not satisfied even with that measure. Lugard (1923), for example, considered that the safest way of teaching English to those who had to have it was at boarding schools where the pupil would be completely under the supervision of the carefully selected staff.

This context considerably complexifies the question of which language policy served whose purposes. The British were determined that language should not be a barrier to maintaining a tight hold on their colonies. Hence, Mazrui and Mazrui (1998: 56) observe, "Throughout the colonial era, European languages served the ends of colonialism, but they did not necessarily do so as the consequence of their imposition on Africans. Sometimes Europeans languages were deemed to serve colonial interests best by being made inaccessible to the African."

Far from forming part of "enlightened education" (Phillipson, 1992: 120), local language education had the very opposite purpose, viz., to cut off the disadvantaged socioeconomic classes from virtually all enlightenment – and the benefits that accrue therefrom, since, as discussed, "vernacular education" was intentionally severely constricted in scope. It is not only in retrospect that such a conclusion is possible. The question was actually addressed in just these terms by the American Philippine commission. That body, quite aware of how different its own policy recommendations were from those in practice in British territories,[7] analyzed the question very acutely:

> If the government were to make the local dialects the media of school instruction, a limited number of the more or less wealthy and influential persons would use the facilities which they can command to learn English for the sake of the additional power or other advantages it would give them in the communities to which they belong, and these advantages or this additional power would tend to perpetuate the prestige and domination of the present oligarchic element in Filipino society. The knowledge of English which the public schools offer to the youth of the islands will contribute materially to the emancipation of the dependent classes. (Philippine Commission, 1903: 881)

Thus, the American Philippine commission accurately captured, as it were, the spirit and purpose of limiting English on the part of the British, the essence of Lugard's policy of "indirect rule" through the perpetuation of the local elite. It was no mere accident that the British rulers promoted this social stratification through language policy. It was integrally tied to the economic structure of the British empire.

At the same time, the containment policy further spurred the desire to acquire English on the part of those oppressed by colonial rule and cemented the struggle for access to English as a pillar of the anticolonial movement. Thus, as Pennycook (1994: 93) has written, "the demand for English education by local people was frequently far stronger than the colonizers' desire to teach it."

It was, therefore, not English education but local language education that formed the cornerstone of the British colonial vision of education. As the Secretary of State for the colonies noted in 1928, "vernacular education . . . is the only type of education within reach of the vast majority" (Ormsby Gore, 1928: 53). Although he did not specify the reason, he knew it well. The very name "vernacular education" indicated what was to be avoided above all, the teaching of English.

"Vernacular Education" as Language Imposition

Given the essential basis of British language policy – to avoid the teaching of English to the vast majority of the population – it sometimes mattered little to them which language was actually used. While the British imperial authorities were not openly hostile to local languages, neither were they actively interested in them. The motivation behind language policy was here, as elsewhere, not linguistic, but practical, as shown by a closer examination of "vernacular education."

There was, for example, a difference between the local language policy of the "vernacular schools" of Ceylon and mother tongue language education as such. The "vernacular schools" of colonial Ceylon, although they employed one of the local languages, did not always use the pupil's mother tongue. Tamil children in "vernacular schools" often had to study in Sinhala and not in Tamil (Ceylon, Commission on Elementary Education, 1906). To say, then, that the principle operating was essentially one of mother tongue education is not entirely correct. It is more accurately described as *a policy of an avoidance of English education*. It is important to realize that, as in the case of a portion of the Tamil population in colonial Ceylon, "vernacular education" in the colonial context did not always mean the right to choose one's mother tongue. "Vernacular education" could in and of itself represent a case of language imposition.

The same policies held true in those colonies where the medium of instruction in the schools was not the child's mother tongue but the local lingual franca, e.g. Malay in Brunei[8] and Swahili in East Africa (League of Nations, 1924a, 1924b, 1925a, 1925b). Similarly, in South Africa selected "vernacular languages" were to serve as the medium of instruction for schooling, irrespective of the mother tongue of the pupil, although these languages were not colony-wide lingua francas (Junod, 1905). Such a policy existed in other African colonies as well. For, as Lugard (1923: 454) declared flatly, "Where a widely-spoken language easily acquired by Europeans exists – such as Hausa in the west and Swahili in the east – it would appear desirable to promote its use as a lingua franca, for natives easily acquire an African tongue."[9]

The central thrust of language policy was evidenced outside the arena of education as well, as reflected in the use of local lingua francas in a number of multilingual colonies. Particularly striking examples are provided by the British territories in East Africa, where Swahili – although not originally the mother tongue of any East Africans – was made the lingua franca, and of the Malay penninsula and surrounding islands, where the Malay language was used for the purpose. Upon returning from a trip to visit England's Malaysian possessions in 1928, Undersecretary for the Colonies, William Ormsby Gore was moved to record that "Malay is becoming increasingly the lingua franca of the peninsula for people of all races, not least the Chinese" (Ormsby Gore, 1928: 53). He noted, for instance, that Chinese residents were more likely to learn Malay than English. Such a development was the product of deliberate policy, both in Malay-speaking colonies and in East Africa. This contributed not a little to the present status of the latter as a "language of the masses" (Mazrui & Mazrui, 1998: 187). Mazrui and Mazrui (1998: 171) comment, "Both the Germans until 1918 and the British afterwards contributed significantly to the triumph of Kiswahili as a region-wide lingua franca."[10]

The case of Uganda was particularly striking. Swahili was declared the official language of the colony despite the fact that it was known to only a small proportion of the people in the colony – and was the mother tongue of none of them (Kabaka, 1929). Moreover, Swahili was given preference to the Luganda language, the most widespread mother tongue among the colony's inhabitants. This situation occasioned a strong protest on the part of the Kabaka (hereditary leader) of Buganda, who believed that this policy unjustly promoted a "dialect found on the Coast of East Africa and adopted and used by foreigners in their daily dealings with the natives of Africa, merely on the ground of conveniency to them" (p. 1) He objected to any attempt to "compel my people to study and use this language against their will" (p. 1). He insisted that the study of Swahili in the schools "should be voluntary and not compulsory" (p. 1) The memorandum concluded, "I am entirely opposed to any arrangement which would in any way facilitate the ultimate adoption of this Language as the Official native language of the Baganda in place of, or at the expense of, their own language" (p. 1).

In several colonies, official languages other than English were proclaimed, e.g. Chinyanja in Nyasaland, although at least six other languages were in widespread use in the country (CO, Nyasaland, 1928: 5). Chinyanja (or Nyanja) was imposed not only on Africans, but on "all [British] officers, civil and military," for whom competence in the language was made "compulsory" and was checked by means of examination (CO, Nyasaland, 1906: 40). And just as importantly, local languages were promoted in the judiciary.[11] In fact, this was essentially an empire-wide policy, motivated by extremely pragmatic concerns, and given surprisingly strong emphasis. As a close observer of British colonial rule warned both the Colonial and War Offices: "so long as responsible officials are ignorant of the languages spoken in the districts committed to their care, they will inevitably be more or less at the mercy of subordinate interpreters, whether European or natives, comparatively irresponsible, on whose accuracy and good faith absolute reliance ought not to be placed" (Transvaal, 1902: 7). Both ministries reassured the writer that they were well aware of this potential problem and that requiring proficiency in local languages for colonial administrators was already long-standing policy (Transvaal, 1902: 10). In addition to avoiding the use of English, the British had a great awareness of the importance of knowing the languages of the peoples they ruled for the purposes of better maintaining control.

The British colonial administrations went to considerable trouble to manufacture the national languages to correspond with colonial boundaries that "linguistically imperialistic" motives should rather have dictated an interest in suppressing. In doing so, they generally confined themselves to using linguistic material found ready to hand – whether a language like Malay spoken by majorities that could be imposed on minorities or by using a non-mother tongue regional lingua franca like Swahili. In at least one case, however, colonial authorities resorted to nothing less than linguistic engineering to accomplish their objectives. In the part of the colony of Southern Rhodesia that the British called Mashonaland, the colonial administration launched a language policy that, it accurately forecast, "should influence many a generation" (Southern Rhodesia, 1929: 18).

The Southern Rhodesian administrative officials and their missionary allies had, by the late 1920s, long been in search of a means to simplify the complex task of ruling the linguistically diverse population of the colony. A committee was formed to advise the government on how best to bring about language "unification." Three alternatives were initially considered. The committee reported, the "easiest would propose to select one dialect and one orthography and impose it by Government decree on all the people in the area. This would mean that in the greater part of Mashonaland the people would continue to possess and use their vernacular speech, while for Government purposes at any rate, and probably for educational work as well, they would have to accept and learn the imposed language" (Southern Rhodesia, 1929: 19). A second option, dubbed "the 'Esperanto' method," was "to make a selection from the various dialects and so to produce fully formed a new language adequate for most purposes, but not possessing any capacity for natural growth and development" (p. 20). Finally, it was possible to choose "one dialect [that] was so clearly dominant and so established as a literary language that it could fairly have been selected as a second language to be taught in all schools and made the language of inter-communication between the various tribes and the Government" (p. 20).

The committee opted for none of these. Instead, they decided that there were in the territory "not four or five languages, but . . . four or five dialects of one language" (Southern Rhodesia, 1929: 20). The committee, composed of missionaries, came to this conclusion on its own, and then commissioned a South African linguist from the University of Witwaters-rand, Clemmons Doke, whose name has been traditionally (and probably wrongly) credited with the language thus created. Although he played a large role in devising its orthographic representation, the decision to pro-claim the existence of this language did not rest with him. And mission-aries who had first taken up the task of teaching the languages of Mashonaland to British civil servants had already gone a good way toward the standardization of the grammar (p. 24). Linguistics, in this case, was brought in to give a scientific stamp of approval to a policy under-taken for expressly "practical advantages" it would afford to colonial rule.

Having decreed the language into existence, the colonial authorities and their missionary allies, aided by Clemmons Doke, reserved to them-selves the task of standardizing it. Not only was a standard grammar to be devised under Clemmons Doke's guidance – despite his complete lack of familiarity with the language – but a vocabulary was to be created "of as many and as representative words as possible which shall include words from all the major dialects" (Southern Rhodesia, 1929: 25). The vocabulary and the grammar would then serve as the basis for the cre-ation of textbooks in all subjects in the language for introduction into the schools. The administration also established plans for the founding of "a Press for the production of a vernacular literature" (p. 25).

The most difficult question the committee faced was what to call this new language it had created – or more accurately, cobbled together. It arrived at the conclusion "that the only possible name for the language" was Shona. Familiarity engendered by time and habit disguises how controversial such a choice was. The committee that bequeathed the name was cognizant of the perils entailed. Its report noted,

> It has been widely felt that the name "Shona" is inaccurate and unworthy, that it is not the true name of any of the peoples whom we propose to group under the term "Shona-speaking people," and further, that it lies under strong suspicion of being a name given in contempt by the enemies of the tribes. It is pretty certainly a foreign name, and as such is very like to be uncomplimentary (like the name "Kaffir") . . . The idea that is a contemptuous name is widespread . . . It is true that the name "Mashona" is not pleasing to the natives, but that may simply because it is a group name imposed from without, and ignoring all true tribal distinctions. Certainly no people in the country claim the name Mashona as their tribal name, and each would prefer to be described by the proper name of his partic-ular group (Southern Rhodesia, 1929: 25–6).

In this, as in all other matters, the wishes and aspirations of Africans and Asians were to be swept aside before the paramount goal of expediting and safeguarding colonial rule. These extensive measures – so contrary to what is usually conceived under colonial language policy – represented part of the *reactive policy of containment*.

Notes

1. Wiley (1996: 110) notes that Cooper's "use of influence suggests that planning is not limited to those who have official power." But Cooper (1989: 183) does not elaborate on this idea. On the contrary, he concludes only: "Language planning may be initiated at any level of a social hierarchy, but it is unlikely to succeed unless it is embraced and promoted by elites or by counterelites." This idea, however, misses the point that a language policy may actually be imposed on the elites by the *actions* of non-elites. The idea of the contested terrain of language policy therefore does more to open conceptual space for conceiving Africans and Asians under European colonialism as "language planning agents" (Ricento & Hornberger, 1996: 402). It should be noted, however, that delimiting language planning as action taken *on others*, as Cooper does, suggests that actions taken on behalf of oneself belong to some other plane of action, a terminology which is far too cumbersome, and, in any case, as yet unnamed.
2. Davies (1996b) points to this weakness of Phillipson's 1992 work. The notion of *hegemony* employed by Phillipson appears to prescribe that the colonized people may only do the bidding of their colonial masters. It discounts the possibility of independent action on the part of the colonized actuated by their own ideas and ambitions, if those acts can be interpreted as beneficial to the colonizing power.
3. This conforms to the observation by Ricento and Hornberger (1996: 404) that it "has long been recognized in the LPP field [that] when governments or states decide to intervene in areas involving language, they usually have primarily nonlinguistic goals."
4. How much this remains the case is shown by the fact that "At the beginning of the 1990s, over half of Lesotho's national income derived from migrant miners working in South Africa" (Crush *et al.*, 1991).
5. K.M. De Silva (1981: 332) notes that the "traditional elite" in Ceylon shared this fear of English education for the working classes, and that its "opposition" to education "was much more comprehensive in scope."
6. "One million is a liberal estimate of the number of Indians who have acquired and retained some knowledge of English; whilst at the last census, out of a total population of 294 millions, less than sixteen millions could read and write in any language ... and this modest amount of literacy is mainly confined to a few privileged castes" (Chirol, 1910: 246).
7. "The effort of the Americans to give the Filipinos a knowledge of English is in marked contrast to the policy carried out by some of the European nations in their oriental possessions" (*Report of the Philippine Commission*, 1903: 881).
8. "[A]t least a quarter of the indigenous population of the State is composed of races whose mother tongue is not Malay. ... The provision of education

in their several languages is obviously impracticable, and it is inevitable that, linguistically at any rate, the other races must be assimilated to Malay" (CO, Brunei, 1938: 32–3).

9. Moreover, the use of the "vernaculars" in education occasioned no small effort and expense. Where the American imperial authorities in the Philippines said that the necessity of so much translation made vernacular education impossible there, the British undertook the immense work, and this should not be lost sight of with respect to claims of linguistic imperialism. At the same time, the American authorities in the Philippines said that the diversity of languages there meant that English was the logical lingua franca, the British made a local language the basis of education, even if it was not the "mother language" of the students. Moreover, it has already been documented in Chapter 2 that the British required their colonial administrators to learn at least one local language as a condition of service.

10. For this reason, it is ironic that Phillipson (1992: 129) should maintain that when the British took over Tanganyika after World War I, "English as established as the dominant language," seemingly unaware that England, in fact, promoted Swahili as a lingua franca above English (League of Nations, 1923, 1924a, 1924b, 1925a, 1925b).

11. For example, contrary to what Phillipson (1992) says, Persian was replaced by English in India only in the higher courts, but by the vernacular in the lower courts, which alone touched the lives of most Indians (Cameron, 1853). The same was true in Nyasaland, where the enshrining of Chinyanja as the official language of the colony was said to have resulted "in a considerable improvement in the Native Courts and dealing with native questions generally" (CO, Nyasaland, 1906).

Chapter 5

Access Denied: Containing the Spread of English

The Economic Basis of Language Policy Variation in the British Empire

One of the results of the reactive nature of British language policy was that, in contrast to American rule in the Philippines discussed in Chapter 3, it varied considerably from place to place depending on local conditions. To form a full view of British language policy in its empire, therefore, the basis of that variation must be considered.

Unlike the US in the Philippines, Great Britain set out with no unified, pre-planned blueprint for colonial administration. In fact, a significant barrier in the way of such an imperial policy was the decentralized organization of the empire. Great Britain did not develop an empire-wide language policy of any kind, and did not even coordinate policy throughout its dominions – or even parts thereof – until the late 1920s (Schilling, 1972: 282). Individual colonial administrations were, rather, left to their own devices.

With the lack of a uniform imperial policy, local conditions and events largely shaped attitudes towards the spread of English and English education in the dependencies (Schilling, 1972). Among other things, colonial administrators felt the pressure exerted by the English merchants and manufacturers, who tended to look to their immediate interests. As Ronald Hyam comments, an overriding goal of British imperial rule was "to avoid spending the British taxpayer's money. Britain's empire was ever an empire on the cheap" (quoted in Schilling, 1972: 26–7). Far from striving to encourage large-scale undertakings on the part of colonial administrations, the British Colonial Office generally confined itself to making significant cuts in the proposed expenditures by the various colonial administrations (Schilling, 1972).

British administrators were not necessarily in a position to look after overarching imperial objectives, such as the linguistic or cultural supremacy of their nation. They were often people who rose through the army and civil service who knew as little of the colony next to them as remote parts of the world. The men like Frederick Lugard who set the language policy of the empire were not imbued with ideas straight out of the boarding schools of England. They were mainly ex-soldiers who, as in Lugard's case, were born and spent their lives in the colonies and were educated not at Oxford but in the military conquest of Asia and Africa (Lugard, 1923). They made policy not as a schoolmaster or ideologue would but as would a soldier and colonial administrator. It was policy arising out of daily political and economic concerns.

The dictates of the local conditions made the spread of English in the colonies uneven. Despite the lack of intercolonial coordination, however, the resemblance of the various educational systems is remarkable. This similarity stems not from the desire to follow a preconceived imperial policy but rather to pursue a course dictated the political and economic imperatives of colonial rule.

As shown in Chapter 3, the requisites of empire created the demand for English-educated Asians and Africans to fill lower and sometimes higher-level positions in the colonial administration and to meet the need for commercial clerks. These needs did not arise all at once at the outset of imperial rule but developed in three main phases. First, there was a period after the colony was founded prior to its extensive imperial economic development in which there was no demand for civil servants, and therefore, education was generally discouraged or simply not addressed. The second stage commenced when the colony became more fully integrated into the imperial economy; at this point, the need for English speaking educated Africans and Asians exerted itself and an emphasis on teaching English followed. In the third and final phase, the concentration on producing English-educated youth outstripped the capacity of the colonial system to absorb them and a strong desire to limit English and higher education ensued. The transition form one stage to another was not uniform across all colonies but depended on the internal economic development of a colony. The economic level of advancement, conditioned by such factors as how long the country had been a colony and the world market price of its chief products, also played a crucial role in determining the educational structure.

The first phase, coinciding with the beginnings of British rule, came during a period in which the British administration concentrated on establishing its power. With insignificant sources of revenue, the government was not in a financial position to undertake vast educational projects. Nor did it feel any particular need to do so.

In Kelantan, part of the Unfederated Malay States that constituted some of the most economically undeveloped portions of Britain's Asian possessions, it was said that there existed no demand for English-educated nationals, so "it has been decided to concentrate for the present on improving the standard of Vernacular education" (CO, Unfederated Malay States, Kelantan, 1929: 20). A report for Trengganu, belonging to the same group of colonies, captured the spirit that motivated the policy (CO, Unfederated Malay States, Trengganu, 1932: 17). Most of its Malaysian civil servants knew no English "whatsoever" – to their disappointment. The administration saw "no obvious reason" for them to acquire it, and therefore had no inclination to pay for their education. In its words, there was little commercial demand for English "in a State which still looks to the padi-field and the fishing boat for its livelihood" (p. 17). Sounding the familiar warning, it continued, "The State does not want its people to gravitate to the towns and to acquire a smattering of English such as is represented by the winning of a Junior Cambridge Certificate and with it a contempt for manual labour. Rather is it to be desired that the peasant be equipped mentally and physically to carry out the work of his forefathers more efficiently and with better results" (CO, Unfederated Malay States, Kelantan, 1932: 30–31). For the disappointed "Malay parents who wish to give their children a better education than they received themselves and think that better education necessarily connotes English education," the British administration had this chilling warning:

> [P]ossibly they forget their own proverb which says that however high the padi-bird may soar, he ends by settling on the buffalo's back: and many a Trengganu youth who struggles up to Standard IV in an English school will find that he has after all to make his living by work in which his English (such as it is) will not help him. (p. 17)

The same situation obtained in much of British southern Africa. That a significant number of people in Basutoland, for example, would speak English was said to be "out of the question" (CO, Basutoland, 1909: 44). Colonial education officials praised missionaries for promoting the teaching of Sesotho, thus keeping education "in touch with the people" (CO, Basutoland, 1909: 42). The teaching of English was practically nonexistent. For this reason, at least at the early period of its existence, no two-tiered system of education developed in which English was taught in the upper standards, as in other African colonies (Lugard, 1923; Schilling, 1972). Instead, the educational policy for the lower classes stands forth in its classic form, as it were. Industrial training for southern Africa went hand in hand with mother language education.

Once a colony reached a certain level of development – particularly if it experienced significant urban growth – the need for a definite number of English-educated persons was inevitably felt. The Archbishop of Colombo echoed this view, "In large towns . . . knowledge of English is a necessity for almost every child" (quoted in Casterelli, 1905: 308). Although this exaggerated the true situation, considerably, it nevertheless explained the focus on the development of English education as a concomitant of urbanization. In the early years of British rule in Africa from the 1890s through the World War I period, particularly in tropical colonies with major trading centers, there was still "unlimited demand" for qualified members of the indigenous population to fill governmental and technical posts. The demand was so great that often pupils who did not finish their education left to assume government posts that called for higher qualifications, which led to some discontent on the part of the British (Lugard, 1923: 442–3). In these circumstances, English education tended to be emphasized in some British West and East Africa possessions even while it was being curtailed in other parts of the empire.

If American imperial policy insisted on teaching English to every student, the British policy limited the number of the students exposed to the formal teaching of English to meet the local demands for English-educated subjects of the empire. It left the bulk of the population to be educated in the local language or, at most, to acquire the rudimentary elements of the English language. In the main, economic interests within the colony controlled the spread of English. As a result, it created an uneven spread of English among different colonies within the British empire, and within a single colony. In the commercial centers of the colonies alone was there significant English education. In the more rural districts, a vernacular education was thought sufficient.

The Socioeconomic Lines of Language Access

The linguistic division of education ran alongside socioeconomic lines. This was the case not only as between rural and urban persons, but also within the urban population. As government reports detail, the fees charged for attendance at government English schools made them inaccessible to the less affluent classes, while "vernacular schools" were free throughout British Asia (CO, Ceylon, 1938). An official in Kedah (Unfederated Malay States) noted that high fees were instituted in English schools (and periodically raised) "to discourage boys of promise insufficient to secure the limited number of appointments open to those with English qualification from continuing their education beyond the age when they are pliable enough to turn to other than sedentary occupations" (CO, Unfederated Malay States, Kedah, 1936: 32). Thus we find, as in Ceylon, that the "purely vernacular schools" in the large towns were "for the poor and lower classes" only (Cull, 1901: 772). The same held true in British Malaya: it is the "better class of Malay boys who are able to attend an 'English' school. These are confined to the towns" (Federal Education Office, Federated Malay States, 1905: 16). In the Unfederated Malay States, English school enrollments were fixed "in accordance with the number of posts, available for boys with an English Education, in Government or private employment" (CO, Unfederated Malay States, Johore, 1930: 16).

The point emerges very prominently from an examination of the numbers of "vernacular schools" versus "English schools" in the British empire. Since educational statistics kept for Asia were much more comprehensive, an in-depth statistical portrait of educational language policy for Asia only will be given.

Educational Language Policy in British Asia: A Statistical Overview

As shown in Appendix A, there were some 4,000 vernacular schools in Ceylon from the last decades of the nineteenth century through the end of colonial period in the 1930s. In contrast, the number of English schools, which numbered 124 in 1889, reached only 255 by 1927. In the latter year there were sixteen times more vernacular schools. The growing emphasis upon non-English education is shown even more clearly by the effort of the government to directly support local language education. As shown in Appendix B, while the total number of vernacular schools remained almost constant over the period considered, the number of such schools that were government-supported increased from 1254 in 1889 to 3117, a rate faster than that of the expansion of government-supported English schools.[1]

The picture is much the same in British Malaya.[2] There, due to a later commencement of British rule and institution of the educational system, the growth in the number of vernacular schools is far more dramatic: over the period of 1900 to 1936, the number of vernacular schools increased from 174 to 1332, while the number of English schools grew from 24 to 48 (see Appendix C), so that in 1936 vernacular schools outnumbered English schools by a ratio of 28: 1. The development of an educational system lagged even further behind in the Unfederated Malay States, but by the year 1928, for which full figures are obtainable, there were 294 vernacular schools to only 9 English schools (a ratio of 33: 1) (see Appendix D).[3] Thereafter the proportion appears to have remained fairly constant, although comprehensive statistics are not available. In the similarly economically undeveloped territory of Brunei during the same period, there were only vernacular schools and no English schools (CO, Brunei, 1929).

In the Straits Settlements, exact numbers of English schools are more difficult to come by because there were transient small private English schools in Singapore. If government schools and government-aided schools alone are taken, the picture is as follows: in 1900, there were 171 vernacular versus 39 English (4.4: 1) (Eleum, 1905); in 1928, 567 vernacular as against 84 English (6.75: 1) (Ormsby Gore, 1928); in 1938, 297 vernacular and 58 English (5.1: 1) (CO, Straits Settlements, 1939). There was in the Straits Settlements a further division between Singapore and Malacca that will be discussed subsequently.

With respect to British Pacific Island territories, it appears from Colonial Office records that, for most of the colonies, almost all the schools were vernacular (CO, Fiji, 1923, 1926, 1933; CO, Tongan Islands Protectorate, 1916, 1926). In early years some of them taught English as a subject but later abolished it. In later years, a few secondary English schools were established.

The Solomon Islands represented something of an exception. There were no government schools in the pre-World War II period (CO, Solomon Islands, 1932: 11). Education was entirely in the hands of missions with some support from the government for technical education in the early 1930s. English was taught as a subject in that territory. The official reason given for this was the lack of a "universal language in the Solomon Islands. Numerous dialects are spoken, and it frequently happens that natives living in villages a few miles apart are unable to understand one another. There are many parts of the Protectorate where a form of broken English is spoken and understood by the natives, especially in the eastern parts of the Group" (CO, Solomon Islands, 1930: 3). The small size of the British Pacific Island possessions, in which student populations were as small as a few thousand, influenced educational policy. Unlike in the colonies of larger population, local authorities sometimes did not think it worthy of instituting the expense for vernacular education.

Taking British colonies in Asia as a whole, the large number of vernacular schools shows that they were scattered throughout the countryside, and were therefore the only kind of school available to the vast majority of the population, as Secretary for the Colonies William Ormsby Gore (1928) noted. The vast number of vernacular schools, therefore, signified a policy of limiting the educational, and thereby the economic, opportunities of the rural population, and thereby serving the goal of maintaining a labor force on the land. For this reason, English schools were for the most part only located in towns, where they served the purpose of educating a small section of the population to carry out the necessary functions of empire.

Moreover, the small enrollments of the vernacular schools are strong evidence, confirmed by the descriptive sources, that these schools were in their vast majority village vernacular schools. The educational statistics from British Asia demonstrate that the policy of vernacular education for the rural population was implemented by colonial authorities throughout British possessions in Asia. Such a policy contrasts starkly with the American policy in the Philippines where English education was made the basis of even the village schools.

In analyzing the data, it should be noted that the ratio of vernacular to English schools, therefore, correlates strongly with the degree of urban development in the colony. In general, the more agricultural the colony was, the greater was the ratio of vernacular to English schools. Hence, the ratio is highest in the Unfederated Malay States, and lowest in the Straits Settlement (where, however, the same ratio is manifested as among the different constituent colonies according to their level of urbanization) (Eleum, 1905). In many colonies devoted purely to agricultural production and whose products were transshipped through other colonies, including Perlis, Brunei and some of the Pacific Island colonies, there were no English schools at all (CO, Brunei, 1931).

The situation was just as apparent in India. A colonial official reported in 1907 that fewer than 15% of the money spent on Indian peoples in the civil service in his district (the Punjab) went to the rural-born Indian population. He commented, "the sons of agriculturalists are almost excluded from clerical posts worth more than a shilling a day" (Thorburn, 1907–08: 140). Just as revealing of the socioeconomic basis of education were statistics collected with respect to caste, the lowest of which the British called the "depressed classes." The colonial authorities acknowledged in 1930 that "It is only in rare cases where members of these classes have through education raised themselves in the economic scale . . ." (*Indian Statutory Commission*, 1930: 395). For example, only one female in 30,000 among the "depressed classes" attended school beyond the primary level.

Students Learning English versus Local Languages

An examination of the figures for students learning English versus those studying in local languages exclusively completes the statistical picture of British educational language policy in Asia. As is implied by the figures on the number of vernacular versus English schools, the vast majority of children in British colonial India received education in local languages only. A small minority received education in English. In 1882, 92.4% of all students enrolled in schools at all levels learned indigenous languages, while 7.6% studied English. By 1919, the proportion of students learning vernacular languages only had dropped slightly to 84%. A more revealing measure is provided by taking the proportion of students learning English to the total school-age population of India. The figures are 1.3% for 1882, and 3.3%[4] for 1919 (Montgomery, 1919; J. Russell, 1887). In the context of the tremendous commercial development of the nation in those years, together with the "Indianization of the civil services" (*Indian Statutory Commission*, 1930, vol. 1), this rise in the number of Indian youths learning English is easily accounted for. It should be noted that total English literacy in India was still substantially smaller than these figures imply. In 1901, a bare 0.68% of all males and 0.07% of all females in India were recorded as literate in English by the census (*Census of the British Empire*, 1906).

As shown in Appendix E, from the late nineteenth century on, the overwhelming majority of students in Ceylon received their schooling in the vernacular schools in which local languages, primarily Sinhala or Tamil, were taught exclusively. The percentage of children who attended "vernacular schools" remained between 80 and 90% from the last decades of the nineteenth century to the end of the colonial period. Even this statistic over-represents the actual number of youth who were learning English, since a large proportion of the children of Ceylon received no schooling at all. In 1904, less than 40% of children of school age (as defined by the colonial administration as children between the ages of 6 and 12) were enrolled in schools (Ceylon, Commission on Elementary Education, 1906), and in 1927 this figure had reached no more than 50% (Ormbsy Gore, 1928).[5] The division between those students receiving education and those not tended to reflect the division between urban and rural Ceylon. As a government report commented around the turn of the century, "The children who are receiving no education at all are mainly those living in outlying country districts" (CO, Ceylon, 1901: 27). In 1904, while 63.8% of students in the Western province were under instruction, under 11.5% of those in the rural province of Uva were so classified (Ceylon, Commission on Elementary Education, 1906: 6–7).

The percentage of children attending vernacular schools was very similar in the Federated Malay States, as shown in Appendix F.[6] The percentage educated in local languages, primarily Malay, remained between 77.3 and 85.3% over the period of 1900 to 1936 even while the total number of students under instruction increased almost 20-fold (Appendix G). For the Federated Malay States, however, more exact figures on the number of children receiving local language versus English education exist. As shown in Appendix H, among all Malay boys in 1928, 6.6% received English education, while 75% attended Malay-language schools only. For Malay girls, virtually no English education existed and a mere 9% attended Malay-language schools.

Local language education dominated in the Unfederated Malay States to an even greater degree. In 1928, by which time education has been established on some basis, fully 93% of school-going children attended the primarily Malay vernacular schools[7] (CO, Unfederated Malaly States, 1928; Johore, 1928; Kedah & Perlis, 1929; Kelantan, 1929; Perlis, 1928; Trengganu, 1928; Ormsby Gore, 1928). Subsequent to that point, while statistics for the whole of the Unfederated States are not available, in the most populous of the states, Johore, 91.8% of the students attended vernacular schools in 1938[8] (CO, Unfederated Malay States, Johore, 1939), and this despite the fact that English education was the most developed in this state. Although statistics on the number of children of school-going age who were not able to attend school are not available, anecdotal evidence suggests that they still constituted a sizable number in the late 1930s.

Only in the comparatively small Straits Settlements were students educated in English and local languages in roughly equal numbers from about 1900 through the 1930s[9] (Eleum, 1905; CO, Straits Settlements, 1923, 1933). There was, however, a great discrepancy as between the different settlements. Whereas, for example, in Singapore in 1900 students at English schools outnumbered those at vernacular schools by a ratio of 4:1, in Malacca the ratio was about the same proportion in favor of vernacular school students. In Penang, the ratio was approximately 1:1 (Eleum, 1905). The unusually high number of students studying English is explained by Singapore's status as a commercial center for all of British Malaya, and to some extent for the larger Southeast Asia region. The demand for English-educated commercial clerks outstripped the supply for virtually the entire colonial period in Singapore, which was reflected in the educational system. On the other hand, Malacca like other parts of British Malaya, was primarily agricultural. And, as has been shown, the outlook of the British colonial authorities in the Straits Settlements was in substance no different from that in the other Asian colonies; the high incidence of English education, therefore, stemmed from commercial need alone.

The difference in quality of education was reflected in the length of education as well. While English schools included standards all the way through secondary school, the vernacular schools extended only to the fifth standard. Moreover, the average pupil probably did not attend that long. In Ceylon, statistics for the year 1898 show that the number of students "presented for examination" for the fourth standard was less than 40% of that for the first standard. By 1928, officials still reported that the "vast majority" of students in Ceylon did not advance beyond the "elementary stage" (CO, Ceylon, 1929). In India as late in the history of British rule as 1923, only 19% of boys and 10% of girls who attended school reached the fourth class (*Indian Statutory Commission*, 1930, vol. 1: 392–3). Therefore, a large percentage of school children, as many as 40%, relapsed in illiteracy as adults (Montgomery, 1919). Furthermore, most Indian children did not attend school at all. As late as 1921, only one third of male and one thirteenth of female children of school age were enrolled in schools. As many as three out of four rural villages still had no educational facilities at all (Mayhew, 1926).

With the reservation of English education for the wealthier classes, the majority of the population, particularly in rural areas, could not climb the socioeconomic ladder. The Ceylon case was typical. Its colonial administration was reluctant from the first to allow the inhabitants of rural areas "the means of attaining [even a] *modicum* of" English, reported the Director of Public Instruction, a refusal the colonial authorities justified "With the cry that this little knowledge of English has an unsettling effect on the mind of the native *goiya* . . ." (quoted in Cull, 1901: 800). In short, the colonial administration institutionally limited access to English for what they considered the "useful class" (Ceylon, Commission on Elementary Education, 1906: 19) – that which was to carry out the manual labor.

Estate Schools: The Education of Migrant Workers

The system of estate schools, perhaps, best exemplifies the inextricable link between industrial/agricultural education and indigenous language education in the colonies. Within the British colonial empire, indentured labor was not at all uncommon (Buell, 1928). In the case of Ceylon, a significant number of persons from the Tamil region of southern India migrated there to work on the large colonial plantations (K.M. De Silva, 1981), or what the British called estates. In 1901, Tamil workers employed on estates were 42% of the entire Tamil population in Ceylon (Ceylon, Commission on Elementary Education, 1906: 58), concentrated on large farms as "indentured" workers providing cheap labor. In addition to men and women, who worked in about equal numbers, children were extensively employed as "tea pluckers," as soon as they were old enough "to reach over the top of a tea bush" (quoted in Ceylon, Commission on Elementary Education, p. 55). On top of the other hardships that life as an indentured laborer entailed, it meant the necessity of frequent migration from one estate to another, although the majority of those who came to Ceylon as indentured laborers settled there permanently (Ceylon, Commission on Elementary Education).

When pressed by members of Parliament in London to address the question of education on the estates in the early twentieth century, the Inspector of Education of Ceylon declared that the children of Tamil indentured laborers had not "yet reached a stage of civilization which makes it necessary to treat them as English children are treated" (quoted in Ceylon, 1906: 55). He added, "Indeed, it must be refreshing to the philanthropist to know that their present condition is far healthier and happier (if less intellectually forcing) than that of a large majority of the children in England" (p. 55). Intellect was to be reserved for others.

This educational official knew firsthand, however, that the indentured Tamil workers themselves were not at all satisfied with such conditions. He detailed in his report that much of the education accessible to the children of indentured workers was organized and financed by the efforts of the indentured workers themselves (Ceylon, Commission on Elementary Education, 1906), a circumstance that was found still to be the case two decades later (Ormsby Gore, 1928).

These Tamil efforts notwithstanding, colonial education officials deemed the "question of intellectual aspirations" of Tamil children "irrelevant" (Ceylon, Commission on Elementary Education, p. 55). Indeed, they cynically concluded that "every coolie who comes to live and work on a tea estate is subjected to educational influences of a disciplinary kind" (p. 55). More than this, the educational experts of Ceylon did not deem wise: "It is not a matter of urgency to the interests of the state that they should spend several years in an organized school" (p. 19). Should such a requirement be introduced, it might only amount to a "mistake that has been the cause of a great deal of mischief already" (p. 56). The government of Ceylon was decidedly against "direct Government interference" in the matter (p. 57). Government policy more or less left education on estates to the discretion of the planters. Colonial officials made no attempt to hide their reasons: "There is an undefined but very real feeling that education will prevent the children from following the vocation of their parents." (CO, Ceylon, 1904: 45). Education was defined as that which encourages the estate worker to go on being an estate worker and did not interfere with production.

Instruction was therefore of the most rudimentary nature. It was confined to two hours daily of basic mother tongue literacy and hygiene (Ormsby Gore, 1928: 103). For the vast majority of the children, "education" did not go beyond the second standard (Ceylon, Commission on Elementary Education, 1906: 55). In "line schools," more or less organized instruction given in the fields, the rudiments of literacy in Tamil and arithmetic constituted the whole of the curriculum. The report on estate education asserted quite straightforwardly, "There is no question of the teaching of English" (p. 55). The children of the estate worker were to learn, above all, the "habits of industry" (p. 19), and it was made clear that school should not be allowed to interfere with the day's labor of children on estates (CO, Ceylon, 1904; Ceylon, Commission on Elementary Education). Education of the children of estate workers was not made compulsory; rather, the planter was left "free to organize this instruction in the way which he finds most suitable" (p. 19). Such instruction was not required to exceed two hours in the day.

Even this most rudimentary education was not available to the majority of the children living on the estates of Ceylon. In 1904, only 16% of the 46,200 children aged 6 to 12 years were in any sort of schools (Ceylon, Commission on Elementary Education, 1906). By 1928, the proportion had grown substantially, to 46% of the 81,858 children (Ormsby Gore, 1928); still, the majority of children remained outside the estate schools such as they were.

The foregoing discussion demonstrates that British language policy developed in piecemeal fashion in accordance with the dictates of the local conditions found in each colony. The imperial authorities in London were almost wholly removed from the picture – so much so that the Secretary of State for the colonies was dispatched on a fact-finding mission in the late 1920s to discover just what constituted British colonial policy (Ormby Gore, 1928). If an impression has been created to the contrary, it owes to developments quite late in the history of the empire, commencing only in the 1920s. It remains only to trace those events to round out the investigation of British language policy in its colonial empire.

Language Policy in the International Political Arena: The League of Nations Mandates Commission and the Phelps-Stokes Fund in Africa

The League of Nations Mandates Commission

By the end of World War I much more uniform conditions had begun to emerge in Britain's colonial empire. The point was reached at which a centrally administered language policy had become possible, albeit precisely for that reason almost wholly superfluous. The similar albeit largely independent responses to colonial conditions throughout the empire ensured that a common policy was in place before an official imperial one was formed in the 1920s.

After World War I, international politics would, for the first time, enter as a prominent factor in determining educational language policy in the British empire, exerting its first effects on the colonies taken over by the victorious Allies from the defeated Germany. England constituted the pre-eminent power in the post-World War I League of Nations formed out of the peace treaty ending the war and as such the most powerful voice on questions of colonial policy. Within the League Mandates Commission, the body charged with distributing and overseeing former German territories, such as Tanganyika (present-day Tanzania) and Cameroon, British representatives wielded the power to ensure adequate representation of their views on colonial rule in Africa. Nevertheless, the process of oversight of those new British possessions by the international imperial body helped institute a process of formation of empire-wide policymaking on the part of the British for the first time in the history of British colonialism. Despite its complete lack of authority over the vast dominions of Great Britain, the League Mandates Commission from its foundation in 1921 marked a new chapter in the history of the British empire – one which, for reasons to be made clear, made its impact felt first in British Africa.

The League of Nations Mandates Commission constitutes a neglected chapter in the history of British colonial language and education policy. The existence of the League Mandates Commission, which interested itself in all aspects of colonial administration, created a forum in which British language policy in various colonial settings would be considered jointly. It also gave Britain a platform from which to attempt to influence other colonial powers. It constituted, therefore, a step toward the conscious coordination of British colonial policy, which had hitherto developed in each colony more or less independently.

Since the League of Nations became a meeting ground for the chief imperial powers – only the US among major colonizing nations failed to join – the Mandates Commission provided a forum for each of the colonial powers to promote its own policy. What is perhaps most interesting about the history of the Mandates Commission is how each power represented its objectives and the clashing philosophies that became manifest over the approach to language policy in the colonies. On one side stood Great Britain and its allies, on the other France and Belgium.

As Great Britain and France were the two largest colonial powers, together holding the majority of the League Mandates, these two powers dominated the Mandates Commission, each striving to exert the most influence on smaller imperial nations. It did not take long for the essential difference in their approaches to emerge. The British, represented by Frederick Lugard from the third session onward, advocated a policy of "vernacular education at the base and English at the top," as had become the popular means of expressing this idea. In this they were joined by the Portuguese delegate (League of Nations, 1923, 1924b) and eventually by the one for Sweden, not itself a colonial power. In the Swedish representative, who interested herself particularly in educational matters, the British made an invaluable ally. She became a Lugard convert, commenting, "Sir Frederick Lugard's *The Dual Mandate* [was] the most helpful book I have ever read about colonial administration" (League of Nations, 1924a: 183). She adopted the British view of the purpose of education being "character-training" (ibid. p. 184) and she sniped at the opposite camp continually in the course of the back and forth exchanges on educational policy in the early and mid-1920s (League of Nations, 1924a, 1924b, 1925a).

The French made clear very early that they regarded the imparting of the French language in all educational institutions, including village elementary schools, to be "indispensable" (League of Nations, 1923: 29) – a view shared by the Belgians. This philosophy, they insisted, entailed the use of French as the language of instruction. The French variously justified their policy, at one time complaining that too many different "dialects" (League of Nations, 1923: 245) existed in a particular country, other times that "the knowledge which [the government] wishes to impart can only be given in French" (League of Nations, 1923: 285). It might, of course, seem more "logical" to use the mother tongue, the Belgian representative allowed, but that would involve the use of "debased languages," popular jargons with "small vocabularies . . . inadequate for the expression of general ideas" (League of Nations, 1925a: 35).

The British were undeterred by these objections. To the first, they countered that a lingua franca would answer the problem, such as Swahili in East Africa. The Belgian representative observed that in this way Swahili would necessarily become the dominant language of the country in question. Nothing was more objectionable to proponents of French than according a "native language" such status. For the last thing the European power should do, the French believed, was to permit a potential rival to the supremacy of the language of the colonizing nation. The British were unmoved by this objection. The Belgian representative tried another tack: were the British not concerned that the spread of Swahili would mean the spread of Islam? The British countered that they had not noticed any such tendency (League of Nations, 1925a).

As to the second objection of the French to the unsuitability of an indigenous language for spreading European culture, the British made it clear that they had no intention of imparting "general ideas" by means of the educational system under their control. To Lugard, education had one overriding objective, to ensure "that natives should work" (League of Nations, 1925b: 206). If education "using that term in its broadest sense" (p. 206) were properly structured, it should bring about that goal, he argued.

Lugard made it clear that from his standpoint – that of training for labor – what counted was the imperative that the "language of the country" must serve as the language of instruction in the schools. It was only a secondary question whether the European language were taught as a subject (League of Nations, 1923). However, as the Swedish representative noted, teaching a European language in the "village schools properly so-called" involved "a great waster of time." While she "quite realised that the elite of the population must be acquainted with French," for the elementary schools it was necessary to concentrate on the "usual branches of knowledge," which she listed as "agriculture, hygiene and manual and agricultural work." She lamented that in a French mandate, as many as 21 hours out of 30 per week were given over to the study of French in elementary schools, leaving no time for the "really essential part of teaching" (League of Nations, 1925b: 34–5). Lugard joined her in her objections to the system of education in French-speaking colonial Africa. For his part, Lugard took exception to the curriculum of education in the territories under Belgian mandate: it was too "literary" (p. 70).

So little could the advocates of French and the British and their allies agree on these questions, that the Belgian representative found himself defending the right of each colonial power to "decide . . . on the spot whether it was in the native's interest that he should be taught his own or a European language" (League of Nations, 1925b: 36). "The matter must be left to the local administration" (p. 36) and not the Mandates Commission, he concluded, ironically vindicating the British policy in their own colonies against the British as the dominant power in the League of Nations. They would simply have to agree to disagree. As the reports of the individual mandated colonies attested, the French followed a policy of instituting French education in their mandated territories,[10] while the British followed a policy of "vernacular education" as the basis of their educational policy.

The Phelps-Stokes Commission

The British position on educational policy in the League of Nations found support from an unexpected source, the Phelps-Stokes Fund, an American philanthropic society directing its resources towards African Americans and heavily interested in education. The Phelps-Stokes Fund previously concentrated much of its efforts on the education of African Americans in the southern states of the US, vigorously supporting the policy of industrial education for southern African Americans of educationalist Booker T. Washington. The attention of the philanthropic society was first turned to Africa by American missionaries there, who feared that political developments in British Africa would lead to the loss of their influence over education. As the colonial governments increasingly asserted their control over the education system in Africa, missionaries sought leverage to ensure their representation in the evolution of educational policy (Jones, 1921; Schilling, 1972). Having determined to take up the question, the Phelps-Stokes Fund appointed a commission of enquiry to look into the current state of education in certain parts of Africa. The commission was set up under the leadership of Dr Thomas Jesse Jones, a sociologist from Columbia University and education director of the Phelps-Stokes Fund.

Prior to their departure for Africa, Jones and other members traveled to Europe, where they consulted with officials in the colonial departments of the European powers with African possessions, as well as with leaders of missionary groups (Phelps-Stokes, 1921: xiii). The Committee left for Africa on 25 August, 1920 and within one year visited the British possessions of Sierra Leone, Gold Coast, Nigeria, Cameroon and much of southern Africa; it also toured French Cameroons, Portuguese Angola, Belgian Congo and the independent states of Liberia and South Africa. The primary means of collecting data were field-trips and interviews with Africans, including women, men, school-age children, teachers, missionaries and farmers. The commission also visited schools and held conferences with Chambers of Commerce and European merchants located in Africa (Phelps-Stokes, 1921: xix).

The detailed recommendations that the Commission made regarding education in the colonies were subsumed under a policy labeled "adaptation." The goal of education in the colony was to "adapt education to the needs of the people . . . as the first requisite" and to "adapt school work to African conditions" (Jones, 1921: 11). According to Jones, "the bulk of the African population lived in small, rural villages and engaged in agricultural pursuits; therefore, African education should be permeated with a strong agricultural bias, with hygiene, health, child care, housekeeping, and handicrafts as other basic subjects" (Schilling, 1972: 245).

The Commission considered the question of language critical to the policy of adaptation. It made recommendations to guide governments in most African colonies, which, however, hardly departed in kind from the previous language practice in the British colonies. The Commission emphasized "vernacular education" (mother tongue education) for the majority of people: "The local school must make all possible provision for instruction in the vernacular" (Jones, 1921: 61). It also recommended the teaching of a lingua franca of African origin in the middle classes in the areas "occupied by large Native groups speaking diverse languages" (Jones, 1921: 26). Finally, in the upper standards, it suggested that the language of the European colonial power "should be taught" (Jones, 1921: 26).

Despite the fanfare that accompanied the commission, the recommendations made by the Commission did not depart significantly in content from the then existing practice – at least in the British case. The entire thrust of the Phelps-Stokes Commission, like that of British policy, was bound up with the economic and political goals of colonialism. As historian Donald Schilling has summed up the Phelps-Stokes Commission's recommendations with respect to Kenya:

> The advocates of adaptation were fully conscious of the colonial situation and were using this policy to insure its perpetuation. Practically, the policy of adaptation served to undermine the development of an African challenge to British rule in Kenya. (Schilling, 1972: 373)

Given the common goals and outlook of the Phelps-Stokes Commission and British imperial administrators and missionaries, their cooperation in the sphere of education in the British empire is not surprising. Officials like Lugard saw in the Phelps-Stokes report the embodiment of their own program, and eagerly seized upon it to spur the Colonial Office, hitherto more or less silent on these questions, into action. The result was the formation of the Advisory Committee on Native Education in British Tropical Africa (Schilling, 1972: 252), later expanded into the Advisory Committee on Education in the Colonies. This Committee, founded in 1923, was under the direction of Lugard and Secretary for the Colonies William Ormsby Gore, both of whom had served as British representatives on the League of Nations Mandates Commission, and both of whom were already advocates of the British policy as it had developed in Asia and most of Africa to that point. Although the Advisory Committee issued a number of policy statements of a fairly detailed nature, it never violated in spirit or substance the educational language policies already in place, nor did it add much in point of detail. Its main function was to provide guidance along these lines to those parts of the British empire, mainly newer colonies in Africa, then still in the process of developing administrative and educational policy, and to bring those colonial administrations whose policies differed substantially into line with the bulk of the empire.

This orientation of the Committee was made clear from the first meeting by Ormsby Gore:

> There are few subjects on which greater uneasiness is being felt at the present time than education, not only in Europe but in other parts of the world, such as India, where it is now admitted that mistakes have been made in the past. The object of the present Committee is to avoid a repetition of such mistakes in Africa and by collecting the truth of experience from all over the world, to build up a sounder system of education, which should be less productive of causes of legitimate discontent. (quoted in Schilling, 1972: 298)

As Schilling (1972: 298) observes, "Ormsby-Gore was advocating a policy which would derail the beginnings of nationalism in Africa and facilitate the continued exercise of British rule. Thus from its very inception the Advisory Committee had an overtly political object."

The Committee's policy recommendations were outlined in its report on Education Policy in British Tropical Africa of 1925. The Memorandum contained 14 broad educational principles that were presented to (and approved by) the Secretary of State for the Colonies and which were to constitute the basis of educational policy for local governments in African colonies. The Committee made use of the philosophy and discourse of the Phelps-Stokes study. Still, its policy more closely demonstrates, perhaps, the influence of the thinking of Lord Lugard, one of its principal authors.

Stressing a favorite Lugard theme, the importance of assuming greater control and supervision on the part of the governments, the report couched its conclusions in the catchphrase of the Phelps-Stokes commission, the principle of "adaptation" of education to "native life": "Education should be adapted to the mentality, aptitude, occupation and traditions of the various people, conserving as far as possible all sound and healthy elements in the fabric of their social life" (Advisory Committee on Native Education in the British Tropical African Dependencies, 1925: 4). In making this conclusion more specific, the report sounded the theme so familiar in British imperial education history, declaring that education must "counteract the tendency to look down on manual labour" (p. 7) that education directed toward producing clerks was thought to produce.

On the question of language policy, the Committee followed the long-standing policy of placing "primary importance" on "the educational use of the vernaculars" (p. 6).[11] A supplementary report specifically addressing this question, drawn up a few months later, made explicit what was envisioned thereby: "The aim of education in Tropical Africa should be to preserve and develop a vernacular as a medium of expression and of communication in adult life and as the vehicle of native thought and culture. Therefore the mother tongue should be the basis and medium of all elementary education in Tropical Africa" (quoted in Schilling, 1972: 310).

That the Advisory Committee's policy should be in line with that of the main portions of the British empire is already shown by the analysis of the Phelps-Stokes Commission, which provided the direct impetus for its creation. The close connection of the two, however, has been misunderstood to indicate the adoption by the British of an "alien" policy (Phillipson, 1992). That such an interpretation is misdirected not only follows from the account of British policy provided above but also from two salient circumstances:

(1) Lord Lugard was a prime mover within the Advisory Committee. As shown, he had already formulated precisely the policy it adopted before the Phelps-Stokes Commission performed its work in Africa, taking it from British Asia, where it was already long-standing policy.
(2) In the American colonies themselves (e.g. the Philippines), the policies advocated by the Phelps-Stokes Commission were never put into place, but English education constituted the basis from the first throughout American rule.

At most, the Advisory Committee brought a somewhat more articulated and unified policy regarding language policy in British dependencies.

It did not, however, essentially alter the longstanding British colonial practice and view on education in general, and language policy in particular. Even in the great majority of West and East African colonies visited by the Phelps-Stokes Commission, subsequent developments produced only minor adjustments of policy.[12] Indeed, because of the very congruity between the goals of the British colonial governments and the recommendations of the Commission, perhaps, the latter's work experienced unchallenged acceptance by the colonial administration.

Thus when the Advisory Committee expanded its scope to include the entire British empire, it was not so much to establish an imperial policy as to stamp with the name of imperial policy what had already developed throughout the colonies as local policy. When, therefore, Great Britain finally developed an "imperial" policy it was not what advocates of imperial policy had understood by its term, nor what is today called the policy of linguistic imperialism, but rather precisely the opposite. It was a policy of limiting the spread of English to what was minimally necessary to running a colonial empire.

Notes

1. While English schools received government support from the beginning, vernacular schools were divided between those receiving government support and those independent of the colonial administration. However, as shown by a comparison of Appendixes A and B, the latter category had become relatively insignificant by the late period of British colonial rule.
2. There is a complicating factor in calculating the number of vernacular schools in that the number of such schools for Chinese or Indian children is sometimes specified and sometimes not. On the other hand, "English Schools" were mostly open to all children. The general picture is not altered. For the Federated Malay States, the number of vernacular schools includes Chinese and Indian in addition to Malay.
3. This total refers only to Malay vernacular schools. There were, in addition, at least three Chinese schools and 14 Tamil schools in Kelantan; other colonies do not give such figures for that year.
4. This number is actually the percentage of students attending all post-primary schools. Since not all secondary schools were conducted in English, the figure overstates the percentage of students actually learning English.
5. The classification of school age had been slightly extended evidently.
6. The total for students at vernacular schools includes Malay, Chinese and Indian students.
7. This figure includes only Malay vernacular students. The actual figure must have been somewhat higher when Chinese and Indian vernacular students are added in. It should be noted that Chinese and Indian students are included in the totals for English schools.
8. This includes Chinese and Indian students in vernacular schools.

9. This includes, for the most part, Chinese and Indian vernacular schools, in the latter of which some English instruction was provided. However, there were few such schools in comparison to the "purely vernacular schools" (Eleum, 1905).

10. The only major class of exceptions were the Arab countries under French mandate, where instruction in Arabic was permitted, but French was made compulsory alongside it.

11. Schilling comments that "it was natural for the memorandum to reflect what had become established practice in African education" (p. 307). And, as is shown in the previous chapter, this policy was also that followed in Asia.

12. For a detailed account, see Brutt-Griffler (1998: 118–26).

Chapter 6

The Becoming of a World Language

Agency in Language Spread

In the phrase "English spread," it is only natural to take *spread* as a verb – and a transitive one: the British (and Americans) *spread* English. Indeed, a central contention of the theory of linguistic imperialism (Phillipson, 1992) is that English spread in the postcolonial world represents the cultural hegemony of the most powerful English-speaking nations.[1] English is therefore an imposed language in the periphery. An important implication follows from this notion: World English is the product of the "mother-tongue" English language nations, particularly the UK and the US. That narrative could be aptly entitled "the world language imperialism made."

When agency in spread is taken one-sidedly, it contributes to the writing of an imperial narrative of English spread. Just as in language planning, in which agency has been traditionally viewed as invested in the powerful, so too in language spread, agency is widely viewed as inhering in the dominant nations. The conceptual lens of linguistic imperialism obscures the role of Africans, Asians, and other peoples of the world as active agents in the process of creation of world English.

There are various reasons to question such an approach. Most important among them, recognition of the agency of Africans and Asians in particular is crucial to a conception of the development of World English. The empirical data presented in the preceding chapters demonstrate that the spread of English was not simply a unidirectional, top-down process. Rather, Africans and Asians have significantly shaped the process of English spread. The formation of language policy in British colonies shows the centrality of the struggle *against imperialism* to the creation of World English.

This account does not start from the assumption of Western hegemony through imperialism, but, as with the containment policy, the codetermination of the social and linguistic environment. In the realm of language, this paradigm means that non-Western agency does not lie exclusively in the domain of the indigenous languages of Asia, Africa and Latin America. Just as crucially, it is found in what are usually called "Western languages," including English.

Taking the construction of World English in its historical process, therefore, requires a shift in perspective. The model of English language spread put forward here does not view English as something imposed by the "Center" on the "Periphery." In presenting evidence of the active historical role of Africans and Asians in the development of World English, the present explanatory framework emphasizes their agency and historicizes their will. In this conception, World English is not simply made *through* them but made *by* them.

The idea has already been discussed under the notion of *the postcolonial in the colonial* (see Chapter 4). It reconceptualizes the binary through which our world is often constructed: the conflict of the "traditional" (generally taken as non-Western) and the "modern" (Western and often imperial). The idea of the postcolonial in the colonial argues that the "modern" world has been constructed not only by imperialism but just as centrally by the struggle against imperialism. In this conception, the historical role of non-Western peoples does not consist simply in the traditional, in what has been carried over from the past. Its agency, rather, lies in its historical role in the creation of the world as we know it.

The idea of postcolonial in the colonial is not one limiting non-Western agency to resistance of Western imperial oppression (cf. Said, 1993) – one in which the "center" acts and the "periphery" reacts. Rather, it is more generative. In this conception, non-Western nations are not "peripheral" but take equal part in the creation of the world econocultural system and its linguistic expression, World English.

A Theoretical Perspective on World English

The global spread of English exhibits complexities that have yet to be brought under a unifying theoretical perspective. Among the questions that remain to be answered, the most important may be why English tended to *replace* local languages in most of the British Isles, North America, and Australia, while becoming established *alongside* them in much of Asia and Africa. In the absence of such an explanation, the disappearance of indigenous languages in the British Isles, as in other parts of the world, in the face of the encroachment of a "dominant" language might be used to imply that the same dangers face many, perhaps most, languages as a result of the global spread of English. Such unproven assumptions have conditioned a conception of World English as a threat to linguistic rights and that has even prompted linguists to involve international agencies against the onslaught of globalization (cf. Maffi, 1999; Phillipson, 1999).

The present account is intended to provide a more complex analysis of such global issues. Rather than aiming at the promotion of a monolithic conception of English as the *only* language operating in the modern era, it attempts to account for the maintenance of societal bilingualism within the international context. The framework developed here seeks to explain the conscious preservation of culture and identity within an acquired language and the evolution of multiple literacies within multilingual speech communities in English in the postcolonial period (cf. McKay, 1996). In doing so, it attempts to overcome the limitations of existing theoretical perspectives and to subsume the various strands in the development of World English under one unifying theoretical framework. In conjunction with the process of macroacquisition (Chapters 7 and 8), the framework put forward in this chapter aims at a unified theory of World English.

In particular, with respect to the essential differences of English spread leading to the replacement of indigenous languages versus the establishment of stabilized bilingual communities, the present account distinguishes language spread within a national or regional context from the growth of world language. From the historical vantage point, the development of English has moved through two essential phases. First, via the formation of the domestic market and the evolution of a national language and culture, English developed into the *national language* of England. Second, by virtue of the creation of the world economy and culture together with accompanying sociohistorical circumstances, English evolved into a *world language*, an international lingua franca that evolves under definite conditions and displays a number of distinguishing features.

Three Premises

Three essential conceptual bases underlie this explanatory framework for World English:

(1) That language spread must be understood in the context of language change, in a unified conception of *language spread and change*;
(2) That the understanding of the development of World English requires a theoretical approach employing a world, rather than a national, scope[2];

(3) That there is need of a paradigm shift from monolingualism to bilingualism reflecting an historical shift in language use.

The last of these corresponds to a recent trend toward an emphasis on
the study of bilingualism. Romaine (1996: 571) notes that "modern linguistic theory generally takes the monolingual individual as its starting
point in dealing with basic analytical problems such as the construction
of grammars and the nature of competence." Romaine and other scholars,
on the contrary, favor those emphasizing the centrality of multilingual and
multicultural contexts, such as those that increasingly constitute the setting of English-using communities (cf. S.N. Sridhar & K.K. Sridhar, 1994).

Romaine (1996) points out that monolingualism and monolinguals
represent neither the typical cases from which linguistic theory must
generalize nor the normal modus vivendi of language users and speech
communities. To the contrary, "It is . . . monolingualism that represents
a special case" as a condition pertaining to a minority of the world's
population (p. 573). As conceptualized here, bilingualism is taken as
central to processes in language evolution, making use of the shift from
monolingual to bilingual/multilingual paradigms.

Differentiating Features of World Language

The explanatory framework developed here identifies four central
features of the development of global language. These are:

(1) Econocultural functions of the language;
(2) The transcendence of the role of an elite lingua franca;
(3) The stabilization of bilingualism through the coexistence of world
language with other languages in bilingual/multilingual contexts;
(4) Language change via the processes of world language convergence
and world language divergence.

The Econocultural Features of World Language

The distinguishing feature of a world language is encapsulated in what
Quirk (1988) has called the econocultural features of a language, that is,
its combination of economic or commercial centrality and its cultural/
intellectual role in the world community.[3] World language is a product
of the sociohistorical development of the *world econocultural system*, which
includes the world market, business community, technology, science and
cultural and intellectual life on the global scale. The emergence of World
English has accompanied the development of the world econocultural
system.

Since the world economy develops so as to increasingly unify both the world market and the production of commodities on which it relies, it simultaneously creates the conditions for world language. The world econocultural system, however, includes more than the world economy in the strict sense. To the extent that science and technology become international, so does a world language tend to emerge to fulfill world intellectual and scientific functions. The world econocultural system has its cultural component as well.

It is important to separate the world econocultural system from one of the phases of its existence, imperialism. As scholars such as Wallerstein (1980) and Frank and Gills (1993) have demonstrated in great detail, the tendency toward a world economy constitutes the driving force in modern historical development and predates and postdates the system of colonialism, which is nevertheless often taken as its most essential feature. Hence, although imperialism plays a role in creating the *world econocultural system* that lies at the basis of world language, it does not constitute by any means the whole of its necessary conditions. As Pennycook (1994: 225) cautions, "it is important not to assume a deterministic relationship of imperialism" and English spread. World language is not essentially an offspring of imperialism. In fact, while the phase known as imperialism helped create the conditions of world language, it simultaneously attempted to undo those conditions.

Imperialism facilitated the development of world language by contributing to the creation of a language of trade. Nevertheless, it also held up the development of world language by confining the language to the elite and commercial classes, by subordinating the spread of language to its own political and economic ends through the containment policy. This other side of the relation of imperialism to world language – the extent to which it retards as well as promotes the spread of English – is overlooked by linguistic imperialism. In contrast, the notion of postcolonialism in language (B. Kachru, 1997; Mazrui & Mazrui, 1998; Pennycook, 1994) has served to call attention to this point.

A central contention of this work is that the spread of English, which coincides with British imperialism and colonialism, is nevertheless the result of the more fundamental tendencies toward global econocultural integration. Imperialism is only the unwitting, even unwilling, *instrument* of the spread of English. As evidenced in Chapter 4, the spread of English is as much a product of the struggle against imperialism, as experience taught the British (cf. Mazrui, 1973; Mazrui & Mazrui, 1998). Frantz Fanon described such a process with respect to French in Algeria: "Paradoxically as it may appear, it is the Algerian Revolution, it is the struggle of the Algerian people, that is facilitating the spreading of the French language in the nation" (quoted in Mazrui & Mazrui, 1998: 63). Mazrui and Mazrui (1998) point out that English also emerged as such an "instrument of liberation," to use Fanon's term, in the British colonial empire, both in Africa and Asia.

The evolution of world language tends to coincide with at least the incipient decline of political hegemony of the nation of origin rather than its rise. The classical period of Latin, for example, comes after the fall of Roman political supremacy, although that constituted its basis. In the same way, English has progressed greatly as a world language since the fall of territorial imperialism, and especially since the decline of British and American hegemony on the world market. That world market is now less dominated by the US and England than in the past, certainly in the case of England, which has fallen back to a second rate world power (Wallerstein, 1980). The current period, for example, has featured the growing importance of Asia in world commerce. Not coincidentally, the same period has witnessed the development of what has been referred to as "English as an Asian Language" (B. Kachru, 1997). World language, then, takes more definite shape when the hegemony of the major mother tongue English speaking nations is challenged by a number of emerging powers.

The spread of English as an intellectual and scientific language also coincides with the rise to prominence of the non-Western world, or nations outside North America and Europe. The last half century has seen the tremendous growth of the middle and professional classes in Asia, Africa, and Latin America and Central and Eastern Europe. Indeed, these sections of society, and with them science and technological innovation, are growing fastest in those areas (Widdowson, 1997). At the same time, Western (European and American) hegemony has receded. Interestingly, the coherent theoretical standpoint of "cultural imperialism" (Phillipson, 1992) has emerged just at the historical moment that old modes of imperial control have been challenged. That perspective, however, reflects that in a declining period of imperial rule, the conditions that characterized it are of recent memory and still exert their effects in the interpretation of contemporary sociopolitical processes. A more persuasive and nuanced argument has been put forward by such scholars as Mazrui and Mazrui (1998) and B. Kachru (1981; 1997) that "indigenized languages" are not carriers of imperialist cultural hegemony. In this respect, it is easy to conflate the development of English in the global arena with one of those lingering effects, or even to see it as the last bastion of imperialist hegemony.

To contrast econocultural spread to the other means by which English has spread, the next section considers the history of English spread in various contexts.

The spread of English in the British Isles

The spread of English began in the British Isles themselves. Its progress there was slow, its expansion to its present state of supremacy commencing no later than the eighth century and lasting throughout the ensuing millennium (Hindley, 1990; Wakelin, 1975).

This period of the spread of English is often overlooked today in considering World English. Its vital importance lies in the fact that, first, it took place in the context of the establishment of a regional economic and political system encompassing the British Isles, and, second, that English to a large extent displaced the Celtic languages that had existed there (Baugh & Cable, 1993). The main exception was Welsh for reasons to be discussed later. It is quite true that many of these languages have in the last century experienced attempts at a revival, particularly Welsh and Irish (Baker, 1985, 1996; O'Riagain, 1997). Nevertheless, the vast majority of the population, between 95% and 98%, throughout the British Isles speaks English as a mother tongue. In this essential respect, therefore, the spread of English in the British Isles – although integrally connected to the extension of English political control – differs significantly from the later spread of English in the British empire.

This first phase of the spread of English did not extend the language beyond the confined geographical area surrounding the home nation. This phase of English spread, therefore, did not involve the creation of a world language, or even the origins thereof. It was no different from other similar examples throughout the world of regional language spread. It shows, nevertheless, that what Quirk (1988) calls the "imperial" model of language spread dates back very far in history and is a model that, as will be shown, includes forms of language spread that are quite different in nature.

The spread of English to North America and Australasia

The second phase of the spread of English commenced around the beginning of the seventeenth century, with the founding of British colonies in North America, and lasted until near the end of the eighteenth century, with the establishment of a British colony in Australasia. Here, for the first time, English spread beyond the confines of the British

Isles in an extensive and permanent diaspora (Baugh & Cable, 1993). There were many ramifications of this spread of English, including in the Caribbean, but underlying the complex result is the basis of this spread of English to America, and later Australasia, in the speaker migrations of English speaking peoples from the British Isles. This basis has led Quirk (1988) to refer to this type of language spread under the "demographic" model. It should be noted, as well, that this model is not unique to English. At the same time English was spread to North America by these means, so were Spanish, French, and Portuguese. What is less often noted is that this episode in the spread of English was confined to a relatively well-defined period, and virtually ceased thereafter. It resulted, moreover, not in the creation of World English, anymore than the simultaneous spread of Spanish, French, and Portuguese made those the language of the entire world; rather, its essential result was the establishment of English as the national language of a number of new nations, including the United States, Canada, Australia, New Zealand and others (see Fishman, 1977). These nations adopted English as a direct result not simply of *the political control of England* but also *the large numbers of English colonists who brought their language with them in their movements.*

Nevertheless, taking this kind of spread of English via speaker migration alone, we cannot account for the development of English into the world language it has become. It does not tell us why English rather than French, Spanish or Portuguese (let alone Arabic, Chinese, Turkish and other languages that had attained a perhaps greater world presence, especially Arabic, when measured both in terms of geographical spread and number of speakers) should attain that position (Brosnahan, 1973; Fishman, 1977).

The spread of English to the Rest of the World

To answer that question we must examine what has been put forward as yet a third model of language spread and contextualize it within two crucial political and economic developments of the eighteenth century. That model is what Quirk (1988) calls the econocultural model, in which English spreads for the economic and cultural/intellectual reasons discussed earlier.

For such an econocultural development to take place, two historical processes had to converge: first, the transition from colonies as a refuge for Europe's surplus population to the establishment of economic and political hegemony over entire peoples; and second, England's attainment of domination over the world market. The form of colonial control differed essentially in European outposts in the Americas and Australasia from its dominant form in Asia and Africa (Hilferding, 1981; Hobson, 1902). In the Americas and Australasia, political and economic hegemony was established mainly by means of the migration of European peoples, who over a period of time established themselves as the majority populations, or at least significant components thereof, in those parts of the world. Political and economic hegemony on the world-scale, however, required an extension of control or at least influence into Asia and Africa, and this required a different form of colonialism. There were necessary limits to the scale of migration-based colonialism. A world economy (Wallerstein, 1980) and a world market required the establishment of economic and political hegemony on the world scale by *conquest of peoples*. It was, therefore, the newer form of colonial control that took root in Asia and Africa in the eighteenth century which established the essential conditions of world language – the evolution of econocultural functions of language on a decidedly global scale, and populations who retained their mother tongues.

Had this system merely produced a series of largely unconnected national dominions, competing empires in a state of equilibrium, no one language could have come to embody econocultural functions. Just as important as the transition to the new type of colonial hegemony of the eighteenth century was the establishment of domination over the world market which England wrested from France in a series of colonial and European wars (Wallerstein, 1980). The more England gained control of the world market – in part a function of the industrial revolution there – the more the international extension of trade and production relations inevitably transmitted English, rather than French, Spanish, Portuguese, Arabic, Chinese or Turkish. Europe subjugated the world, and England subordinated the other European powers. Hence, while French, Spanish, Portuguese, Arabic, Chinese and Turkish remained imperial languages, none of them became a world language, because none of them acquired world econocultural functions.

This result was something that no one nation, culture, or people willed. Noting the British opposition to the "'reckless' spreading of the English language" in contrast to French efforts to promulgate their language, Mazrui and Mazrui (1998: 21) comment that "English gathered its own momentum and rapidly outstripped French both in the number of countries in the world that adopted it as a major national medium, and in the number of speakers. The British who did not want their language to become a universal language ended with precisely that fate, while the

French had to embark on a determined attempt to stop French from receding in importance." Such an outcome was the result of historical processes of development, rather than a conscious policy of linguistic or cultural imperialism, however much we may find elements of the latter within it. Neither linguistic imperialism nor the econocultural model of language spread by themselves can explain how English came to take on the econocultural functions that made its transition to a world language possible.

The Sociohistorical Basis of Stable Bilingualism in Asia and Africa

To fully understand this process, we must consider more closely how the conditions in South Asia, and later other parts of Asia and Africa, differed from those of other places to which English spread. Such an examination holds the key to explaining why English replaced the languages of such nations as Ireland while in places like India and Nigeria English functions alongside other languages.

If we examine the three periods of the spread of English referred to earlier – first within the British Isles, second to America and Australasia, and finally to Asia, Africa, and the rest of the world – we find that three quite different processes were at work, and in this we find the explanation for the replacement of the indigenous languages in the earlier episodes as opposed to the establishment of bilingualism/multilingualism in the most recent. In the first period of the spread of English within the British Isles, it was in part accompanied by and in part carried out by means of a migration of English-speaking peoples during the establishment of English political and economic hegemony in Great Britain (Hindley, 1990; Wakelin, 1975). A direct and substantial English presence existed in the form of English enclaves or English-speaking communities. The same took place in the migration of English-speaking peoples to the Americas and to Australasia; but in the latter case, the transition to English as the dominant language was immediate, as the English-speaking community formed itself into the dominant political force through displacement of the indigenous population. This was possible because the people who formed the laboring population were imported to the New World, particularly from Africa (Blassingame, 1979). Since these forced migrants came from numerous different language groups, the English of the numerically dominant part of the population became the most likely medium for them to adopt, however much they adapted it to their own use.

The reasons behind the language spread within the British Isles and the English diaspora in the Americas and Australasia aside, the cases are really quite different. For the colonization of America and Australasia was a spread of the language by means of population movement, whereas in the British Isles English was spread primarily by its supplanting of the mother tongues of the indigenous populations. The more interesting question is why English supplanted most of the languages of the British Isles and not the languages of Asia and Africa. The proximity of England to its neighbors played a crucial role, and we must keep the substantial migration of English-speaking peoples in mind. The result of this migration, as mentioned, was the establishment of English-speaking communities, e.g. in Ireland in the sixteenth to eighteenth centuries (Hindley, 1990). Given English economic hegemony, these communities, or English enclaves, were necessarily the most economically, including industrially, advanced regions in Ireland. As the Irish population was drawn to these centers from the countryside, English spread to the working classes; it first became the language of the migrant workers from the countryside. By these means, it began to spread even throughout the countryside, until by the mid-nineteenth century Irish had become a minority language (O'Riagain, 1997). In contrast, in Wales, where much of the rural working class retained Welsh, the language has retained a much higher proportion of daily users (Baker, 1985, 1996; Romaine, 1996).[4]

In English colonies in Africa and Asia, on the other hand, the great distance and the vastness of the empire compared to the metropolis made only a small, insignificant migration of English-speaking peoples possible (Lugard, 1923). The English language spread to Africa and Asia by political and economic means, not demographic (Quirk, 1988). There was, consequently, no establishment of large-scale English-speaking communities in such nations as India. Hence, English-language dominated areas did not emerge. In short, English never became the language of industry and of the major agricultural districts; instead, it was the language primarily of the colonial administration.

Within this distinction lies the crucial factor in the establishment of English as the dominant language of a nation versus its spread as a world language. For purposes of understanding this question, to Quirk's conception of the econocultural functions must be added a conceptual distinction between *internal* and *external* functions, that is, those that have reference to the domestic economy and those that pertain to the world economy. Distinguishing between the national and world realms of econocultural functions helps define the basis on which world language arises.

To replace the indigenous languages, it is not enough that English should become the language of external commerce or world trade; it must also become, as in Ireland, the language of the domestic economy – or at least, to begin with, its essential centers. A monolingual mother tongue English context is formed when the language is necessarily transmitted to the working classes by economic life itself. Otherwise, the indigenous languages are not supplanted. It is this distinction between purely internal and external economic functions that must be attached to Quirk's (1988) econocultural model to make it serviceable for the explanation of the development of world language.

A world language is more than a widely – even internationally – dispersed population of language users. The emergence of a world language requires not merely regional macroacquisition, as in the spread of English within the British Isles, and certainly more than speaker migration, no matter how far-reaching. It entails widespread macroacquisition on the global scale. That process was set off by the development of the new type of colonialism in Africa and Asia. For that reason, the roots of World English lie in the spread of the language to Africa and Asia beginning in the eighteenth century, rather than in earlier episodes of English spread, or in the policies of the British empire beginning in the nineteenth century.

With the distinction in forms of language spread between speaker migration and macroacquisition (see Chapter 1), it is possible to construct a model of the outcomes of English spread in the world. The fundamental division between speaker migration and macroacquisition accounts for the distinction between contexts in which English replaces other languages as the mother tongue of the speech community and those in which stable bilingualism/multilingualism develops. Where English spread by speaker migration, it was established as a mother tongue variety, generally assuming the role of a national language. The same outcome has tended to characterize macroacquisition settings in which there was a significant mother tongue English speaker migration component, with the exception that a second language remained rooted in the context, experiencing different degrees of decline and reemergence.

The macroacquisition context without significant speaker migration of mother tongue English users, on the other hand, divides into two distinct cases. In multilingual nations, English has generally tended to emerge as a national lingua franca in addition to its world language functions, creating what is variously called the "New English" or "indigenized variety of English" setting, such as Nigeria or India. In these nations, the language serves both internal as well as international functions, and its existence is often formally institutionalized. In contrast, where macroacquisition occurs in the context of an already existing and firmly entrenched national language (such as Egypt or China), English tends not to be seen as playing such a formal societal role, and no "New English" is recognized. These two different macroacquisition settings are analyzed in Chapter 7.

The three different settings in which English has established itself via language spread have become familiarly known as English as a National Language (ENL), English as a Second Language (ESL) and English as a Foreign Language (EFL). When used to denote these distinct contexts, the terms may provide useful abbreviations. It is to be noted, however, that ESL is often used in two distinct senses: (1) the language environment in which a New English arises, and (2) to describe the English language learner in the ENL context.

The framework employed here provides an explanation of these three functional settings via exploring the sociohistorical *context* of English spread. As Figure 6.1 illustrates, English (represented by the darkly shaded core of the figure) spreads into the three different contexts (represented by the arrows pointing outward from the core through the lightly shaded area): (1) where English spread by means of speaker migration of mother tongue English users; (2) that in which English spread via macroacquisition to multilingual settings without significant migration of native speakers; (3) where English spread via macroacquisition to linguistic settings with an entrenched national language. These contexts divide into two essential subsets, those in which the means of spread is both imperial and econocultural in nature (Cases 1 and 2, represented by the top half of the diagram), and that in which it is predominantly econocultural (Case 3, shown in the lower portion). Although macroacquisition takes place in both cases, the national functions that attach to English in the multilingual national settings in Africa and Asia produce a strong sense of national identity in the language acquired that manifests itself in the recognition of a New English (illustrated by the dotted arrow). In contrast, the weaker sense of national identity in the "foreign" language context tends not to lead to such a result (as in Western Europe, East Asia, etc.). Why the sociohistorical context of language spread, or macroacquisition, produces differences in linguistic outcome will be explored in Chapters 7 and 8. In the context of the *speaker migration* of mother tongue English speakers (North America, Australasia), English acquires the function of a national language (represented under linguistic outcome in the figure).

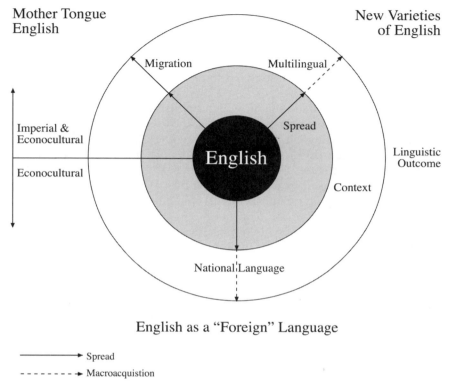

English as a "Foreign" Language

——————→ Spread
- - - - - - - - → Macroacquistion

Figure 6.1 A model of English language spread and change

The Transcendence of the Role of an Elite Lingua Franca

Unlike an international lingua franca, such as Latin and later French represented in Europe at one time, a world language is more than an exclusive language of a socioeconomic and intellectual elite. It has an economic role in the world that induces its spread independently of the political and cultural hegemony of any one nation or nations. World language combines economic and cultural/intellectual roles.

A world language exhibits the tendency toward breaking out of the confines of the elite, and that has already occurred throughout the world (cf. Mazrui & Mazrui, 1998). It is estimated that the world's English-using population has reached nearly 2 billion (Crystal, 1997); it would be hard to claim the existence of 2 billion members of the world's elite.[5] The very surge of demographics that has taken place in the postcolonial world shows that it is no longer a language for exclusive use of the elite.

The imperial legacy alone could not have brought about this result. The cooptation of English as a means of resistance led to its spread beyond the bounds of an elite lingua franca. As even recently in South Africa, where the opposition to apartheid included the demand for access to English (see Chapter 8), the non-elites of the world have not been content to be excluded from a knowledge of the language and have insisted on the right to its acquisition. It may appear to some that post-colonial governments have imposed these policies as a "colonial inheritance" (Phillipson, 1992); but that represents a one-sided reading of which legacy this policy embodies.

The Coexistence of the World Language with Other Languages in a Multilingual Context with Bilingual Speakers

The framework of world language recognizes that English spread has established bilingual/multilingual contexts. The development of World English commences with the establishment of English alongside other languages without replacing them. For example, Bamiro (2000: 36) writes, "In Zimbabwe ... the English language has become a stable second language, functioning side-by-side with Shona and Ndebele." This mode of development distinguishes world language from national language development, in which a dominant political language suppresses all rivals over time within a limited territory. Instead, a crucial component of world language is that the majority of its speakers are bilingual or multilingual. Bilingualism, therefore, assumes a place of centrality in the present framework. In understanding World English, it is necessary to consider how bilingual contexts *condition* the development of varieties (Chapters 7 and 8) and the evolution of the language (Chapter 9).

It is interesting to note that the principal non-English speaking areas of the British Isles went through a transitional period of bilingualism before English supplanted many of the indigenous languages, e.g. Cornish, Manx and Gaelic. This might suggest to those who adhere to the framework of linguistic imperialism that the encroachment of English in many parts of the world will continue until the same process takes place. At this point at least, there is no indication that English is supplanting other languages where it has spread as a world language. Moreover, where displaced languages have made a comeback, it is not by the attempt to supplant English but through bilingualism. For example, bilingualism has been crucial to the "fight for the maintenance and restoration of the Welsh language" (Baker, 1985: 41; cf. Romaine, 1996).

Why does world language not replace other languages?

Unlike the case of a national language, a world language seems not to displace other languages. If World English tends not to be limited to the elite, it may be asked why a world language does not replace the languages of the nations to which it spreads. Once it reaches lower socioeconomic classes, it might be thought that, as in Ireland, it should supplant the languages of the given nation to which it spreads. This does not occur, however, so long as the world language does not become the language of the internal (domestic) economy (market).

Unlike the case of the spread of English to Ireland, a world language spreads by its establishment in multilingual conditions and is spoken by bilinguals. The situation of the Irish type occurs in the immediate vicinity of a hegemonic power, and only where a large speaker migration of mother tongue users takes place as well, as distinct from the spread of English to colonies of the newer type in Asia and Africa. Hence, even where the language serves certain functions of national language, its spread to the working classes also involves bilingualism. World language, therefore, does not replace other languages, but serves as integral part of what S.N. Sridhar (1994: 802) has called "the composite pragmatic model of bilingualism, one that recognizes that a bilingual acquires as much competence in the two (or more) languages as is needed and that all of the languages together serve the full range of communicative needs." This type of bilingualism allows English to assume certain important functions without usurping the domain of other languages. English in these "second language contexts" fulfills certain intellectual/cultural functions that it develops alongside the purely political and economic without thereby establishing itself as the basis of the local economy (the internal market). Hence, even in its spread to classes outside the elite, it does not do so as the language of the domestic economy, but in the econocultural functional realm of world language. Throughout Africa, for example, as Mazrui and Mazrui (1998: 78) note, "More and more now learn it simply because it is the most important language *globally.*" Its role has already been established by means of the particular type of spread behind the establishment of world language.

Bisong (1995: 123), writing about English in Nigeria, seems to capture the essence of the spread of world language. Bisong describes that in

Nigeria, the "linguistic and cultural picture is one of multilingualism and multiculturalism." Directly tackling the concern sometimes voiced by proponents of linguistic imperialism that English represents a threat to Nigeria's indigenous languages, he remarks:

> There is no way three or four hours of exposure to English in a formal school situation could possibly compete with, let alone threaten to supplant, the non-stop process of acquiring competence in the mother tongue. .... The parent sends the child to the English-medium school precisely because she wants her child to grow up multilingual. She is also not unmindful of the advantages that might accrue from the acquisition of competence in English. Why settle for monolingualism in a society that is constantly in a state of flux, when you can be multilingual and more at ease with a richer linguistic repertoire and expanding consciousness? To interpret such actions as emanating from people who are victims of Centre linguistic imperialism is to bend sociolinguistic evidence to suit a preconceived thesis. (Bisong, 1995: 125)

Indeed, the concern over English spreading too widely and too rapidly has tended to obscure a grave problem that needs to be addressed. Language rights advocates should be alert to the important implications of this condition and would be well advised to insist that bilingualism/multilingualism, at least that form which includes English, no longer be the preserve of the privileged and powerful.

Language Change via the Processes of World Language Convergence and World Language Divergence

In positing that World English finds its basis not in speaker migration but macroacquisition, this explanation of World English connects language spread as a sociopolitical process to linguistic change, an element of the question generally overlooked. To this point, the present study has concerned itself with spread. It will now turn its attention to the process of English language change.

Like the process of spread, language change does not take place in a vacuum. Rather, it is integrally tied to the same world-historic forces that have been traced throughout this book: colonialism, the anticolonial struggle, and the emergence of political and economic independent nations as outgrowths of the collapse of colonialism. The development of World English is part of the transition from language spread as a function of national language development to language spread as the expression of world language development.

As such, there can be said to be two historical processes of politico-linguistic development: national language and world language. Language spread in the modern era, therefore, takes on a political determination, national and world, which are political and economic categories rather than linguistic ones. Hence, neither national nor world language develops for linguistic reasons, but for sociohistorical reasons. They are manifestations of, respectively, the development of the nation-state and the development of the world economy (Wallerstein, 1980).

National language implies the development of one language for a nation-state, although, as Quirk (1988) points out, this ideal case has seldom been realized in practice. Nevertheless, national language has historically exhibited something of this tendency, and has, for that reason, become the basis for monolingualism or the destruction of various and competing languages. World language, on the other hand, implies the existence of a language in addition to national languages, hence bilingualism. World language, then, is a process of the superseding of national languages as the dominant sociopolitical language form. This process has coincided with the continuous growth of the world economy over the last few centuries, and is tied, in particular, to the dominance of the UK and US within the world market. In this respect, World English is not the product of a policy, but a world historical process, similar to, in a different era, the development of national languages.

World language thereby becomes a meaningful unit of analysis as much as national language. It allows an understanding of how English has changed as a result of its becoming a world language, and how language change can now be as much driven by processes outside the mother tongue English nations as within them.

These two levels of language conditioned by extralinguistic circumstances find their reflection within the process of language change of World English. Within the development of world language, I identify two fundamental processes of language change: (1) world language divergence, or the creation of new varieties of English; (2) world language convergence, or the maintenance of unity in the *world language*. These two processes comprise the topics of Chapters 7, 8 and 9.

Notes

1. If English were not both an essentially "foreign" language as well as an imposed language, it would make little, if any, sense to call those from the

"periphery" who advocate the use of English there agents of a linguistic imperialist policy who have "internalized" its essence, as Phillipson does (1992: 57).

2. A parallel transition from a focus on the national to one on the global has taken place in other social sciences as well, particularly political economy and sociology. See Frank and Gills (1993).

3. This point is discussed further in Chapter 9.

4. Census statistics reveal a different picture. In the case of Irish, for example, 32.5% of the population (Central Statistics Office, 1996) claims knowledge of the language, whereas, in the case of Welsh, only 18.7% (Williams, 1997) claim knowledge. It appears, however, that Welsh might be used more as an "everyday spoken language" (Baker, personal communication).

5. Just as socioeconomic status at one time determined access to English, it now often governs the level of proficiency in English ultimately attained – the highest levels generally found in the social elite. (I am grateful to Sandra McKay for calling my attention to the importance of this issue.)

Chapter 7

Macroacquisition: Bilingual Speech Communities and Language Change

Methodological Considerations in Language Change

To this point, the major focus of this work has been to trace the process of English language spread. In accordance with the approach adopted, it remains to take up the other side of that question, the English language change that has accompanied its transformation into a world language. In particular, the new varieties known collectively as the "New Englishes" (Platt *et al.*, 1984) must be accounted for.

It might appear that this change of topic requires a corresponding change of approach, since the investigation has shifted from the broader sociohistorical plane to the more narrowly linguistic. In place of historical factors such as colonialism, anticolonialism, and language policy, language change moves into the realm of phonological, semantic, morphological and syntactic alterations (Labov, 1994; McMahon, 1994). The lexical borrowings, changes in sound, and semantic restructuring seem to have little to do with the topics that have been considered in the present work to this point.

And yet, upon closer inspection, a convincing reason to revise these apparently logical methodological assumptions presents itself, and from, perhaps, an unexpected source. Indeed, prominent linguists specializing in the study of language change via second language acquisition (SLA) processes have become the strongest voices for combining the realm of the "linguistic" with that of what they call the "extralinguistic," or the sociohistorical conditions that have been under investigation. Weinreich's (1974) seminal work on language contact highlights the centrality of such "extra-linguistic factors." He comments, "The linguist who makes theories about language influence but neglects to account for the socio-cultural setting of the language contact leaves his study suspended, as it were, in mid-air" (1974: 4). He cites approvingly the words of Haugen, "Talk of substrata and superstrata must remain stratospheric unless we find it solidly in the behavior of living observable speakers" (p. 4). Other linguists are even more forceful in their conclusions. Romaine (1995: 70) reports that "Thomason (1986) says that all of these attempts to formulate linguistic constraints on contact phenomena have failed because both the direction and extent of linguistic interference is socially determined." At most, concludes De Graff (1999: 527) in a wide-ranging study of linguistic factors in language change, "internal (morphosyntactic factors and . . . cognitive constraints)" form the "space of possibilities" within which "contingent external factors (e.g. sociolinguistic, demographic, and historical factors, which vary in complex ways on a case-by-case basis) determine the actual outcomes of language creation and change." Lanham (1996) also contends that the causes of language change are "social, and can only be accounted for when we have adequate information about the uses of language in the society that maintains it." In other words, the very attempt to account for language change through linguistic processes alone has convinced some linguists that the sociohistorical setting of language change must be considered.

To take just one example, Mufwene (1993a, 1993b) and other creolists have greatly advanced the study of the development of New World creoles in the sixteenth to eighteenth centuries by means of a detailed study of plantation slavery. They have concentrated on how its organization affected the access of Africans and their creolized descendants to the various languages (lexifiers and substrates) that came in contact in the formation of English and French creoles. Mufwene (1993a, 1993b) has persuasively argued that many assumptions present in the literature as to the formation of creoles – including the existence of antecedent pidgins and the rapid abandonment of African languages – have to be significantly modified. His work demonstrates how in the study of processes of speech community second language acquisition as processes of language change, the researcher must consider "sociohistorically grounded hypotheses" (1993b: 203–4). Mufwene's detailed study of the context of creolization in the New World has led him to the same conclusion that others have who have looked into the question: that the explanation for the emergence of these new varieties lies in the sociohistorical or "extralinguistic" realm and its interrelation with linguistic processes.

In the attempt to integrate the "linguistic" and "extralinguistic," a fundamental theoretical limitation of models of SLA-induced language change – or *language contact* – is that, from the time of Weinreich, linguists have accepted as an essential "premise that the individual is the ultimate locus of contact" (Weinreich, 1974: 6). According to this assumption, the individual embodies only abstract, perhaps universal, linguistic laws that are conceptually isolated from the realm of the historically-grounded social (the "extralinguistic"). The linguistic laws are held to be such because as linguistic universals they hold in any circumstances and thus are not contextual or historical. The social, on the other hand, is contextually bounded, limited and limiting (of the linguistic). There is thereby a conceptual gap between the realms of the linguistic individual and the "extra-linguistic" social. The theoretical cul-de-sac provided by this dichotomous standpoint is not accidental. For, as D. Cameron (1990: 84) has commented, without a "satisfactory account of the relationship between social and linguistic spheres, sociolinguistics is bound to end up stranded in an explanatory void."

Language Contact and the Explanation of New Language Varieties

The problems inherent in the explanatory framework of language contact appear to derive from its assumption that the linguistic sphere is inherently that of the individual speaker. So long as language is approached as arising out of the individual speaker, it remains detached from the sphere of the social. In particular, there is a contradiction in attempting to account for the emergence of a new language or language variety by employing the outlook of individually based models of SLA.

Theories of contact-induced language change

Hitherto attention in SLA, following the general orientation in linguistics, has focused on the development of language within the individual L2 learner. Drawing on this work, Weinreich (1974) sets out to discover how "linguistic interference"[1] operates to affect the performance of the second language speaker, thus altering the language that emerges from their learning. Similarly, Thomason and Kaufman (1988) build their theory around the notion of "imperfect learning" of the second language.

In describing the kind of social process that gives rise to language change in SLA settings, Thomason and Kaufman (1988) argue "if shift occurs rapidly, and if the shifting group is so large numerically that the TL [target language] model is not fully available to all its members, then imperfect learning is a probability, and the learners' errors are more likely to spread throughout the TL speech community" (p. 47). Thus, contact-induced change is conceptualized in terms of:

(1) the TL model;
(2) perfect/imperfect learning;
(3) "errors" in the shifting group.

The fundamental problem with this conception is that it denies language change. All change is deviation and can, therefore, be described as error. Modern linguistics works from the assumption that change initiated by a "native" (or mother tongue) speaker is not error. Theories of SLA, on the other hand, begin from the opposite premise, change introduced into the language by L2 learners constitutes error. As long as we take the standpoint of the individual speaker, these conditions appear not only to conform to common sense but also do not seem to present a theoretical problem.

Conceptual limitations of native speaker-based explanatory frameworks of language change

What if, on the other hand, this question is referred not to individual speakers but to speech communities? Here a contradiction does arise. Linguistics operates from the presupposition that any language is the linguistic expression of the speech community that speaks it. It is thereby contradictory to claim that a speech community can speak its own language in error. What holds for the individual speaker does not hold for the speech community.

There are only two means by which such a conclusion can be denied. Either (1) it must be claimed that the same native/nonnative dichotomy applies to speech communities as to individual speakers, or (2) it must be held that the altered language spoken by the speech community is somehow not a language in the usual sense.

As to the first point, such a claim results from the familiarity of the categories and their overextension rather than any meaning that would attach to the resulting construct. Speech communities (as opposed to the individuals who comprise them) do not have critical or sensitive periods. They are not distinguished from some other norm-establishing group (a second speech community) as "nonstandard."

To describe a speech community as "nonnative" involves, rather, a process of reverse derivation. The construction of speaking a language natively is first constructed as a qualitative differentiation of *individual* speakers within a speech community. There are those who are said to speak the language "natively," having learned it as a first or only language, or according to other definitions perhaps before a certain point in their linguistic development (Davies, 1991, 1996a). On that basis, the speaker is said to have a *native language*. Suppose this individual then learns a second language? His or her speech is then called "nonnative" – and by extension we derive the notion of *native speakers* as opposed to those *nonnative speakers*. The distinction pertaining to individual speakers has now to be superimposed on its own premise, the language of a speech community, for it to be claimed that there are "nonnative" (and "native") speech communities. Such a distinction, however, cannot be perforce said to apply to speech communities.[2] On the contrary, it is the differentiation of the speech of an individual learner from an existing speech community that underlies the classification of the former as a *nonnative speaker*. Against what standard can the language use of whole speech community be adjudged *nonnative* – that is, *sub*standard – while still preserving the premise of modern linguistics that the language use of different speech communities is not hierarchically determined ("better" and "worse"; more or less "advanced")?

As to the second possibility – that the language spoken by the speech community is not a language in the usual sense – similar conceptual problems present themselves. In particular, such a conclusion follows not from the characteristics of the language but from the mode of creation of the language (the means by which the speech community acquitted it) and the condition that its usage differs from that of the language's other speech community or speech communities. For this reason, the purported difference between this language and others reduces to the idea that the speech community in question is using not "its own" but some other speech community's language.

We might use any number of means to try to differentiate this "nonnative" language, but such attempts all reduce to the a priori assumption that its speakers are "nonnative." Such justification puts us in the midst of an explanatory circle, since the native speaker presupposes a language of which s/he is a native speaker. The assumption of the existence of the language gives a basis for the determination of the native speaker – not the obverse. And so this tells us nothing about the nature of any language qualitatively.[3] That must be the case so long as linguistics takes a language as the linguistic expression of its speech community. Given this construction of language, we are left with no basis to distinguish categorically the language of one speech community from another. Such a differentiation would require some other construction of language, one permitting a hierarchy of languages by their qualitative characteristics. For example, languages such as Russian that have zero copula (the absence of the verb *to be*) or those such as Spanish that exhibit pro-drop (the omission of subject pronouns) would have to described as less "developed" (or, alternatively, more "developed") than languages without that feature.[4] Such a construction of linguistics, however, is one that modern linguistics has emphatically denied. From a relativist notion of no inherent distinction among languages, we would now require precisely such a distinction that was explicitly ruled out, "higher" and "lower" languages – and that conclusion would have been reached by invoking categories for speech communities that pertain solely to the individual speaker.

The conceptual limitations of native speaker-based linguistics becomes manifest in the discussion of language variation – "languages in the making," as Weinreich (1974) aptly calls them. In such a case, the language itself cannot be presupposed as the basis on which native speakers can be constructed as a point of reference for solving theoretical difficulties, or as a norm by which other speakers can be referenced. This conceptual dilemma is only compounded if this language takes shape by an SLA process. In that case, the language appears as a deviation from some other language, the "TL" of the SLA process, from which it takes rise. We cannot speak of deviation without positing a norm – the *other* language. These two languages, however, according to the fundamental assumptions of linguistics, do not differ qualitatively. Each is the composite whole of the speech of a speech community, and a whole cannot be said to deviate from itself. On the other hand, all languages deviate from *other* languages: that is just what makes them (distinct) languages. What is distinctively Polish will seem like error to a Czech speaker, and vice versa. This is the condition of their determination as two different languages. The qualitative difference between the new language (or variety) and the old says nothing about that new language other than that it exists. Nor does it help if we substitute another word, such as *dialect* or *variety*, for the word *language*. The new language (or variety) deviating from the old is the condition of its existence as a separate linguistic entity.

In the whole, there can be no error determined, for all variety on the social level (as between the language of two different speech communities) translated to the perspective of the individual appears as error. Error is not determined for the domain of the social in language. The appearance of error is created by a particular interpretation placed on variation. There cannot be *error* as between two separate speech communities but, rather, *difference*. Or, put another way, difference does not connote error in the social realm of language (when speech communities are considered). When we speak of error, we speak of the individual as opposed to the group, but never one group as opposed to another.

The notion of error in the determination of the language of a speech community is filtered through the lens of linguistics taking root in the individual.

The inadequacy of theoretical models of individual SLA for explaining the New Englishes

The assumption that all variation introduced by speech communities of L2 learners constitutes error – a view taken over from approaching the question from the individual standpoint – cannot be accepted as valid for social groups, speech communities. For this reason, we cannot superimpose the understanding derived from processes of individual SLA to "languages in the making." Individual SLA invokes the category of errors, expressed variously as *imperfect learning* (Thomason & Kaufman, 1988) or *interlanguage* (Selinker, 1972). The terminology (or linguistics) of "error," "fossilization," "interlanguage," is poorly chosen to describe the emergence of variation reflected in the New Englishes. Language contact-induced change as a function of learner error takes from the idea of individual SLA an assumption of a fixed target language (in relation to the L2 learner) that is incompatible with the conditions that hold in language change – not a fixed target but a language or variety "in the making" as Weinreich (1974) puts it. Indeed, in this sense, theories of language contact have encountered the results of this problematical starting point in their incapacity to explain what transfers and what does not.

These shortcomings are characteristic of explanations of newly emergent language varieties in L2 settings that draw on theories of individual SLA. For example, Selinker (1992) has applied his theory of interlanguage (IL) to the understanding of the emergence of new varieties of English. According to this model, individual learners progressing along an interlanguage continuum toward a target language coalesce around a variety somewhere intermediate between their first language and "native speaker" English. There are numerous inherent problems with such an explanatory framework. First, its starting point is the analysis of the language as acquired by the individual through an examination of the stages of her/his interlanguage development. Compared to the target language as the goal of individual SLA, we arrive at the notion of "error" and deviation in language development. Here, however, the classical assumptions of SLA models do not hold.

Once again we encounter the same problem – how does *language* as a social realm take rise from the processes of the linguistic individual?

IL theory attempts to explain the development of language variety at the microlevel, as a process taking the individual as its unit of analysis. It is generally acknowledged, however, that a comprehensive theory of SLA has to account for both internal and external (societal) factors (Ellis, 1994). The same conditions apply to the explanation of the emergence of new English varieties. External factors have to be taken into account to derive a better understanding of why a particular linguistic form develops. The application of IL theory, with its notion of fossilization, employs different terminology in putting forward the same underlying explanatory basis as language contact.

The problem consists partly in explaining how individual "errors" become general – in other words, how we move from an individual's imperfect learning of a given language to a social standard involving an entire speech community. On the one hand, the individual speaker constitutes the unit of analysis. On the other hand, what is to be accounted for is a language that represents a phenomenon apart from the speech of any given individual speaker. For example, many linguists working within the generative framework take it as axiomatic that the individual errors of a speaker do not belong to the language, for which purposes they invoke the category of *competence* as opposed to *performance* (Chomsky, 1965). In the case of a second language, however, such a distinction proves very difficult to draw. In addition, if we have in question the development of a new variety, then where this variety differs from the source language it must appear to be in "error." That error, paradoxically, constitutes the necessary basis of its existence.

Conditions of the explanation of the emergence of New Englishes

When considering the development of a new language variety, with its own system and standards, it is not enough to study the learner and assume that the target language remains the same. The results of its being learned must also be considered. Nor are these changes to be found within the speech of the individual learner alone, or in the interlanguage, but in the language variety that takes shape as the essential result of the SLA process.

The context of the emergence of New Englishes differs from the classical SLA setting as defined by Larsen-Freeman and Long (1991: 7): "A second language is one being acquired in an environment in which the language is spoken natively." The context is one in which the SLA process takes place in a "nonnative" setting, with limited input from native speakers. Moreover, there is no fixed target language, but the language variety rather develops from the SLA process itself.

What makes the process of development difficult to account for under the existing theories of language change is that the new varieties develop explicitly as second languages, rather than as varieties, such as American English, which are presumed to be the mother tongues of monolingual speakers. The target language only *develops* as the result of the SLA process, rather than preceding it.

The distinction between the New Englishes and pidginization/creolization context

The theory of pidginization/creolization, to some extent, covers the same conditions, but the New Englishes have not developed as either pidgins or creoles (cf. S.N. Sridhar & K.K. Sridhar, 1994). The term pidgin refers to a minimal L2 "which barely resembled the masters' language as they spoke it" (Anderson and Shirai, 1996: 527). A creole is the "new natural native language" (527) arising from a pidgin spoken by the second generation of native speakers. Mesthrie *et al.* (2000: 281) define them as "languages which developed out of pidgins to become the first language of a speech community."

The context of the development of new varieties differs from that of pidginization/creolization in the following ways:

(1) The new variety is not a restricted language, or a minimal language, as is a pidgin, but a language showing full linguistic and functional range (cf. S.N. Sridhar & K.K. Sridhar, 1994; B. Kachru, 1997).

(2) The new variety does not serve as the mother tongue of the descendents of the speakers of an English-based pidgin, as would a creole. It is not the mother tongue of its speakers. New Englishes remain second languages.

(3) Acquisition of the new variety does not take place in a "natural" setting of first language acquisition, but primarily in an *educational* setting after the L1 has been acquired (cf. Platt *et al.*, 1984). This finding is confirmed by the historical data presented in previous chapters of this work.

(4) New Englishes do not exhibit the same degree of differentiation from English that English-based creoles do.

(5) There is no empirical evidence of an antecedent English pidgin transformed into a creole by a second generation using it as a first language. In the New Englishes contexts, pidgins that have developed

have been separated from the New English proper by a wall of class and education.

Some linguists claim that the conditions of pidginization/creolization and the development of New Englishes are essentially identical (Mufwene, 1994). Such a condition, however, overlooks a crucial difference. Pidginization/creolization, at least as traditionally used, conceives language change via a process that on the front end involves what Mühlhäusler (1986: 5) calls "non-targeted second language learning" – in which the acquiring learners do not specifically target any existing language. On the back end, the creolization component is either thought to develop via first language acquisition by a second generation that transforms the pidgin into a native language or by a gradual process of expansion of the pidgin over many generations (Mesthrie *et al.*, 2000), in either case no longer involving SLA processes. The formation of New Englishes, in contrast, is wholly one of SLA, as a speech community acquires English as a second language and, primarily, not a "native" one. It is, in fact, just this condition that has led to their problematic description as "nonnative languages." As such, the assumptions of pidginization/creolization theories do not hold in the New Englishes contexts and cannot be held to offer a compelling explanation for their development.

Justification for Social SLA (Macroacquisition)

Language contact implicitly depends on a theory of SLA (cf. De Graff, 1999); importantly, it takes such a theory as involving the linguistic individual. Yet if SLA theories tend not to apply to groups, then language contact does not really explain how new languages take shape. It merely says that it *involves* SLA. What is needed is a theoretical understanding of how SLA works as a social process.

To explain how second language varieties develop requires a paradigmatic shift. Rather than imperfect learning, "language contact" situations involve language development. The notion of social SLA (also referred to as macroacquisition) introduced in this work conceives the process in this way; it posits that the result of SLA as a social rather than an individual process is *language change*. Macroacquisition locates the basis of language change within SLA processes that arise out of the sociohistorical conditions of language spread. The reinterpretation of language spread that has been put forward in this work, which distinguishes language spread as *speaker migration* (the geographical movement of mother tongue speakers establishing new mother tongue contexts) from *macroacquisition* (the spread of language to new speech communities via a process of second language acquisition) not only integrates language spread and change but provides a new way of understanding language change. It conceives language change through the process of second language acquisition by groups or speech communities rather than the individual L2 learner. It also posits that the primary input is not coming from native speakers.

To account for such complex linguistic processes as the development of new language varieties during SLA, we cannot simply look at the process of acquiring an L2 one-sidedly, from the individual learner's perspective alone, but must look at the relationship of *learner populations* and language in the process of the development of second languages.

Macroacquisition does away with the problematical dichotomy of the linguistic individual as against the extralinguistic social by making the locus of change not the bilingual individual but the historically grounded speech community undergoing the process of macroacquisition. In this conception, therefore, the "point of language contact" is the *bilingual speech community*. For purposes of conceiving this SLA process, bilingual speech community must be taken in a broad sense as any community of learners that begins and carries out to some extent the process of SLA. It should be noted that this definition essentially equates the macroacquisition context with that of language contact. To that degree, language contact is, at least in part, reconceptualized as macroacquisition, or social SLA.

The present account of social SLA focuses neither on the acquisitional stages of individual learners nor their progress along the interlanguage continuum. It does not seek to provide an explanation of the ultimate cause of language transfer, whether from substrate influence or Universal Grammar. Rather, it seeks to answer only the more limited question of what changes stabilize in the formation of new language varieties – particularly the more standard varieties. This account suggests that while individual SLA gives rise to *interlanguages*, social SLA gives rise to *language varieties*. Without doubt, these two sets of questions are related and an integrated explanation must constitute an ultimate goal of SLA theory. For purposes of this discussion, however, each of the two explanatory realms presents a distinct set of questions. The reasons behind language transfer and other qualities that distinguish a learner's interlanguage from the target language does not alter the conditions of the explanation of their *stabilization within a speech community as a language variety*. So while it may be true that individuals acquire languages, it is also true that, in certain sociohistorical circumstances, *they do so not alone but in speech communities*.[5] For this reason, the result of this process (if not its form) is different.

Taking second language acquisition as a social process requires requisite conceptual changes in the relation of language and learner. SLA becomes a dynamic process, in which the language no longer appears as a static category, a fixed target, but alters as a result of its acquisition by the learning population. The speech community not only acquires the language but also makes the language its own (cf. Widdowson, 1996).

This view draws on the work of Weinreich (1974) and other language contact theoreticians. Weinreich (1974: 83), for example, asserts that "When a group of some size brings two languages into contact, idiosyncrasies in linguistic behavior tend to cancel each other, while socially determined speech habits and processes characteristic of the group as a whole become significant." It is precisely these "processes characteristic of the group" that this account seeks to uncover. Thomason and Kaufman (1988: 4) maintain, "The key to our approach – and the single point on which we stand opposed to most structuralist (including generativists) who have studied these issues – is our conviction that the history of a language is a function of the history of its speakers, and not an independent phenomenon that can be thoroughly studied without reference to the social context in which it is embedded." I contend that these objectives can be achieved in a model of social SLA.[6]

As asserted above, the present conception contends that while individual SLA might be said to give rise to an "interlanguage" rather than a language, macroacquisition (or social SLA) necessarily gives rise to a new language variety. They constitute distinct linguistic realms with distinctive linguistic outcomes. Social SLA endows the process and the product with the social quality – the "extralinguistic" side of the question – that is the basis of construction of a new language variety.

Within the reconceived parameters of the problem that forms the basis of this study, certain categories finding their basis in the individual speaker no longer apply: *native speaker, target language, imperfect learning*. The present study, therefore, will distinguish not between native speaking and nonnative speaking communities, and it also thereby breaks with the recent argument over the existence of native and nonnative varieties of English (R. Singh, 1996). Instead, a central distinction will be made between monolingual and bilingual communities. This categorization is perhaps not only more concrete, but also more linguistically meaningful.

Defining Macroacquisition and the Emergence of a Bilingual Speech Community

Macroacquisition is the acquisition of a second language by a speech community. It is a process of social second language acquisition, the embodiment of the process of language spread and change, or language change through its spread. This approach to World English has the potential to explain how a language can be "appropriated" by its speakers. It ties resistance into language change by anchoring the process of language contact to the realm of the extralinguistic, or the sociohistorical.

Macroacquisition as a theory of language contact starts from the opposite premise from that taken by Weinreich (1974) (see also Romaine, 1995). Rather than conceiving the bilingual individual as the locus of language contact, it takes the bilingual speech community, thus doing away with the dichotomous understanding of the (individual) linguistic versus the (social) extralinguistic realms.

At the same time, macroacquisition emphasizes that the impetus for change lies in the process of social SLA – not in the static condition of a bilingual community, but within its process of that *speech community in the making*. This condition coincides with that of a new language or variety, providing the key to explaining this process. The explanation for language change as a result of its spread is found within the genesis of the bilingual speech community, which is itself both a sociohistorical and a linguistic process (both "linguistic" and "extralinguistic").

Two forms of the emergence of bilingual speech communities

A bilingual speech community can emerge in two ways:

Type A

- Through a process of macroacquisition that coincides with the development of a new speech community. This occurs when speakers of different mother tongues simultaneously take part in the acquisition of a common second language, as in the case of the spread of English within "second language" settings in Africa and Asia. Thus, Type A macroacquisition takes place in a multilingual setting in which the acquired language serves as a unifying linguistic resource, the speakers otherwise belonging to separate mother tongue speech communities. Examples of nations in which this type of macroacquisition of

English have taken place include Nigeria, South Africa, India, and Singapore.

Type B

● Macroacquisition that takes the form of the transformation of a monolingual mother tongue speech community (or a section thereof) into a bilingual speech community. Type B macroacquisition takes place, in general, in a formerly predominantly monolingual setting – one in which one mother tongue dominates. With respect to English, this process has taken place, for example, with respect to incipient speech communities in Japan, Mexico, and Jordan.[7]

The following are the differentiating features of two types of macroacquisition:

Type A macroacquisition		*Type B macroacquisition*	
Multilingual setting	+	Multilingual setting	−
Monolingual setting	−	Monolingual setting	+
New speech community	+	New speech community	−
Existing speech community	−	Existing speech community	+

Although in a general sense, this distinction appears to coincide with that of the ESL and EFL contexts of English spread, there are significant differences. In fact, the underlying basis consists not in the functions that the language plays in the given setting, but in the division of macroacquisition speech communities into those that share a common mother tongue and those that do not. Sociohistorical rather than linguistic processes determine whether the speech community undergoing macroacquisition shares a common mother tongue. The sociohistorical conditions of language spread are reflected as functional uses of the languages – e.g. as an intranational lingua franca, or as a means of international communication (the defining features of the ESL and EFL contexts).

The sociohistorical conditions of the emergence of new speech communities

While SLA as traditionally conceived describes the acquisition process of the individual L2 learner, *macroacquisition* involves that of L2 learning populations, whether national, regional, "ethnic," or otherwise. This acquisition of the language by entire social groups is not merely a linguistically but also a historically bounded process. What separates macroacquisition conceptually from a simple aggregate of simultaneous but discrete individual SLA processes is precisely this historical context which transcends the level of structural alterations in a language. In this conception, SLA has a historical component. The process of macroacquisition, in contrast to the model of language contact, fulfills the goal suggested by Tollefson (1991) and echoed by Ellis (1994) that a sociohistorical approach to the study of language be integrated into SLA. The construct of macroacquisition lends conceptual consistency, since the historical process is represented both in the methodological foundations and in SLA. The outcome of the SLA process needs to be conceived as more than acquisition by the L2 learner. It also involves development of languages. In the present study, macroacquisition is central to the development of World English.

In entering the domain of the sociohistorical as it relates to the linguistic, however, it is necessary to clarify the relation of the two, particularly as it concerns the domains of social groupings, *community* and *speech community*.

Community and speech community

Although community and speech community are widely used terms, pinning down their precise meaning has proven difficult. Consider the definition of community offered by Gomez (1998):

> [C]ommunity is used here to convey the concept of a collection of individuals and families who share a common and identifiable network of sociocultural communications (for example, kinship, dietary patterns, labor conventions, artistic expressions, language) that have their origin in either a particular geographic area and period of time or a unique system of beliefs and rationalization. (p. 6)

Gomez uses language to refer to a possible form of sociocultural communication. Yet its place is in certain respects more central than the other elements. For kinship by itself is not enough (since members of a community need not be related) while such constructs as dietary patterns and artistic expressions are too vague to serve as a useful basis and too diffuse to define a coherent social structure (the tomato, for example, being characteristic of Italian cuisine even though it made its appearance in Italy centuries after an identifiable Italian community existed). As for origin in a particular geographical area, that would go little way toward identifying the basis of modern communities such as the American (would we take Native American, European, African or Asian?) while many systems of beliefs may exist within one community (e.g. China or India).

The meaning of *speech community* has been equally elusive. As commonly used, it refers to a group sharing a particular language. Should we inquire what *language* here refers to, however, we must base its definition in circular fashion on the existence of a particular community that shares it. Such an explanatory circle renders Chomsky's (1965: 3) idea of a "completely homogenous speech community that knows its language perfectly" not only an idealization (Wardhaugh, 1998) but conceptually problematical. Hymes (1962: 30), one of the first to attempt a scholarly construction of the term, defined it as "a local unit, characterized for its members by common locality and primary interaction." This attempted geographical basis ignores the condition that speech communities may cross national boundaries and span continents, as with the French, Spanish or English. On the other hand, what constitutes a local unit? Indeed, at the least, we need a definition that is flexible enough to recognize levels of speech community affiliation, as well as the potential for multiple affiliations (cf. Saville-Troike, 1996). Throughout the world, people interact on a daily basis, even primarily, with people with whom they do not share a language, or do so only partially. If they belong to the same speech community, they do so not so much because of language, but due to other social factors. In other words, they belong to the same *community*.

For this reason, most definitions of speech community focus not on the basis of its definition, but on the boundaries that demarcate one from another. They are located not in the linguistic, but in the social, within the condition that they belong to the same community. Labov (1972), for example, emphasizes that a speech community is not constituted by "any marked agreement in the use of language elements, so much as by participation in a set of shared norms; these norms may be observed in overt types of evaluative behavior, and by the uniformity of abstract patterns of variation which are invariant in respect to particular levels of usage" (pp. 120–1). Such elements are similar to what Gomez (1998) has in mind as distinguishing a community. Gumperz (1971) declares that the usual categories of social analysis, "be they small bands bounded by face-to-face contact, modern nations divisible into smaller subregions, or even occupational associations or neighborhood gangs, may be treated as speech communities, provide they show linguistic peculiarities that warrant special study" (p. 114). In other words, the speech community is merely the linguistic (or a linguistic) expression of the community.

All of these analyses leave an underlying question unanswered. If the definition of *community* versus *speech community* each necessarily invokes that of the other, what is their relation? Are they identical? Clearly we find cases where community can be said to exist without there being a speech community. A religious community may exist, for example, in the absence of a common language. On the other hand, the speech community is by its nature a kind of community, so there cannot be speech community in the absence of community.

As such, *community* and *speech community* must find their basis in the same kind of meaningful social grouping. To make this possible, I suggest, first, that the speech community be viewed as a sort of strong case of community. Second, rather than mirroring flawed conceptions of the natural (such as ethnicity), community is usefully constructed as rooted in *shared subjective knowledge*.

The concept I choose to call shared subjective knowledge has been termed many different things. For example, Gee (1999) favors the term *Discourses*. The *shared knowledge*[8] to which it refers has been used as the basis of definitions of culture (cf. Y. Kachru, 1999). Quinn and Holland (1987: 4) define culture as encompassing the knowledge content that members of society "must know in order to act as they do, make the things they make, and *interpret* their experiences in the distinctive ways they do." I prefer to place the emphasis on the knowledge, rather than removing the discussion to the more amorphous realm of culture. *Knowledge* in this case includes norms of interaction (pragmatics), value systems, and beliefs, alongside of other kinds of knowledge about the natural and social worlds we inhabit.

At the same time, I add the term *subjective* to *knowledge* to stress that human cognition does not differentiate forms of knowledge according to its alleged objective content (belief and "fact" are treated no differently by subjective experience), despite claims of the Western positivist tradition to the construction of such objective knowledge or objective truth. The "common-sense knowledge"[9] (Weedon, 1997: 73) derived from social experiences is, perhaps, held onto most tightly. In general, beliefs, values, common-sense knowledge, together with the products of science and often pseudo-science (e.g. astrology) reside virtually indistinguishably juxtaposed in our minds. To a much greater degree than is usually conceived by the Western positivist tradition, we do not and for the most part cannot distinguish between the idea that the earth is round (or spherical, albeit slightly constricted at the poles) and our particular conception of self, the spiritual realm (e.g. religion), or the rules of social interaction.

Shared subjective knowledge, therefore, characterizes what is, in general terms, held in common by a particular social group. These are the ties that bind communities and demarcate them from one another. It is to be noted that such ties do not require advocacy of a given notion or belief – familiarity suffices. For example, even the critic of particular "cultural assumptions" (let us say, gender roles) is intimately familiar with them. Thus, a member of the feminist movement in Poland is well aware of the expectations and assumptions toward women in Polish society, while she in no sense acquiesces in those she finds oppressive. It is the set of shared assumptions that permits ready communication among people who have never met, the sense of the familiar even in the stranger who is perceived to belong to one's own community. It is the basis of the "insider status" that a member of the community experiences, and which a non-member does not (cf. Gee, 1999).

Although we have become accustomed to the attempt to demarcate social groups through the appeal to the natural (often employing terms such as "race" or "ethnicity"), none of these categories have proven to have any sort of biological or physiological reality (Asante, 1993). What separates, for example, Serbians from Croatians is nothing more than the idea held by both groups (buttressed by religious beliefs) that they are distinct. On the other hand, Bulgarians are considered part of the Slavic "ethnicity" despite "ethnic characteristics" that might appear to distinguish them from Russians or Czechs.

Communities can take shape on the basis of other kinds of shared subjective knowledge that is external to language, such as religion (as in the Muslim, Christian or Buddhist communities). Such communities, however, are less immediate, more remote, and more abstract. The speech community is stronger and more coherent, because it alone facilitates the ready communication of the shared knowledge via a common language. The speech community thereby constitutes the strong case of community as *that type of social grouping in which shared subjective knowledge exists and can be linguistically communicated easily and readily among the members of the group*. This conception of speech community and community not only makes the common basis explicit in differentiating the two but also allows for different levels of both community and speech community, including multiple affiliations (to be discussed in Chapter 9).

Macroacquisition as a Sociohistorical Process

Taking this construction of *communities* and *speech communities*, macroacquisition of Type A (e.g. Nigeria) and Type B (Japan) differ in a crucial sociohistorical respect. What is manifested linguistically as the creation of a new speech community in Type A macroacquisition takes root in the larger sociohistorical process of *community formation*. In macroacquisition of Type B, since the community and speech community antedate the process of macroacquisition, the latter entails the transformation of an existing speech community into a bilingual speech community.

This distinction contains important implications for the sociohistorical context of English spread and its effect on language change. In the first place, what appears from the politico-linguistic side as *resistance* to linguistic imperialism in the spread of English coincides with the process of community formation as nation-building. It has been shown in this work that much of the spread of English took place within the context of the anticolonial movements of Asia and Africa. And, as has been noted by many scholars, English language change has been tied to this resistance. This process has culminated in what have been called the "indigenized varieties of English" (B. Kachru, 1986, 1992; K.K. Sridhar & S.N. Sridhar, 1992) of Africa and Asia.

Both the notion of resistance and "indigenization" suffer from the essential flaw that they start from assumptions taken over from the theory of linguistic imperialism (Phillipson, 1992). The construct of "indigenization" assumes a genetic relation between a language and its speakers, so that a previously "alien" language goes through a process of "decolonization" – thereby yielding a language that has become "indigenous." If indigenization is intended to mean more than the process of second language acquisition – as its association with decolonization implies – then it implies a natural relation between certain groups and certain languages. Davies (1997) has called this the linguistic essentialist implications of linguistic imperialism.

The idea of resistance within language spread as factoring into "indigenization" (cf. Canagarajah, 1999) also relies on the assumptions of linguistic imperialism. According to this notion, the linguistic imposition of a language is accepted, but it is displaced through the transformation of the language concomitant with the struggle against linguistic imperialism. Such an explanation makes language change dependent upon a purely political process, the rejection of ideological assumptions about language. In this vein, resistance is operationalized as a political construct, one that is only tenuously linked to the process of language change. As such, we might expect to find that language change would cease with the end of colonialism, and we would be at a loss to explain why the same kind of process should occur in non-colonial contexts.

The foregoing is not intended to deny or minimize the importance of resistance as a sociohistorical category. On the contrary, the role of resistance to colonialism has been emphasized within the concrete history of English language change presented in this work. Before resistance to colonialism – which has been transformed into resistance to linguistic imperialism (Canagarajah, 1999) by the notion of indigenization – can be placed within a general account of language change, however, it must be examined for its underlying sociohistorical content.

When resistance is conceived as directed toward colonialism rather than linguistic imperialism, its immediate objective and result is not the transformation of language but of social relations of power. In particular, the anticolonial movement gave rise, via the overthrow of external colonial rule, to new postcolonial nations. Such a process, in its general social shape, is simply the process of community formation – taking in this case the particular historically determined form of nation building. Hence, while resistance constitutes the particular form in which this process manifests itself, it is not the underlying sociohistorical content. Hence, resistance is not the key itself, but the formation of the new communities that take shape out of the resistance.[10] Herein lies the link between resistance to colonialism as a historical condition discussed in the earlier part of this work and the linguistic process of macroacquisition.

As the present-day South African context (considered in Chapter 8) shows, the process of macroacquisition as community formation is not at all delimited by colonialism. Macroacquisition as the formation of new speech communities (Type A macroacquisition) occurs whenever community formation and social second language acquisition take place simultaneously. It sets the general sociohistorical condition of macroacquisition Type A, which therefore has no inherent connection to colonialism or imperialism. Type A macroacquisition is not limited to the colonial time frame, and so is not a colonial/postcolonial question at root, as it appears when the theory of linguistic imperialism is taken as the frame of reference. It occurs in multifarious circumstances, and is to be seen today, for example, in South Africa (Chick & Wade, 1997). There is in South Africa the formation of a new national community (what is often referred to as nation building in the post-apartheid era) that coincides with the formation of a speech community in English.

Macroacquisition thereby has much wider applicability than the process described as the "decolonization" of a language. It coincides with community formation, or it is speech community formation that is also community formation. Macroacquisition Type B, in contrast, is not linked to community formation.

The linguistic outcome of macroacquisition

The linguistic outcome of macroacquisition differs also with respect to the type of bilingualism of the given bilingual speech community. In both Type A and Type B macroacquisition, there is the formation of a bilingual speech community. These bilingual speech communities, however, differ in a central respect, thereby dividing into separate kinds of speech community bilingualism. In the case of the bilingual speech community that arises out of Type A, the speech community, although made up of bilinguals, shares only one language, the second language. In Type B, the speech community shares both languages. Speech community bilingualism, therefore, may consist of speech communities that share either one or both languages.

This analysis of the types of bilingualism differs from the usual division between individual bilingualism and societal bilingualism. Scholars of bilingualism have generally distinguished forms of the bilingualism of individuals (e.g. balanced, functional) and what has been called *societal bilingualism* (Baker, 1996; Baker & Prys Jones, 1998). While a significant amount of work centers on the bilingualism of individual speakers, societal bilingualism has been used to examine the presence and role of more than one language in a given geographical space, e.g. a multilingual nation such as Canada or Switzerland (Romaine, 1995). This usage serves explanatory purposes without representing a linguistic condition as such. In contrast, speech community bilingualism refers to languages (co)existing in the same linguistic space, i.e. in the same speech community. Here the (co)existence is from the linguistic point of view essential rather than accidental.

Because a speech community, unlike a society, may undergo a process of SLA, either of Type A or Type B macroacquisition, the distinguishing feature of that speech community's bilingualism is that it consists either of the sharing of one or both languages. The fundamental criterion that differentiates the two different bilingual speech community contexts is the shared first language (Type B) or the lack thereof. For instance, the bilingual Spanish/English community comprised of Hispanic Americans in California, Texas, and Florida (among other places) typically shares both languages. Insofar as this community (or part thereof) has undergone or is undergoing a process of macroacquisition, it is of Type B. In South Africa, on the other hand, there is a process of macroacquisition of English within a multilingual setting – including Zulu, Xhosa, Venda, Tswana and Afrikaans – thereby constituting a community of Type A. It should be noted, however, that in such cases, there exist as well within the whole subsets of Type B, e.g. of Zulu speakers. Chapter 8 takes up the implications of the two types of macroacquisition for language change.

Notes

1. Odlin (1989: 26) notes that "the term *interference* implies no more than what another term, **negative transfer**, does." In his work, he provides a discussion of this construct and offers a more extended definition of language transfer. He defines it as "the influence resulting from similarities and differences between the target language and any other language that has been previously (and perhaps imperfectly) acquired" (p. 27).
2. The extension of these qualitative distinctions among speakers that are not present in the basis of language do not end there. Suppose that a whole group of such "nonnative" speakers comprise the speakers of a particular language? That language can then be called, by analogy, a "nonnative" language (see, for example, Trudgill & Hannah, 1985). In this case, however, it is unclear what the meaning of this term may be. For there is not present in the notion of language any such qualitative distinction on the whole.
3. The argument that X is not a language because it does not have native speakers is thus logically invalid. For the native speaker is derived from the language, not vice versa. That is, a native speaker presupposes a language, but a language does not presuppose native speakers. If it did, it could never develop in the first place, since the native speakers would thereby have to precede the language of which they are native speakers.
4. These examples have been chosen to illustrate that although there has been an attempt to define New Englishes by such structural features, all such features are also found in other languages. As such, their features in no way differentiate them categorically from other languages.
5. See the quote from Weinreich below. S.N. Sridhar (1994: 801) has also emphasized this point:

   The central images in SLA are those of the "transplanted learner," a rather lonely individual. Little reference is made to the learners' speech community. This paradigm . . . leaves out vast millions of L2 users who learn and use second languages in their own countries, from their own (nonnative) teachers, for use primarily with other nonnative speakers, and who may never come across a native speaker face to face.

6. Macroacquisition is called a process of social SLA as distinguished from individual SLA, by which means SLA has traditionally been approached. As used in this work, social SLA is macroacquisition.
7. To clear up a potential misconception, let me just make clear that I am not calling these *nations* bilingual; I am simply calling attention to the existence of bilingual speech communities within them. Nor does bilingual here refer to so-called "balanced bilinguals" who possess equal fluency in each language.
8. That such knowledge can be shared is something taken for granted not only by theorists of culture but also by linguists. Such an assumption, for example,

underlies Chomsky's (1965) construction of the "completely homogenous speech community," as well as forming a starting point of the field of sociolinguistics. Although we are still some way from understanding the dynamics of such networks of cognition, as Diller (1998: 1) has argued, "recent work on complex systems and artificial life gives us tools to deal with 'externalized' languages as (partially) shared systems of cognition hosted in individual agents." Wardhaugh (1998) also employs the term shared knowledge as central to the study of language. He points out that we "must assume that every individual knows the grammar of his or her language by the simple reason that he or she readily uses that language and also some kind of shared knowledge, that is, knowledge possessed by all those who speak the language" (p. 2).

9. "Common sense consists of a number of social meanings and the particular ways of understanding the world which guarantee them. . . . [I]ts power comes from its claim to be natural, obvious, and therefore true" (Weedon, 1997: 74).

10. Hence, rather than viewing such formations as *imagined communities* (Anderson, 1983), I prefer to conceive them as sociohistorically determined communities.

Chapter 8

The Macroacquisition of English: New Representations in the Language

Macroacquisition and Language Change

The language change referred to in "New Englishes" literature as "indigenization" or "nativization" (B. Kachru, 1965; 1981) that occurs as a concomitant of social SLA is centrally linked to the bilingualism that it entails. I propose an explanation of language change resultant from macroacquisition that centers on the process of bilingual speech community formation, of the two kinds considered in Chapter 7. From this standpoint, the central question that needs to be answered is why in the case of Type A macroacquisition a new language variety develops while such a process does not apparently take place in the case of Type B.

To understand how the process of social SLA finds expression in language change, I suggest that a particular view of bilingualism is needed which does not divide the bilingual's linguistic knowledge into two separate and inviolate systems. I draw on Cook's (1993, 1999) understanding of the *multicompetence* of bilinguals. Multicompetence refers to "the compound state of a mind with two languages" (1999: 190). Cook's understanding of multicompetence supports the notion that languages do not reside in separate compartments in bilingual speakers. Cook concludes that "the minds of L2 users differ from the minds of monolinguals" (p. 192) in the "way they know and use the L1 and the L2" (p. 194) – a conclusion that has found support in studies of bilingualism and language processing (Baker & Prys Jones, 1998). It also accords with other recent work in sociolinguistics, including Nagy's (1999) understanding of multi/bilingualism as entailing "multiple expressions of one identity" rather than the "expression of multiple identities."

Although Cook's contention pertains to the individual bilingual, it has important implications for the understanding of *bilingual speech communities*. The defining characteristic of a bilingual speech community is that the linguistic communication of the shared subjective knowledge that bounds and demarcates it finds its expression not in one language but in more than one. In adapting multicompetence to the analytical level of the speech community, I will designate as *multicompetence of the speech community* the condition that these languages represent not separate and complete systems each unto itself but rather parts of a composite reservoir of meaning that expresses the shared subjective knowledge of the community. The construction of the bilingual speech community as multicompetent contrasts with a view that treats the two languages it employs as separate and independent systems.

Code switching and code mixing constitute particularly important evidence of multicompetence. Cook (1999: 193) remarks, "Code switching is the most obvious achievement of the multicompetent user that monolingual native speakers cannot duplicate, as they have no language to switch into. It shows the intricate links between the two languages systems in multicompetence." As such, we would expect it to play a central role in the multicompetence of the speech community sharing an L1. This supposition is borne out by the observation that code switching is a very common occurrence (or communication strategy) among speech communities that share an L1 (Bhatia and Ritchie, 1996; Chick and Wade, 1997; Kieswetter, 1995), functioning as a "valuable communicative resource" (Chick & Wade, 1997: 276).

Romaine (1995) observes,

> Although it is popularly believed by bilingual speakers themselves that they mix or borrow because they don't know the term in one language or another, it is often the case that switching occurs often for items which people know and use in both languages ... Mixing and switching for fluent bilinguals is thus in principle no different from style shifting for the monolingual. The bilingual just has a wider choice – at least when he or she is speaking with bilingual speakers. (p. 143)

This multicompetence of the speech community provides a key conceptual link in unlocking the reasons behind language contact, hitherto conceptualized in terms of reproduction of learner error (Thomason & Kaufman, 1988; Weinreich, 1974).[1] Alongside code switching and code mixing, the process known as "language transfer" or "cross-linguistic influence" (Odlin, 1989) represents part of the same linguistic process, the formation of bi/multilingual systems of communication, or the multicompetence of the speech community. All of these processes need to be brought under a general explanatory framework, rather than being treated as separate and discrete processes. In the present framework, they are conceived as taking root in the *shared subjective knowledge* and the *multicompetence* of the bilingual speech community.

Language Use in Bilingual Speech Communities

Like the speech community bilingualism from which it derives, multicompetence of the speech community has two varieties: that in which the linguistic expressions of the community's shared subjective knowledge are identical and that in which they are different. A premise of the explanation of language change concomitant with the two different forms of macroacquisition follows from this analysis:

- *The L2 (in the present study, English) is used differently as between bilingual speech communities that share an L1 and those that do not.*

Taken in light of the notion of multicompetence of the speech community, the concrete embodiment of this difference comes in the ability of the bilingual speech community that shares an L1 to resort to code switching and code mixing, and the need for a parallel process in the case of bilingual speech communities that do not share an L1.

From the standpoint of the speech community, code switching as a manifestation of multicompetence requires that the community as a whole (as opposed to subsets of that community) share both languages. In comparison to the Type B bilingual speech community, that of Type A has fewer linguistic resources available to it, since it lacks a common L1, thereby motivating its speakers to express *shared subjective knowledge* in the L2. While multicompetence of the speech community finds expression (in part) in code mixing and code switching for Type A bilingual speech communities, it is expressed for those of Type B in language change via processes of "language transfer."

In the case of Type B, shared subjective knowledge is easily communicable in the first language. For Type A, on the other hand, the multicompetence of the speech community finds its expression not in code switching and code mixing, but in stabilized language change, the creation of a new variety.

The multicompetent speech community and language change

Since multicompetence of the bilingual speech community serves the function of communicating shared subjective knowledge, it is bound up above all with the expression of meaning, since meaning is rooted in shared subjective knowledge. It follows from this condition that the language change that arises out of the multicompetence of the speech community will be manifested above all in transformed meaning.

Evidence for such an explanation is found in work on borrowing in situations of language contact, a phenomenon that has been noted but not adequately accounted for. Silva-Corvalan (1998: 226) has found that "what is borrowed across languages is not syntax but lexicon and pragmatics."[2] She lists, in particular, "lexical items, subcategorizations, discourse constraints and pragmatic uses borrowed or modeled after the source language" which are expressed as "crystallized fixed patterns characteristic of the language use of a community of speakers" (p. 227). Similarly, in her discussion of the bilingual speech community, Romaine (1995) synthesizes the literature on borrowing in the context of language contact. On this basis, she develops a hierarchy of borrowing: items that show highest ease of borrowing are lexical items, followed in order by morphology (especially those morphological elements that are less bound, i.e. derivational morphemes) and finally syntactic structures (p. 64).

While this hierarchy of borrowing may be explained in terms of ease of transfer, such an interpretation begs the question. It shows that elements of language conveying the highest content of meaning are most likely to transfer. That is to say, the more meaning is overtly represented, the more it transfers. For this reason, lexical items, as units of meaning, stand atop the hierarchical structure. Morphological elements, although meaning at root, also contain a measure of structure. And the more structural the morpheme, the less likely it is to transfer. Syntax, which is meaning in its most abstracted form, is the least likely.

The greater likelihood of the transfer of meanings occurs because it is the primary (most surface-level) expression of the community's shared subjective knowledge.[3] The more structural elements of language do not convey the same kinds of social meanings. What actually "transfers" are the community-bounded (or speech community embedded) subjective meanings, or the particularizing factors of community. This phenomenon is reflected, for example, in what has been termed the "grammar of culture" (Bright, 1968; D'souza, 1988). Interestingly, even phonological processes may become bound up in such areas of subjective meaning, as, for example, in the case of Thai English speakers transferring the prestigious trilled /r/ from Thai to English in formal contexts (Beebe, 1980).

It also appears in the realm of stylistics. Gough (1996: 68) writes, "With regard to stylistic features, formal written [Black South African English] shares with other new Englishes the 'penchant to the florid' – a tendency toward ornamental English [including] circumlocution" – usage that does not sound authentic to the American or British ear because it is out of step with current notions of style in the West. Explanations for this usage have included, Gough notes, "lack of exposure to the formal conventions of academic literacy" (p. 68). Although other explanations exist, descriptions such as these clearly connote that such usage represents substandard English. Other scholars have come to different conclusions. They attribute it to what we might call cultural preferences. Sey (1973) mentions that in Ghana "flamboyance of English prose and style is generally admired" (p. 7). The Indian English writer Raja Rao (1938) looks at the question quite differently: "The tempo of Indian life must be infused into our English expression even as the tempo of American or Irish life has gone into the making of theirs" (p. 10; cf. B. Kachru, 1983).

It is a contention of this account that the stabilization of language change into new varieties as a result of the process of Type A macroacquisition mirror the hierarchy of borrowing, or that meaning-based changes are most likely to stabilize in the new variety. There is a growing scholarly consensus among those who study the "New Englishes" that the greatest level of difference lies in areas of "high ease of borrowing." Bamgbose (1982) characterizes the differentiating features of Nigerian English as consisting mainly in lexis, idiom, and meaning, a conclusion with which Adegbija (1998) agrees.

I draw on Bamgbose (1982) in identifying lexical items and idioms as the most prominent differentiating feature of new varieties of English.[4] To understand this process fully, greater importance must be attached not to borrowings but to transformed meanings,[5] a phenomenon that is much more difficult to investigate. As Hymes (1996: 9) has pointed out, "The overt forms may be familiar – the words, the attire, the buildings – but the interpretations given to them is subject to shift, to deepening, to fresh connecting up." It is in the nature of meanings to be subject to change, re-interpretation, recreation.

What Diller (1999) has linked to the "negotiation of meaning," D. Cameron (1998) refers to as the process of *(re)naming* and *(re)defining* (p. 148), or the "struggle to create new meanings" (p. 153). According to D. Cameron, "Precisely because meaning is not fixed, there is no end to the struggle over 'the power to name and define'" (p. 154). While such a process appears difficult, as D. Cameron notes, when the question is one of altering meanings within a community, it represents a more likely occurrence with respect to meanings from the source language acquired during the process of social SLA. In this case, the shared subjective knowledge of the speech acquiring community transforms the language.[6] As

Malinowski (1923) postulates, word meanings across contexts cannot be studied in isolation from the context in which they arise. The presence of lexical items from the source language cannot be taken in isolation from the social meaning. Transformed word meaning, then, is likely to constitute a more general phenomenon than borrowing from a local language, and represents a clear manifestation of shared subjective knowledge as an agent of language change as well as constituting an overlooked question within language change.

Chisanga and Kamwangamalu (1997), writing about English in Southern Africa, distinguish three separate processes of the transformation of meaning: lexical transfer (or what is usually called lexical borrowing), hybridization, and semantic extension. Lexical transfer, the most obvious of these, involves the incorporation of words from African languages – such as *lobolo* (roughly "dowry") into the new English variety. Hybridization takes the borrowing a step further by attaching English morphemes to the root word from the African language. For example, the word *bulala* (meaning "to promote") becomes *bulawa-ed* in the following sentence: The man will be *bulawa-ed* soon (Chisanga & Kamwangamalu, 1997: 93–4).

Finally, in semantic extension, the "English word is assigned a new meaning which is more relevant to the new users" (p. 94). The examples of the latter are as varied as they are instructive. Thus, in Southern African English the adjective *ripe* applied to a young female indicates "ready for marriage" while the noun *damage* can be used to refer to the impregnation of a young female (Chisanga and Kamwangamalu, 1997: 95). In Nigerian English, the verb *settled* used intransitively ("He has been settled") means "receiving some gratification or favor to keep [one] quiet" (Adegbija, 1998: 5), while *town council* refers to the department of sanitation (Bokamba, 1992: 136).

Shared subjective knowledge is contained, in particular, in idiomatic expressions, since in such cases the focus is on contextual meaning. Thus, in Nigerian English *to put to bed* means "to give birth to a child" while *to take in* connotes "to become pregnant" (Adegbija, 1998: 21). The expression *white–blackman* indicates a "black intellectual who behaves as a white man" while a *European appointment* is a "high-level white collar position" (Bokamba, 1992: 136).

Shared subjective knowledge also enters into the performance of speech acts. As Gough (1996) shows of Black South African English,

> In requesting, a deferential form in African languages is to use the performative equivalent *I ask* . . . or *I request* . . . as a marker of deference

in unequal encounters, as in *I ask for an extension*. . . . Such uses indicate the African norm of acknowledging the status of granting a
request to a subordinate petitioner. This is different from the Anglo-
Saxon norm in which there is often the expectation, witnessed by the
use of modal forms (as in "Could you please give me an extension"),
that a person in authority may have the ability but not the desire to
grant a request. (pp. 65–66)

Shared subjective knowledge includes knowledge of the norms of interaction, which can be important in language change. To take an example
from a recent change in American–English, the use of the pronoun
they/their has replaced the role of *he/his* as a supposedly gender-neutral
marker, even when the context clearly involves a singular subject (e.g.
"To each their own" rather than the traditional "To each his own"). In
such cases, the substitution of a formerly exclusively plural pronoun for
the masculine singular facilitates the communication of shared subjective knowledge, although it might be perceived as a violation of a
consistent application of the syntactic rules of a particular description
of English grammar. In this case, shared subjective knowledge of an
increasing number of American–English speakers includes a notion that
the use of an all-encompassing masculine form to include women is no
longer socially acceptable – despite a strong and long-standing prescriptivist tradition to the contrary (cf. Cameron, 1985).

In fact, as Bodine (1998) shows, the history of this usage is more complex than usually believed. *They* as singular, sex-indefinite pronoun was
present, if not common, in English usage through the end of the eighteenth century, at which time pressure from prescriptive grammarians
undercut its acceptability within standard American–English, even while
it retained to a considerable degree its currency in British standard usage.
Changes in shared subjective knowledge of speakers of Standard
American English in different periods have both eliminated and reintro-
duced the singular, sex-indefinite *they*, in the former cases for reasons of
perceived "logical consistency," in the latter for those of gender equity in
language. Moreover, there might very well be said to exist at present a
condition of varying usage within Standard American–English reflecting
an attempt on the part of the user to show awareness of the shared subjective knowledge underlying one (or both) of the conflicting usages. If
the speaker conforms to the prescriptivist usage, "they" commit[7] what
appears to be a violation of "English syntax" in order to avoid specifica-
tion of the gender for a hypothetical situation (as above) or where the gender is unknown (*Did that person get the bag they left in the office?*).

Given such variation of usage, linguists would not claim that such examples are the result of errors or lack of knowledge of English syntax. Rather, they recognize that they reflect an intentional choice on the part of the speaker to avoid a linguistic utterance that would be regarded as worse than a "grammatical mistake."[8] Nor is the fear on the part of the speaker in this case that she would be misunderstood. In each of the specified cases, the contextual meaning is quite clear. Rather, the speaker is concerned she should appear to violate shared subjective knowledge that governs gendered discourse.

Interestingly, the avoidance of the use of *he* to cover *she* has developed despite the fact that *he* constituted the base of all Old English third personal pronoun forms, including the forms for she (*hio, heo*, the feminine forms of *he*) (*Oxford English Dictionary* (1989), vol. 7: 34). In other words, the convention has developed despite the particular circumstances that may once have dictated the development of the word choice in the source language.

In exactly the same manner, syntactic rules of the source language of these varieties are often violated to facilitate communication of shared subjective knowledge. Trudgill and Hannah (1985) report this basis for the use of could/would in place of can/will: Indian English "speakers feel the past forms are more tentative and thus more polite" (p. 109). Such pragmatic considerations also seem to govern the usage of tag questions. The standard American/British English use of such forms as "Did/didn't you? Has/hasn't she? Was/wasn't he?" have given way to tag questions of the kind "is it?" or "isn't it?" across numerous new varieties (Bhatt, 1995; Chisanga & Kamwangamalu, 1997). In this case, it is often perceived that the direct questioning of an interlocutor violates community-bounded language use. Such constraints of shared subjective knowledge can override considerations of syntactic rule-governed use.

Shared subjective knowledge pertains as much to what is generally referred to as pragmatics (norms of interaction) as it does to any other form of community-bound subjective knowledge. For language conveys this knowledge as much in the pragmatics of its use as in the meaning conveyed by overt means. When syntax becomes a *barrier* to the communication of shared subjective knowledge, it leads to language change. As demonstrated by the case of *he/she* versus *they*, this phenomenon need not be limited to macroacquisition. The latter form of language change, nevertheless, particularly entails the need to convey shared subjective knowledge overriding purely syntactic concerns. In such cases, I argue, not only will the change occur but will also stabilize even in the most "standard" varieties of English.

Such situations cover a rather large category of what are usually classified as syntactic transfer. These include answering negative questions in the affirmative and rules of negation, both of which derive from culture bound conceptions of "logic." Chisanga and Kamwangamalu (1997) give the following example from Southern African English:

Question: Didn't the college send you an application form?
Answer (a): "Yes," meaning "the college *did not* send me an application form"
Answer (b): "No," meaning "the college did send me an application form" (p. 96).

In these cases, if nothing other than "yes" or "no" are given in answer, the usage is precisely the opposite of British or American, but necessary to convey the meaning to the speaker of the New English (a phenomenon also true for English in South Asia, as B. Kachru (1990) notes). Likewise, while the shared subjective knowledge of many or most American and British English speakers regards double negation as rendering a positive meaning, other cultures recognize an intensity of negation.

Similarly, Trudgill and Hannah (1985) cite as an example of West African English usage the construction *They like themselves* ("they like each other") (p. 104). A related case from West Africa is cited by Platt *et al.* (1984): *They speak to themselves in English* (p. 119). In this case, the meaning of *liking themselves* or *speaking to themselves* is used as a characteristic of the entire group, rather than the group being constructed as a number of individual identities. Here we see at work a different shared subjective knowledge as to the relation of individual and community, once again rendering an opposite meaning than American or British-English.

In like fashion, "dummy" *there* may be supplied with meaning, as in Indian English: *What do you want to eat? Meat is there, vegetables are there, rice is there* (Trudgill & Hannah, 1985: 109). Another category of changes that Platt *et al.* (1984) categorize as syntactic appears to involve meanings as well. The conversion of nouns that are singular in form but apparently plural in meaning into plural nouns – such as *furniture* into *furnitures* and *luggage* into *luggages* (pp. 50–51) – involves an alteration of the meaning of the word. Rather than a collective noun standing for the category, the word is altered to a countable noun of the more typical variety (after the pattern *chair – chairs*). The use of the word by itself now connotes a different meaning (a possibility noted by Platt *et al.* (1984) as a potential explanation), e.g. *luggage* as a singular becomes equivalent to *a piece of luggage*.

In contrast, numerous scholars (Adegbija, 1998; Bokamba, 1994, Chisanga & Kamwangamalu, 1997) of new varieties of English report that such syntactic conventions as the omission of *to be* are found in colloquial speech but not the more standardized variety. The question with respect to macroacquisition is not so much what types of transfer may *occur* in the speech of individuals, but what kinds of "transfer" will *stabilize* in the new variety. The work of Gough (1996) also lends support. He finds that while lexical extensions and forms such as *a luggage* have become "entrenched and perceived as standard by educated speakers [of Black South African English] even in monitored situations," structures representing linguistic interference at the syntactic level such as "the extended use of the progressive and the use of resumptive pronouns (at least in relative clauses) are not as entrenched or 'fossilised' as has traditionally been thought" (p. 64).

Macroacquisition, therefore, would appear to tend not so much toward the syntactic alteration of the language so much as what Silva-Corvalan (1998) aptly describes as the "gradual loss of discourse-pragmatic restrictions as well as incorporation of new uses of existing structures, all of which produce a slight foreign quality, comparable to what happens at the phonetic level" (pp. 240–41). Thus the changes that stabilize are not those of the interlanguage of an individual learner and so should not be attributed to fossilization of language transfer or be described in terms of deviance and error.[9]

What is often called "syntactic transfer" constitutes neither haphazard nor automatic transfer, language interference or even imperfect learning, but often represent efforts toward the maintenance of the context of meaning (Malinowski, 1923). Such changes maintain shared subjective knowledge, or context of meaning, of importance to the community, e.g. norms of social interaction. A syntactic form (or apparently syntactic form) that impinges on shared subjective knowledge (e.g. how to address people in conversation) will transfer, whereas those forms that do not are far less likely to do so. Hence, tag questions become part of the stabilized variety, while merely formal types of transfer disappear. Where the syntax hinders (or creates a barrier to) the communication of shared subjective knowledge, language change is more likely to occur. As Silva-Corvalan (1998) has argued, "What is borrowed is not a syntactic structure, but the semantics or the pragmatics of a construction, which is then linked to a close structural parallel in the borrowing language" (p. 242).

In certain cases, the basis of the syntactic variation might not be obvious to a structural-level analysis. For example, Bamiro (2000: 111) attributes such forms as *thematization* (*Things* he despises. *People* he despises.),[10] *double subjects* (*This woman she is needing help*), and *resumptive references* (*They are clever, the strangers*), or what he calls *focus constructions*, to "communicative strategies used to achieve emphasis and thematization." He maintains that "their use underscores the logic of many African languages," enabling "speakers to reorder the English language to reflect their thought channels" (p. 111).

It has been argued that language change is meaning-bound for the stabilization of new varieties out of Type A macroacquisition. In this respect, it is important to note that the parallel process available to Type B macroacquisition situations not available to Type A – code mixing and code switching – is also meaning-bound. Bhatia and Ritchie (1996) have called attention to the centrality of semantic restructuring to syntax in code mixing. With code mixing there may be just the same resultant syntactic changes in order to convey shared subjective knowledge. If, as Romaine (1995) suggests, the boundaries between mixing and borrowing are not always what they appear to be, it follows that code mixing and code switching belong to the same category of linguistic processes as language change – the multicompetence of the bilingual speech community.

The processes are really not different at root, each involving the communication of shared subjective knowledge (or communication bounded by shared subjective knowledge). In the case of Type A macroacquisition, there is a more identifiable result, a stabilized variety that becomes socially and often politically institutionalized. Looked at from another standpoint, it could be said that language change is retarded in the case of Type B because of the greater linguistic resources available to the multicompetent bilingual speech community, particularly the ability to resort to code mixing and code switching. At the same time, as Silva-Corvalan (1998) notes, "In a situation of extensive and intensive bilingualism, bilinguals are called upon to communicate often in one language or the other in rapid succession in response to different interlocutors, different social domains or other factors" – suggesting a possible source of certain tendencies toward language change (p. 228). Such situations are more likely in Type A than Type B contexts. Thus, while all macroacquisition involves language change, it appears in a more stabilized form in the case of Type A.

Macroacquisition as Community Formation and the Question of Language Change

Questions of identity may enter in as well. Since Type A macroacquisition coincides with the creation of communities (as in South Africa), it will tend to be accompanied by its speech community seeking identity within that language. In Type B, on the other hand, the community already exists and lacks any compelling basis to do so. A main difference between the two macroacquisition contexts, therefore, consists in the degree to which the new variety enters into the identity of the speakers. While this does not in principle condition the tendency toward language change inherent in macroacquisition, it does have the potential to affect the stabilization of that change in the form of an institutionalized variety that provides the target for future learners.

As Chambers (1995) has argued, the quest for a shared identity can manifest itself in a tendency toward homogenization – which might be expressed linguistically as stabilization of community-bound norms of language use. Bamiro (2000: 106) argues that "As in other African varieties of English, a Zimbabwean cultural identity is constructed through certain syntactic variations." Similarly, in discussing the roots of African–American Vernacular English, Wood (1974) has called attention to the usefulness for enslaved African Americans of speaking English in a way that concealed their intended meanings from the slaveholding class. The resultant variance between the language of master and enslaved adapted the language to its role of maintaining group identity. James Baldwin has captured the legacy that remains in the language known as African–American Vernacular English: "[A]n immense experience has forged this language, it had been (and remains) one of the tools of a people's survival" (quoted in Mazrui and Mazrui, 1998: 24). When the macroacquisition process coincides with the creation of a common social and political identity, this dynamic expresses itself in the language variety.

The Context of the Macroacquisition of English in Asia and Africa

Language contact theoreticians stress the importance of "extralinguistic" conditions. Yet seldom have these conditions been analyzed historically in detail. Given that the most important category within the development of World English is its spread, the preceding part of this study gives the concrete conditions for understanding the macroacquisition of English.

With the recent attention to the implications of the theory of linguistic imperialism, this context of English language spread to much of Asia and Africa – crucial in the formation of World English – has not received adequate attention in the literature on World English. At the same time, in discussions of language contact, for example, much attention has been paid to immigrant communities undergoing language shift (Thomason & Kaufman, 1988). This trend resonates with the recent interest in linguistic imperialism. Given such standpoints, it is often assumed that communities undergoing language shift will normally experience "bilingualism . . . as a stage on the way to monolingualism in a new language" (Romaine, 1995: 40), thus also undergoing the loss of one identity and the imposition of another. In such cases, the old identity appears rooted in the mother tongue, without any meaningful expression of that identity in the language being acquired.

From that point of view, it seems natural to assume that the community would resist language shift. If, for example, the British had followed a policy animated by an ideology of linguistic imperialism, it might follow that not only would English have been resisted, but it might also prove to be the case that the process of its language change would have been stunted (thereby justifying ignoring this side of the question). For instance, in former French colonies to date, there does not appear to be the same level of seeking identity within "indigenized varieties of French," a fact which might be related to the French language policy of encouraging widespread learning of French.

This model has been common within the consideration of the spread of European languages to Africa and Asia in general. One side has received inordinate attention – the context of conquest, or colonialism (cf. Mazrui & Mazrui, 1998). Another, just as crucial, has been largely ignored: that of resistance, or the postcolonial in the colonial.

Because theories of language contact have most often sought to characterize the process of language change via language spread as a series of purely linguistic phenomena, they have lost sight of the larger sociohistorical processes in which language change is firmly rooted. Historians interested in the process of community-formation, on the other hand, have focused on the larger significance. For instance, Gomez (1998: 14) writes of the formation of the African American community,

> Learning the rudiments of a European language was part of the process, but the language was bent and frayed and stretched and refashioned. The tone of the delivery, the lilt of the voice, the cadence of the words, the coordinated body language were employed to communicate the ideas, emotions, and sensibilities of persons of African descent. As such, Africanized English greatly aided collective, inter-ethnic efforts at resistance.[11]

In the chapters devoted to English spread it was shown that the concrete historical conditions of English language spread consisted of the active contestation that formed the context of the British containment policy aimed at limiting the spread of English. For this reason, the acquisition of English became not only a means for individual social advancement but also a means of resistance as well as a unifying force against colonialism. It was used as a means to further the goal of national liberation from colonialism (Mazrui & Mazrui, 1998). To that extent, the macroacquisition of English coincided historically with postcolonial nations in the process of their formation (both during and after colonialism). Therefore, the language change that took place reflected this process of community building (and often nation building), or the creation of community (national) consciousness.

Small portions of the elite might speak (or attempt to speak) British English (especially those in the colonial administration). Such linguistic usage, however, would necessarily become associated with a comprador elite (cf. Adegbija, 1998). To distinguish their national character, the English-speaking elite would have to turn that language into a vehicle for the anticolonial struggle (in multilingual nations at least), as a medium for the expression of the process of nation-formation and national consciousness (shared subjective knowledge).[12] In so doing they would necessarily put particular emphasis on expressing non-British meanings. For language serves not only as a means of communication, but all social purposes, including political. Such distinctive elements (the stabilized changes constituting a new variety) would embody the notion of a "language of liberation"; English had to serve those purposes (Mazrui, 1976, 1998). Elements emphasizing the national character of the language would thereby tend to gain social acceptance. Within this process, as in the sometimes successful struggle of the women's movement to alter language (D. Cameron, 1998), deliberate efforts at language change cannot be ignored. Wole Soyinka (1993) describes this process in the African context,

> Black people twisted the linguistic blade in the hands of the traditional cultural castrator and carved new concepts on the flesh of white supremacy. The customary linguistic usage was rejected outright and a new, raw, urgent and revolutionary syntax was given to this medium which had become the greatest single repository of racist concepts. (p. 88)

Mazrui and Mazrui (1998) refer to this process as the *deracialization* of English, an effort entirely analogous to feminist efforts to purge language of sexism (cf. D. Cameron, 1998). Bamiro (2000: 103) finds that the use of certain "indigenous words foregrounds the politics of race/class and gender" in postcolonial Zimbabwean literature.

The "extra-linguistic factors" – the use of English as a medium of liberation, the context of language policy in which English spread to Asia and Africa – contributed to the stabilization of the new varieties as expressions of new communities in the form of the process of becoming *post*colonial nations.

The Restandardization Toward Black South African English: A Case Study in Macroacquisition

The case of South Africa serves to illustrate the differing results of macroacquisition versus speaker migration in the formation of variety within World English. Scholars of English in South Africa have called attention to one of the most interesting cases of language development – the process of restandardization of standard South African English (StSAE) toward Black South African English (BSAE) (Chick & Wade, 1997; Lanham, 1996). Behind this linguistic process lie "extra-linguistic" factors rooted in the context in which macroacquisition has taken place. StSAE, which has traditionally served as the standard variety in South Africa, both for its 3 million mother-tongue English speakers as well as for its second language speakers (Gough, 1996; Lanham, 1996), was a product of the *speaker migration* of British subjects since Great Britain took control of the formerly Dutch colony in the early nineteenth century.

The large Black (or African-descended) majority, however, together with the overthrow of the system of apartheid (white political, economic and social control) within the last decade have combined to set in motion a process that portends a movement toward a new standard for South African English based on the "New English" BSAE. Lanham (1996: 30–31) writes, "As to the form and meaning of English in future South Africa, there may, in the long run, be profound changes . . . Already there is one report (personal communication) of features of black English appearing in the speech of mother-tongue English-speaking children who are heavily outnumbered in their Model C school. With ideological support for black English, there can be no doubt that it will be maintained and cultivated." Chick and Wade (1997: 279) also call attention to this same linguistic process at work, noting its basis within the "growing demographic strength and status" of BSAE and its existence as a target language for the nation's Black majority that "can simultaneously signal social identity and prestige." Lanham (1996: 27) reports that whereas in previous decades black South African parents wanted their children "to learn and use" Standard British English, "In the 1990s . . . the volte-face in attitudes is patently clear. Black English is the established symbol of identity, solidarity and the aspirations of black South Africans."

Such a restandardization could not be taking place were it not for the existence of an institutionalized version of BSAE. Its development exhibits the classic features of Type A macroacquisition: a second language acquired by a speech community that does not share a first language through the medium of education. As described by Gough (1996: 54), "The acquisitional context and domains of English for typical black learners reveal broad similarities to those described for new Englishes elsewhere." In particular, acquisition has taken place in educational settings that commence with the mother tongue before introducing English, and in which students "have little exposure to mother-tongue speakers of English, or varieties of English other than black English" (p. 54). From the standpoint of function, Gough writes that English, although not the exclusive one, represents the most important *"lingua franca* amongst blacks from different language backgrounds" (p. 54). With respect to its domains of use, Gough notes that the "use of English amongst blacks is typically restricted to formal communicative situations (such as political meetings)," while "the vernacular or vernacular mixed with English is generally used in everyday encounters" (p. 54). Thus, English is "only part of the total linguistic repertoire of black South Africans (and even here variably so) as it is in other multilingual states in which new Englishes have emerged" (p. 55). Finally, he reports, English remains very much entrenched as a second language for Black South Africans, of whom fewer than 0.25% speak English as a first language (p. 53).

Through a closer examination of the process of macroacquisition in South Africa, it is possible to discern close links between the political process of the Black liberation movement (or antiapartheid movement) and the establishment of BSAE and its characteristic forms. Since the stabilization of the language variety created via macroacquisition requires its institutionalization or standardization across domains of use, formal as well as informal, an examination of written sources provides a window into the degree of institutionalization that may have taken place in a particular epoch. In the effort to establish the connection between epochs in political developments (Black liberation movement) and language change, documents from the history of the former have been examined for evidence of language change from StSAE.

Such an examination of the historical record fails to reveal significant variation from the standard within written documents from the start of an English-language opposition movement by Black South Africans at the end of the nineteenth century through the first half of the twentieth century. A number of related developments in the 1950s combined to first introduce elements of an emergent Black South African English into the language of the liberation struggle. Two of those factors were internal to that movement: (1) the rise of the Youth League under Nelson Mandela's leadership, with its more sharply-defined African nationalism and its militant approach to the liberation struggle; and (2) the consequent turn to mass action as a political tactic, resulting in the launch of the "Defiance Campaign" in 1952, which was aimed at civil disobedience in the face of the draconian pass laws (Fredrickson, 1995; Karis & Carter, 1973; Lodge, 1983; Magubane, 1990).

These elements combined with increasingly larger numbers of Black South Africans learning English. Lanham (1996) notes that English usage among Black South Africans had entered a period of steady increase, so that by 1960 approximately one third "claimed some competence in English."[13] Concomitant with this development came a dawning awareness of "African English" – "particularly in educational circles" – "as having a uniform core of norms" (p. 25). The result of the coincidence of these demographic and political developments were substantial changes in the language of the liberation movement, the first step toward the institutionalization of the emerging BSAE as a New English variety.

Among the visible changes was the increasing prevalence of code mixing in political discourse in the form of the widespread use of African-language slogans in English texts. For example, in Albert Luthuli's presidential address to the ANC in 1953, he begins with the words: "*Afrika! Afrika! Mayibuye! Inkukuleko Ngesikathi Sethu! Freedom in our Lifetime!*" (Luthuli, 1977: 115).[14] The same tendency is reflected in such instances as the following: *The forces of "Tokoloho ka nako ea rona" are marching on* (*The Africanist*, 1977, p. 498) and *That, Ma-Afrika, is the meaning of our struggle* (*The Africanist*, 1977, p. 500). Not long thereafter, the use of a new slogan, *Amandla Ngawethu*, immediately followed by its English equivalent, "Power to the People," became the most visible slogan of the ANC for the duration of its fight against apartheid (ANC, 1977: 758).[15]

In appraising the significance of the use of this code mixing, it is important to look into its social context. More than simply a matter of "the linguistic principles that underlie the form that code-switched speech takes," the sociolinguistic tradition of exploring code mixing and code switching behavior investigates the relation of "linguistic forms to function in specific social contexts" (Toribio, 1999). In this case, it is useful to apply the insights of Toribio (1999), who notes that "code-switching requires social knowledge that is culturally specific and acquired only through contextualized practice" (cf. Aguirre, 1977; Valdes-

Fallis, 1976, 1981). Thus, the code mixing of the type that came into widespread usage in the South African liberation struggle can yield important insights into the social meanings being conveyed.

Applied to defiance-campaign-era South Africa, such contextually determined code mixing shows three things. First, it demonstrates the increasing prestige of African languages even in a liberation struggle dominated by English serving as a lingua franca, reflecting a more deeply-seated African nationalism at the root of the movement (Karis and Carter, 1977; Lodge, 1983). Second, it expresses the related underlying notion that certain shared aspirations of Black South Africans can best be expressed in African-language words and their associated meanings. It is important to note that in the strictest sense the use of African-language slogans does not constitute code mixing, but rather borrowing, since only a minority of the Black South Africans whom the liberation movement targeted spoke the languages from which the words were taken.

Since the gaining of freedom and political power is tied to a vision of African nationalism, African-language words are held to be appropriate to express those aspirations. There is something of this association as well in the tendency that emerged at the time to spell Africa with a "k" in liberation movement texts, the word "Afrika" being thought to embody a set of shared aspirations of a nationalist movement.[16] Within this process, African concepts expressed in word borrowings were placed front and center within the discourse of the liberation struggle. That is not to say that goals, strategies, and tactics were not discussed in the press and writings of the liberation movement in political terms familiar to Western society.

Rather, that process became tied up in the third element in the significance of language mixing within the liberation movement. It reflects the intention of reaching the majority of Black South Africans that accompanied the changeover to mass-based civil disobedience. Concomitant with the attempt to convey the message of the liberation movement to large segments of the population, the medium of expression that was adopted (evidently because it was thought to be most suited to the purpose) was a different type of English altogether, full of African meanings, African borrowings, and extended meanings. In this sense, it is significant that the first institutionalization of Black South African English within the language use of the liberation struggle accompanied its transformation into a mass movement at the time of the Defiance Campaign.

The same motivation that underlay the use of code switching and borrowing could be found in the substitution of "Sons and Daughters of Afrika" for the English convention of beginning speeches by addressing the audience as "ladies and gentlemen" (cf. Luthuli, 1977: 115) In fact, the term "son of Africa" came into usage as an honorific title, conveying the meaning of roughly "hero of the liberation struggle."

At the same time, there were extended meanings of English words that traced their origins not to African languages but arose from the context of the struggle itself. Such a case of semantic extension is represented by the permutations of the word *defiance* within the umbrella of the Defiance Campaign. So central was the defiance campaign to the creation of mass liberation movement, that the word itself became imbued with new meanings that led to its use in a number of different ways. Its base form, as in the sentences (taken from a Nelson Mandela speech) *Defiance was a step of great political significance* (Mandela, 1977: 107) and *The tide of defiance was bound to subside* (p. 108), connotes "a decisive period of the liberation struggle." This meaning was transferred as well to the verb, *At the end of the year, more than 8,000 people of all races had defied* (p. 106). Here *to defy* not only acquires the meaning of "to take part in the defiance campaign" or "to resist apartheid laws through non-violent civil disobedience," but this acquired meaning also sanctions its conversion from its more usual use as a transitive verb to an intransitive use, a case of meaning conditioning syntactic alteration. Other forms of the word, such as *defiers* (p. 107), were also formed. The extension of the range of meaning and forms of this visible lexical symbol of the liberation struggle signified the degree to which the emerging BSAE was becoming central to the struggle. Some two decades later, English as a political weapon[17] was tangibly demonstrated in the Soweto uprising of 1976, in which the desire of Black students to learn English was at the center of a school boycott movement that sparked a national crisis (Hirson, 1979).

Macroacquisition as an Explanatory Framework for Language Change

As a consideration of English in South Africa suggests, sociohistorical conditions constrain language change as much as language spread. The conception of macroacquisition presented above implies that all second language acquisition by speech communities tends toward language change. Such a conclusion is widely recognized and reflected in the various theories of language change via language contact, including pidginization/creolization. Some scholars, for instance Mufwene (1993a, 1993b), have concluded that these various manifestations of language change have a common explanation and should be brought under a unifying explanatory model.

The model of macroacquisition makes a fundamental paradigm shift in the understanding of language change via SLA processes. It replaces models of individual SLA as the basis of explaining processes of language change with those that have reference to the speech community level. It conceives the tangible link between the linguistic and the extra-linguistic in the form of the sociohistorical development of the speech community.

As such, macroacquisition is a more comprehensive theoretical framework for considering language change than language contact.[18] By focusing on internal linguistic factors, language contact has been unable to explain adequately the changes languages undergo. Theories of language contact by themselves do not contain a conception of language spread, taking the "contact" as a given rather than a crucial topic for investigation. It addresses only one side of the macroacquisition context; by itself it cannot distinguish between the site of macroacquisition in the ESL and EFL contexts. Macroacquisition, in contrast, contains both of these elements and combines an explanation of processes of language spread with language change. It is language contact as a sociohistorically-determined process. It grounds language contact in its sociohistorical context, since bilingual speech communities undertaking SLA sharing or not sharing a first language constitutes a sociohistorical and not a linguistic condition.

In investigating the process of creation of a language variety from the genesis of a speech community, the study of transfer processes can identify only sources of language forms and structures, but by itself does not constitute an explanation of the process of change. Since the new varieties are often spoken by members of linguistically diverse first language backgrounds, the differentiating elements of the language variety must achieve a status within the collective identity, must express social meaning. They are neither mistakes nor merely systematic deviations that can be catalogued. They are the reflections of the social context that has produced them, produced by a social process of second language acquisition. Hence macroacquisition, social SLA, cannot be regarded as merely the sum total of individual SLA processes such as language transfer.

Thus the advantages to the explanatory account offered here is that it links the sociohistorical to the linguistic via the category of the speech community, which language contact does not do. It explains the same phenomenon as language contact but does away with the conceptual dichotomy between the "linguistic" and the "extralinguistic." At the same time, the framework of macroacquisition provides a model that covers cases more diverse than the limited conditions described by pidginization/

creolization and provides at least a means of understanding the degree of language change that stabilizes. It is an explantory model that supports Mufwene's (1993b: 195) contention that "that all new varieties of English are adaptive responses to new ethnographic and other cultural ecologies."

The potential explanatory power of macroacquisition as a theoretical model can be illustrated by a consideration of English varieties in four historical cases of English spread: American English, Irish English, English creoles spoken in the Caribbean and the New English varieties like Nigerian English (see Figure 8.1). Of the four, the one exhibiting the smallest degree of language change from British English, the source language, is American English. The reason behind the similarity is socio-historically conditioned: American English was not originally the product of macroacquisition, but of speaker migration, a process that does not determine language change as such.[19]

The second case, Irish English, was formed by macroacquisition of Type B followed by language shift – the almost complete abandonment of Irish (or Gaelic) (prior to its recent comeback) as the vernacular of the nation (a condition in part determined by the speaker migration of native English speakers that accompanied the process, as described in Chapter 6). This case demonstrates that Type B macroacquisition can lead to the stabiliza-tion of language change where what, drawing on Mufwene (1993b), I will call *vernacularization* – the transformation of the language into the mother tongue of predominantly monolingual speakers – takes place. Mufwene (1993b: 200) bases his conception of creolization without a necessary pidgin stage on "the stabilization and normalization of a new, pidginlike or pidgin-based language concomitantly with its usage as a vernacular. This normally happens soon after the community born out of the contact of people from diverse ethnolinguistic backgrounds starts using the emerging language as a primary means of communication." In extending Mufwene's usage, I am denoting as *vernacularization* any language undergoing macroacquisi-tion that comes into primary usage, as in Ireland. As a second stage of macroacquisition, this process transforms the bilingual community into a primarily monolingual community using what was originally the second language. Vernacularization thus involves language shift with concomi-tant language change – the development of a new variety.

The other two cases, English creoles and "New Englishes," involve macroacquisition of Type A. The essential linguistic condition that sepa-rates them (and is sociohistorically determined, as discussed in Chapter 6) is the presence or absence of vernacularization. In the case of English creoles, vernacularization takes place – as Mufwene (1993b) stresses in constructing his conception of creolization absent pidginization. In the

	American English	Irish English	New Englishes	English Creoles
Type A	+	−	+	+
Type B	−	+	−	−
Mother tongue English Population	Dominant	Small	−	−
Language shift	N/A	+	−	+
Lesser			⇒	Greater

Figure 8.1 Factors influencing language change resulting from macroacquisition of English

case of the "New Englishes" like that spoken in Nigeria, it does not, instead remaining a second language variety. For this reason, while both exhibit considerable language change, it is considerably greater in the case of creoles thereby leading to a distance from the source language.[20]

Figure 8.1 illustrates how sociohistorical conditions distinguish the three cases of English spread via macroacquisition from the first as primarily speaker migration. In the figure, the category of speaker migration versus macroacquisition is denoted by the size (or absence) of a mother tongue English population. The differentiation of types of macroacquisition further serves to distinguish "New Englishes" and creoles from the Irish case. "New Englishes," products of the process of creation of World English, are finally distinguished from English creoles by the absence of vernacularization. These contextual conditions of language spread all impact the degree of language change.[21]

In macroacquisition as developed in this work, agency is not invested only in languages in contact, but in peoples creating languages as the expression of their self-determination and community-formation. In this sense, the anticolonial struggle discussed in Chapters 3, 4 and 5, has formed a crucial context for the creation of new bilingual speech communities in English and so has been central to the change of English as a result of its globalization. That history gave rise to multiple English speech communities without a common mother tongue, and is therefore reflected in the emergence of new varieties of English that have led to the further development of the language itself, the subject of Chapter 9.

Notes

1. Although it does not pertain to the present subject, multicompetence of the bilingual speech community also provides a basis to explain the phenomenon referred to as convergence of languages in contact (see Romaine, 1989).
2. Silva-Corvalan (1998: 226) adds, "This type of borrowing is constrained by the structure of the recipient language, and by general cognitive principles that have been found to operate in the acquisition of natural languages. In addition, the sociolinguistic circumstances of contact need to be taken into account." She goes on to say, "Mine is an argument against the existence of syntactic borrowing and not against syntactic change resulting from lexical borrowing or from the transfer of discourse or pragmatic constraints" (p. 226).
3. Explanations of borrowing do make tacit use of some notion of shared subjective knowledge, since, for instance, the category of "social prestige" of the languages involved is invoked as an explanatory category (Romaine, 1995: 66; Weinreich, 1974). Prestige belongs to the shared subjective knowledge of the community.
4. Bamiro's (2000) study of Zimbabwean English-language writers lends compelling support to this contention. He concludes, "As in other varieties of English around the world, most differences between Zimbabwean English and British English . . . are to be found in the innovations in lexical items and their meanings" (p. 77).
5. Word meaning has been central to the study of historical linguistics, but due to the structural-generative dominance in linguistics, has not been sufficiently recognized in theories of language contact. The historical evolution of word meaning (a central component of language change) has its spatial analogue – cross-cultural variation in meaning. This important part of language change in the creation of new varieties of English is not accorded sufficient theoretical attention.
6. Note that here and in the discussion that follows throughout this chapter this need not, except in the rare case, involve any intentionality on the part of the speakers themselves.
7. I have deliberately employed this construction to highlight how questionable such usage is "felt" to be. Let it be noted as well that the discomfort does not only stem from the prescriptivist taboo on this usage, but the fact that singular *they*, like singular *you*, takes a verb marked as a plural. Take the following sentence: *A person makes use of the prescriptivist tradition when they employ "he" as a sex-indefinite marker.* The same subject referent (*a person* and *they*) takes in one case a singular verb, in the second case a plural.
8. The alternatives – e.g. *he* or *she* – are often perceived as worse, especially in spoken discourse. It is, therefore, quite common to hear an unidentified author, or one whose gender might be in doubt even if "their" name is known, referred to as "they" in spoken discourse. The usage has become so frequent as to have led to not the infrequent use of "they" for such an author whose work is being discussed, despite the clear and unambiguous knowledge of the conversants of the author's gender.
9. To the objection that such "deviant" structures are found in basilects – nonstandard varieties of New Englishes as well as English creoles – it can be argued that they are equally to be found in the speech of mother tongue

American or British speakers of nonstandard dialects. So much is this true that some linguists have claimed nonstandard British English dialects carried by migrants to the New World as the source of African American Vernacular English (Poplack, 2000).

10. Thematization may involve, "the foregrounding or fronting of clause elements such as initial complements ... or adjuncts that would not normally occur in the first position. Given the fact that many African languages are topic-prominent, speakers have a preference for the thematization of complements and adjuncts" (Bamiro, 2000: 113).

11. It should be noted that there are complications involved in the macroacquisition of English by Africans in the New World, including the mother tongue context in which it occurred and the rapid disappearance of bilingualism of the speech community.

12. Bamiro (2000: 98) suggests that such considerations might lie behind choices of lexical items in New English fiction: "Lexical borrowings from the indigenous languages signify culturally bound objects and systems of belief that have no direct translation equivalence in English. They thus set up hermeneutic tension between the post-colonial and pre-colonial representations in the texts. If the texts are post-colonial in the sense that they set up disidentificatory and oppositional dialectics to colonial discourse, these culturally salient words attest to the pre-colonial status of certain ideas and objects in the novels."

13. A significant indicator of increased acquisition of English literacy among Black South Africans is the condition noted by Lanham (1996: 43) that "English ... since the 1950s has been the dominant language of the black press."

14. Henderson (1997: 117) confirms that "the cry of 'Afrika' as a political slogan [was] first recorded in the 1950s."

15. According to *The Dictionary of South African English on Historical Principles*, the first occurrence of this slogan was in 1961 (Henderson, 1997: 113). Henderson notes that the historical approach of the dictionary makes "The link between language development and political and social structures ... immediately obvious" (p. 117).

16. Such a practice might be compared to the political significance attached to alterations of the spelling of the word *woman* within at least certain segments of the women's movement.

17. Henderson (1997: 113) writes that "particularly for the writers of the Freedom Charter, or the children of Soweto in 1976" English was "a language of liberation." He notes that the *Dictionary of South African English on Historical Principles* calls English "the language of liberation and black unity" (p. 113).

18. Romaine (1996: 572) has observed that "Linguists are giving increasing attention to the systematic study of language contact, and some have used the term *contact linguistics* in a wide sense to refer to both the process and outcome of any situation in which languages are in contact. Linguists who study language contact often seek to describe changes at the level of linguistic systems in isolation and abstraction from speakers. Sometimes they tend to treat the outcome of linguistic interaction in static rather than dynamic terms, and lose sight of the fact that the bilingual individual is the ultimate locus of contact."

19. I would tend to agree with Mufwene (1997) that much of the basis for its distinctive features might be sought in language contact phenomena. For, although the variety was planted in North America by English-speaking migrants, the language was subsequently acquired by Africans, Native Americans, Europeans, Asians, and others. The standard variety, however, has remained relatively close to the British, so much so that Quirk (1985: 5) has virtually denied any essential difference between them, commenting that "the differences between American English and British English are smaller than the differences within either." The large role of initially second language speakers in the development of American English is denoted in Figure 8.1 by the use of parentheses around its characterization as a macroacquisition context.

20. The common basis might explain the structural similarities that numerous linguists have noted (Mesthrie *et al.*, 2000; Mufwene, 1997). It could also be argued that with creoles the basilect becomes more entrenched because as a vernacular it is subject to greater variation as a language learned outside educational settings.

21. An additional consideration might be the degree to which macroacquisition of a language is carried out. For instance, pidginization might be explained as partial or interrupted macroacquisition, as a degree of macroacquisition, or a stage on the way to full macroacquisition (creolization). This would then get rid of the problematic assumptions of child language acquisition, the necessity of antecedent pidgins for creoles, and other theoretical assumptions of the conception of pidginization/creolization that have proven difficult to substantiate.

Chapter 9

(The) World (of) English: Englishes in Convergence

A theory of the development of World English must answer an additional question, one that hitherto has perhaps not been posed: Why have not the linguistic processes that created the diversity of "Englishes" – or varieties of English – proceeded to the point that they should become separate languages as in the case of the emergence of the Romance languages out of Latin? Even those scholars who emphasize the importance of the variety found within global English for the most part concur that while they exhibit the characteristics of language varieties, they remain identifiably English (Bokamba, 1992; B. Kachru, 1981). A model of the emergence of World English must account for the underlying unity of the language as much as the linguistic variety. In the context of world language theory, such an explanation becomes possible. The underlying linguistic unity of varieties of World English owes to the process of *world language convergence*.

Constructing the Speech Community of World English

Just as world language divergence finds its basis in the speech community, so too does world language convergence. At the root of the former is the local (or national) speech community undergoing the process of macroacquisition, resulting in the language change that accounts for the variety exhibited within World English. It might not then seem evident how the notion of speech community can at the same time account for the centripetal tendency that maintains the unity of the language.

The basis for this dual role of speech community lies within the nature of speech community affiliation. Recent scholarship has identified the existence of speech communities on multiples levels. Thus, as Saville-Troike (1996: 357) writes:

Individuals may belong to several speech communities (which may be discrete or overlapping), just as they may participate in a variety of social settings. Which one or ones individuals orient themselves to at any given moment – which set of social and communicative rules they use – is part of the strategy of communication. To understand this phenomenon, one must recognize that each member of a community has a repertoire of social identities and that each identity in a given context is associated with a number of appropriate verbal and nonverbal forms of expression.

Although there is often a tendency to equate speech communities with nations, a speech community may or may not be national. At root, it is a community based on the ready communication of shared subjective knowledge. Whether that community has the status of a nation is a sociohistorical question. It may be a national minority, such as African Americans or Latinos in the United States, or it might consist of a transnational community, such as Arabic speakers spread through the many nations of the Middle-East and North Africa.

To be sure, although language and nation have seldom, if ever, coincided (Quirk, 1988), national language has played an important historical role. Its centrality has resulted not from the circumstance that language naturally pertains to the realm of the nation, but as a reflection of the "national consciousness" (shared subjective knowledge) that has developed out of the sociohistorical tendency toward nation-states.[1]

Despite the historical dominance of the nation-state, however, it is far from the only large-scale determinant of community. Some religious communities, such as Islam, Christianity and Buddhism (sometimes sharing a language), span much of the globe. Ethnic communities (such as Chinese, Arabic or French) also transcend national boundaries, often sharing a language. Nor is the nation-state the only macrohistorical political determinant in the modern world. Rather, the world itself has increasingly emerged as a cohesive economic and political unit, reflected both in the more frequent usage of "international community" and in the subfield of academic studies known as world systems analysis (Frank and Gills, 1993).

In the same way that a form of "national consciousness" – or what has been described in Chapter 7 as *shared subjective knowledge* – took root in the development of the nation-state, so has global shared subjective knowledge been forming on the basis of the historically new world econocultural system (discussed in Chapter 6). What used to be viewed as intercultural contact and communication (e.g. Smith, 1976, 1987) has now assumed the form of a composite, a "culture" of its own. This shared subjective knowledge of what is often called the "international community" includes political and organizational expressions, such as the United Nations (UN), General Agreement on Tariffs and Trade (GATT), and World Trade Organization (WTO) and non-governmental organizations (NGOs) – for instance, Amnesty International – as well. It has moral and legal components, in the form of human rights (and more recently linguistic human rights) and international law. It includes media outlets targeted to a world audience, such as CNN International and BBC World Service (it is important to note that they have been including speakers of numerous varieties of World English).

The shared subjective knowledge that characterizes this developing world community is not so easy to pin down as that differentiating nations. To be sure, not everyone in the world takes part in it – only some fractional subset (and some may take part only partially or marginally). Still, an identifiable shared subjective knowledge is emerging, buttressed by cosmopolitan, multicultural world urban centers, like Singapore, Hong Kong, London, New York, Toronto, Cape Town, Mexico City, Amsterdam and so forth, which, despite their individual characters, all share readily identifiable characteristics. The shared subjective knowledge of the world community also includes expectations or assumptions of cultural pluralism, understanding, and accommodation to diversity. For example, those who take part in the world community tend to realize that they cannot take culture-bound assumptions onto the world stage, such as ethnic or gender stereotypes from local contexts. Technology also plays an important role, including the booming international communication made possible by the Internet. Finally, the process of knowledge-creation has become international and has increasingly included the development of a set of shared expectations of standards. With each passing year, the contours of the shared subjective knowledge deepen and broaden.

In the same way that the development of the nation is reflected in the evolution of a national speech community (that may coexist with various forms of subnational or supranational forms), the world econocultural system discussed in Chapter 6 finds its analogous expression within a *world speech community*.

This development affects how those persons outside mother tongue English-speaking nations who seek to learn English should be viewed. They may be construed as representing a case of "English consciousness" imposed via linguistic imperialism on non-English speakers. That standpoint, however, overlooks what is perhaps a more essential element, a desire to link to the world at large (even if superficially that appears as the attempt to link to the US or UK). Just as in the economic realm there is a definite pull toward the world market, so culturally is there one toward the world econocultural system. Indeed, human rights – and some of its offshoots, such as language rights – are other manifestations. As the world language, English greatly facilitates these purposes. To interpret this cosmopolitan or global element in such cases as reaching out for English/American or European culture might reveal a Eurocentric outlook that places Europe at the center of the modern world and makes it the reference point around which others position themselves.

The Centripetal Force of World Language Convergence

World language divergence and convergence, therefore, reflect the multiple levels of speaker affiliation with the construct of *speech communities*. There are (at least) two contexts defined by speech communities in World English. One is the local (or national) speech community that plays the essential role in divergence. The second is the international speech community that forms the basis for convergence.

Since every particular language (although not language in general) must be defined as the linguistic expression of its speech community, that of the world speech community of English is *World English*. As illustrated in Figure 9.1, countering the process of world language divergence (represented in the figure by mother tongue, *Type A* and *Type B* macroacquisition Englishes), a centripetal force (represented by the arrows) maintains the "Englishness" of world English varieties.[2] The centralizing tendency in World English represents the world speech community as the unity of English speakers internationally. World English, rather than a variety, constitutes a sort of center of gravity around which the international varieties revolve. Their functional relation in the arena of the world econocultural relations discussed in Chapter 6 (business and trade, popular culture, science and technology) serves to ensure their continuous mutual interaction.[3] Hence, unlike the various Romance languages, which evolved into wholly separate languages in the wake of the death of Latin, the varieties of World English retain their essential linguistic unity.

The process by which English has become a world language has exerted important effects on the language itself. One of the processes within the internationalization of English is what I call *transculturation:* the process by which varieties of World English increasingly become multicultural media within pluralistic cultural communities. This process

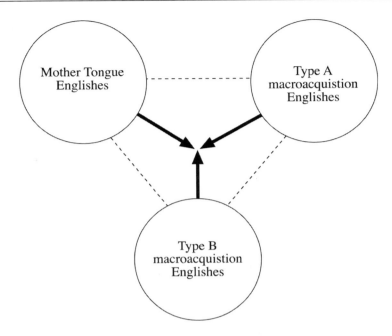

Figure 9.1 Language convergence with World English

contrasts to a degree with national language development, which can be looked at partly as the tendency towards the formation of a *national culture* which encourages homogenization (Chambers, 1995). Transculturation is the process of transcending monoculturalism in language both within the world econocultural system and also within the varieties of World English. There is an interplay of forces in which these varieties influence one another and so each variety becomes itself more and more multicultural.

Examples of such processes include, perhaps, the task of what Mazrui and Mazrui (1998) call the "deracialization of the English language," or "the process by which the language would be tamed and domesticated in the direction of greater compatibility with the dignity and experience of people of African descent" (p. 45) as an aspect of what they call "linguistic counter-penetration"(p. 42). In this sense, the creation of World English involves, in a fundamental sense, the linguistic counter-penetration of the new varieties found in Africa and Asia on mother tongue varieties. Such a project, for Mazrui and Mazrui, constitutes "a first step towards a healthier universalism built on a multicultural heritage"(p. 52).

The Ideological Legacy of Colonialism: Core Languages and Native Speakers

It is not the development of World English as such that represents the legacy of anglophone nation imperial domination, as shown in Chapter 6. It is rather the tendency to view both World English and the new varieties consequent upon its macroacquisition through the lens of the center/periphery dichotomy, which is a political importation into linguistics. Mazrui and Mazrui (1998: 64) criticize the "a historical and artificial contrast that associates European languages with oppression and non-European languages with liberation" which tacitly "accept[s] the racist and undialectical terms of reference imposed by European imperialism itself." Herein, then, lies the main legacy of the inequality of power relations of the colonizing nations and the nations they dominated. Hence, the colonial origins of the macroacquisition varieties are reflected not in the true relations of the languages, but in their perceived relations. As B. Kachru (1997) points out, we must "realize the limitations of . . . colonial constructs . . . in terms of our multilingual and multicultural societies." This discourse of colonialism takes many forms, including the endowing of the speakers of mother tongue Englishes with the status-laden and norm based honorific of native speaker, which in this sense could be taken as a "colonial construct" (cf. Pennycook, 1998). If postcolonial linguistic relations are referenced to the colonial context, new varieties may be denigrated, or their status as varieties of English may be denied altogether (Prator, 1968; Quirk, 1988, 1990).

In the traditional model of English in the international context the "nonnative" user is situated along the interlanguage continuum, with the "native speaker" (a member of the mother tongue speech communities of the dominant English-language nations) as the point of reference. The language of that nonnative user is assessed by this standard, and s/he is considered to be proficient solely with respect to it. There is a unidirectional relationship – authority in English – that inheres in the speech communities thus privileged (whether by age of the variety or power, but always by essentially political criteria). This paradigm is one in which the non-mother tongue user/learner seeks affiliation in the community of native speakers – an affiliation that was either impossible or nearly impossible to attain (Davies, 1991; Medgyes, 1994).

Taking over the conceptual apparatus of linguistic theory based in the individual, that paradigm yields a power relation, which might be represented thus:

Native speaker

↑

nonnative speaker

Disguised as a relationship between individual English speakers, this notion theorizes power relations between different speech communities. The relationship is unidirectional because the "native speaker" community is held to affect the "nonnative" without itself being affected.

The current framework introduces a bidirectional model. It recognizes two essential contexts in which all English users are situated: the local and the international. Each speech community has its own context (local), but also participates in the speech community of the whole, the *world English speech community*. Each affects the other, with the whole representing a space that no one speech community controls. This conception does away with hierarchy among speech communities, so that community relations are better depicted:

Local speech communities ← → world speech community

In this model, the point of reference or grounding of the language (the speech of the local English-using community) is not the mother tongue English communities but the world community. So that the interplay between the speech communities is not direct but mediated by the whole speech community (in the same way that New York and California dialects of American–English affect one another through the medium of American–English).

It is in this interplay of local speech communities in interaction that World English gains its determination, just as do national varieties (American, British). The frame of reference for World English is neither the native English speaker nor solely each individual local speech community. Instead, every speaker has a dual speech community membership or affiliation: the local English speech community and the world English speech community. Of course, the local itself has further divisions within the national, but the essential division remains the local versus world communities.

An important implication follows from this standpoint. There can be by the nature of the case no hierarchy among speech communities on linguistic grounds. Such a construction of language hierarchies belongs to the political realm. That also does away with the notion of standard, for what does standard really have to do with speech communities? It is supposed to inhere in the languages they speak, but that is merely the reflection of the prestige of the speech community itself. So, for instance, educated people are held to be better than uneducated, and this social value is transferred to the language they speak.

English as a national language is only the source of world language, not the world language itself. And it must more and more be reduced to merely one variety of World English among many. World language is the domain in which national distinctions dissolve. There follow from this circumstance important pedagogical implications, with which the volume will conclude.

Notes

1. This account takes communities, including nations, not as imagined communities (Anderson, 1991), but as sociohistorical ones, set apart by shared subjective knowledge.
2. The graphic representation of world language convergence given in the figure bears a resemblance to other such graphic depictions of English that have been put forward, and specifically to that of McArthur's (1998: 95–6) "Circle of World English." The conception represented here differs in that (1) it does not conceive, as McArthur does, a "World Standard English" lying at the center, but rather a centripetal unifying force in English internationally. Second, the model is constructed not on geopolitical lines but on a more specifically linguistic basis, based on the linguistic process that led to the creation of the different varieties.
3. It is not my intention to represent the influence of each variety as necessarily being equal only to say that they all exert, or have the potential to exert, an impact at some level. That is certainly a limitation of the graphic representation I have given to the process of world language convergence, and it should not be interpreted too literally – only as broadly indicative of the process.

Chapter 10

Decentering English Applied Linguistics

The present chapter concludes the book with a discussion of World English with a look toward the future. A comprehensive treatment of World English is not complete without a discussion of English language teaching (ELT) and applied linguistics. The development of English into a world language over the past two centuries stands in an interesting relation to the field of ELT: World English is at one and the same time the *result* of ELT and yet also its *context*. The former stems from the fact that English would not be a world language without the field of ELT. The latter is true because ELT now takes place on an ever-expanding international scale (cf. Graddol, 2001).

As previous chapters demonstrate, ELT has been an active participant in language spread and change. Given that the historical spread of English has taken place overwhelmingly in educational contexts (cf. Platt *et al.,* 1984), important implications follow from this. As Ricento and Hornberger (1996) have pointed out, teachers lie at the center of language policy, and by extension, at the center of language spread, despite the traditional focus on institutional language planning. In addition to the implication that teachers are active shapers of World English, this realization calls attention to the integral connection of pedagogy to the history of the language.

In the conceptual framework developed in this work, World English has been defined as a phase in the history of the English language. This phase has witnessed the transformation of English from the mother tongue of a handful of nations to a language being used by far more speakers in non-mother tongue settings. The changes that have accompanied this spread – the multiplicity of varieties – result not from the faulty and imperfect learning of the non-mother tongue speakers, but from the nature of the process of macroacquisition, language spread and change.

As emphasized in Chapter 9, such an understanding of English language spread and change is far from having gained general acceptance. Even if the mother-tongue context no longer dominates World English use, the period of that dominance is of such recent vintage that it continues to exert a strong ideological force, particularly in influencing notions of how English should be taught and who should do the teaching. Indeed, on the basis of this ideological role of mother tongue English speaking nations, it is possible to arrive at a completely different critical assessment of the ELT profession than the one offered by Phillipson (1992) – who views it as an agent of linguistic imperialism. If the center-driven ELT profession has not *created* English as a world language as an expression of the cultural and linguistic hegemony of "Center" nations, it *has* attempted to dictate the terms on which that world language exists and spreads. Phillipson's impressive evidence relative to post-World War II policy documents – not that the "Center's" policies have played the role of the *cause* of World English – but that mother tongue English speaking nations have attempted to exercise control over the ELT profession. Hence, linguistic and cultural imperialism comes not in the act of teaching English but in the way the language is taught: in the teaching of a *particular* variety, which amounts to the attempt to elevate that variety to the status of an international standard. In failing to distinguish the general structural unity of English internationally and the contingent discourse-pragmatics that differ throughout the English-using world, ELT has sought to associate a particular culture with a multicultural language.

This hegemony is perhaps most evident in the common *perception* that ELT has been (and perhaps *should be*) pursued through relatively monolithic methodology. Holliday (1994: 2), for example, observes that "English language education by its nature extends over a world-wide canvas through an immense variety of social contexts. Largely through aid projects, but also through a variety of other international activity, *a relatively united approach to classroom instruction has been proclaimed across the globe.*" There is much truth in the notion that such a "united approach has been proclaimed," much less in the proposition that the intention has been successful.

The Historical Context of English Language Teaching

ELT methodology is necessarily linked with the international history of English, with the spread of English to British colonies in Africa and Asia beginning in the eighteenth century. ELT, therefore, arose specifically as a product – not simply of English language spread – but of macroacquisition. It does not date from the period of speaker migration to North America and Australia, where an English-speaking population established itself as the majority. Nor was it so much a product of immigration into the UK or the US. As Pennycook (1998: 131) points out, theories and practices were not developed in Britain and "then exported to the Empire but rather . . . the Empire became the central testing site for the development of ELT, from where theories and practices were then imported into Britain." As such, the history of ELT methodology first took shape as formal instruction within a macroacquisition context. Significantly, then, it began its career as an agent of English language change, a role antithetical to upholding the "authenticity" of the language through the native English-speaking teacher from a mother tongue nation.

To be sure, even in the early days there were latent seeds of what was to come. The early English macroacquisition contexts of Asia and Africa had their own particular characteristics, which have been set forth in this study. Driven by the political and economic imperatives of empire, language methodology was subservient to imperial purposes. An important result was that the curriculum tended to be driven by language examinations given by the British government that were used as qualification standards for civil service (and often private) employment. Nor is this practice – so much at odds with the localization of the language – without its legacy in parts of the present world. As an English teacher from West Africa with almost 20 years of experience teaching English there observes:

> [S]ince the colonial times when the inner circle [mother tongue] and the outer circle [second language] schools took the same end-of-year exams (at least in Britain's and France's colonies), the outer circle (former colonies) haven't stopped looking up to the inner circle and emulating their curricula and standards. (quoted in Brutt-Griffler and Samimy, 1999: 424)

Just as important, if not more so, however, were the factors that pointed in the other direction and gave expression to the development of variety in the colonial context. First, the orientation of English education, perhaps surprisingly in light of the later history of ELT, was decidedly not assimilationist. On the contrary, there was great emphasis put on grounding in mother tongue literacy as part of rooting the English student in his/her "environment." English education was also not conducted by immersion, but on the basis of bilingual education. Since, absent the conditions of speaker migration, the British empire had no intention of or capacity for commitment of an extensive native English speaking teaching force, one of the goals was training local English teachers. Indeed, much of the process of language spread was to become dependent on these "nonnative" English-speaking teachers, which from the standpoint of ELT constitutes a significant legacy of the process of creation of World English.

This context for the development of ELT methodology contradicts some more recent assertions based on the notions of linguistic imperialism. Holliday's (1994: 3) notion of "the unilateral professionalism which has carried English language education across the world," while finding its ostensible basis in economic – even neocolonial – relations between the "Center" and "Periphery," is nevertheless ahistorical. It neglects the dynamics of the social context to which he pays so much attention (cf. Canagarajah, 1999). In particular, it neglects the contribution and the agency of the nonnative speaking teachers who have been *doing* the teaching of English in those contexts. A number of scholars who ascribe to linguistic imperialism and cultural imperialism do not acknowledge the historical fact that English spread across the globe and is spreading via the work of local teachers. One of the principal goals of this chapter is to *reclaim* the contributions of the "nonnative" teacher of English within the international history of English.

At the same time, given the history of English spread, it is too facile an assumption to claim that these teachers accept the methodology produced in the UK and US. For example, Brutt-Griffler and Samimy (1999) found a critical attitude toward such methodology was easily awakened and often already latent among international students studying ELT methodology in the US. The idea that "nonnative-English-speaking" teachers rely heavily on the dominant mother tongue English nations for methodology seems to arise more out of ideological notions of an "intellectual dependency" patterned on the economic model than on the actuality. Too many factors present in the sociopolitical context of that spread have dictated otherwise. Since the allegedly hegemonic "Western methods" – which Phillipson (1992) dates from the post-World War II period – had not yet come into existence at the time that English began the process of its spread to Africa, Asia, and elsewhere, ELT methodology relied in large part on the creativity and resources of local teachers.

If the attempt to establish a "unilateral professionalism" – or the perception of one – is of relatively recent origin when placed within the historical scale of English spread, where, then, do the "Center"-driven efforts to redirect English methodology come in? They have played a role in the attempt to exert control over the future course of ELT. They are brought to bear in such constructs as "authenticity," "native" and "near native" proficiency, and notions of what constitute proper goals for learners of English as a second language (ESL). They reach their pinnacle, perhaps, in a central "tenet" of ELT, what Phillipson (1992) calls the fallacy that the ideal teacher of the language is a native speaker from a mother tongue English-speaking nation. Such a conception challenges the authority of the non-mother tongue English-speaking teacher, the very foundation on which World English has been built.

Justifying the Dominant World View of ELT

The portentous project of justifying the alleged centrality of the "Center" in the global spread of English rests on a narrow construction of the conditions in which second language acquisition (SLA) takes place. A central assumption of much SLA theory has been that the second language learner learns the target language in a mother tongue environment (Larsen-Freeman and Long, 1991). As S.N. Sridhar (1994: 801) writes,

> The central images in SLA are those of the "transplanted learner," a rather lonely individual. Little reference is made to the learners' speech community. This paradigm . . . leaves out vast millions of L2 users who learn and use second languages in their own countries, from their own (nonnative) teachers, for use primarily with other nonnative speakers, and who may never come across a native speaker face to face.

SLA has rather conceived its subject as an individual learner who confronts the second language in a "naturalistic" setting, that of a larger mother-tongue speaking population. That is a very natural (although not necessarily correct) assumption to make if the theorist positions herself in the Center and assumes that the language learner has been "transplanted" to that context.

The "relatively united approach to classroom instruction [that] has been proclaimed across the globe" (Holliday, 1994: 2) – or the "Center"-dominated conception of ELT – flows directly out of these assumptions. With SLA conceived as, in what is currently the most widely-accepted model, the progression along the interlanguage continuum toward the target proficiency of the mother-tongue English speaker, there follow definite assumptions as to what constitute appropriate target varieties of English, how they should be taught, and who should teach them. The central image is, indeed, one of a second language learner immersed in and eventually assimilated within the mother-tongue English environment – with the learner waging a desperate struggle to learn the language that provides the key to adaptation and life success. Such circumstances connote the learning of the target culture together with the English variety. Finally, and most centrally, it follows that mother tongue speakers are needed to model the language. The whole process is one referenced exclusively to other mother tongue English speakers, as though this were the only possible referent. Once developed, this model of SLA and the ELT methodology that corresponds to it have been exported to the rest of the world – environs where its assumptions would appear to be singularly out of place.

There is actually surprisingly little empirical basis behind any of these propositions. As S.N. Sridhar (1994) points out, the assumed conditions of the English learner are far from the typical condition in which the second language acquisition of English is today carried out. Given current global trends, the typical English learner acquires the language in a "nonnative" setting – the macroacquisition context. The target languages in such cases are often not the dominant mother tongue varieties (American or British) but new varieties of World English – the "New Englishes." The methods best suited to teaching in these environments are not those emphasizing assimilation to the English mother tongue contexts that may remain remote to the learner even as the language is acquired to a high level of proficiency.

At the same time, there is no reason to assume that the teacher best suited to impart knowledge of the target language is the "native speaker." Despite the recent attempts to enact the proposition that native speakers make the best teachers of English, the question of whether native speakers of English are better suited to teach the language than non-native speakers has only recently been investigated at all. The results of these investigations have provided no support to the common view. On the contrary, such scholars as Brutt-Griffler and Samimy (1999), Phillipson (1992, 1999), Seidlhofer (1999) and Widdowson (1994) have questioned what they see as the problematical application of the notion of authority as traditionally defined to buttress a tacit policy of investing the native English speaking teacher and the mother tongue English speaker with authority in the field of ELT. It must be emphasized that there is no data to show that the former are more effective. Indeed, in theoretical discussion of the question, at least as many good reasons have been adduced to suggest the opposite and highlight the advantages of bilingual teachers of English (Seidlhofer, 1999). The myth that native speakers constitute the ideal teachers of English owes its existence, not to sound scholarship, but to the struggle for control over the terms on which English spread will be carried out in the twenty-first century.

Speech Community Bilingualism and ELT

Implicitly, in concerning itself with the "transplanted learner," SLA has tended to focus on cases of individual bilingualism. In contrast, a crucial implication of the framework of macroacquisition is that in conceiving the process of SLA it is useful and necessary to distinguish between the contexts of individual bilingualism (the isolated individual learner approaching the mother tongue of the larger society) and speech community bilingualism (in which whole communities of learners may be acquiring the language). The historical evolution of English into a world language has conditioned the predominant ELT context as increasingly one of speech community bilingualism rather than individual bilingualism.

This distinction between individual and speech community bilingualism supersedes the usual one between the mother tongue, second and foreign language contexts. Those settings represent the outcome of a historical process, but they do so from a standpoint that attaches the importance to geography and to societal language functions rather than to speech communities and to learners and teachers. Because the spread of English is not only an historical but also a linguistic process, the results are expressed not in essentially geopolitical terms but in the form of language users. Yet when we speak of mother tongue, second language, and foreign language contexts, we tend to reference them to particular nations (for example, the US, India or China), rather than to either particular learners or speech communities.

To illustrate this, we can consider ELT in a seemingly homogenous context, that of a mother tongue English nation such as the US. While ELT (or ESL) in the US, at least at the conceptual level, is often thought to address the needs of the second language learner who might be in the process of assimilation to the mainstream culture, an increasingly significant component of English language teaching is comprised of second language learners who do not conform to this model, since their language learning is directed both to the mother tongue and their home contexts. A model of ELT that ignores the home context cannot be held fully to serve their needs.

Take the following separate English-learning settings, all of which are found in ESL programs in the US:

(1) A community-based ESL course located in a small town consisting of adult learners, each of whom speaks a different mother tongue;
(2) International students from diverse L1 backgrounds studying at a university;

(3) Elementary school-aged Latina and Latino students whose home language is Spanish attending school in such places as California, Chicago, Florida, and Texas.

For group (1), in the absence of a large speech community of their mother tongue, the main English speech community to which they might belong is the larger American one. If that were true, their English learning, therefore, might with some justification be geared toward the end of acculturating to that speech environment. The same cannot be said for groups (2) and (3). For many, perhaps most, of the international students of group (2), there are two distinct English-using contexts, the American and the home. Although these students intend to remain in the US for the duration of their higher education, the vast majority of them will return home upon completion of their studies. As such, the home English using context remains fully in the picture throughout their academic career in the US. For group (3), although they constitute a part of the American English speech community, their English cannot simply be assumed to be identical with that of the larger American society. As members of a large bilingual speech community, their English using context differs from that of the larger monolingual population of the US. Even within the mother tongue English context – leaving the international speech community out of the picture for the moment – it is impossible to deny the existence of other English varieties alongside "standard" American.

The current dominant conceptual frameworks in SLA are not adequate to the task of grappling with the complexities attending the acquisition of a world language. Ignoring the diverse experiences of English second language learners, these models place them all into the dichotomized space of *L2 learner/nonnative speaker* as opposed to the *mother tongue/native speaker*. Such an approach loses sight of an enormous range of questions crucial to understanding how SLA takes place.

For example, the traditional model of the "transplanted learner" excludes the multitude of cases (crucial, for example, to the ESL classroom in the US, Canada, and the UK) in which the second language learner first begins studying English in a non-mother tongue English setting and only then comes to where it is spoken as a mother tongue. This condition is particularly important when it is considered that the identity of a non-native speaker does not spring to life automatically with any attempt to learn a second language. It results essentially from the linguistic shock the learner experiences upon entering the mother tongue setting of the target language. SLA needs to study the process of transformation of a *second language learner* into a *"nonnative speaker,"* a non-elective identity that confronts the second language learner, in order to understand the obverse process to which it aspires – the transformation of a less proficient learner into a fully proficient speaker of a second language.

To aid the learner in accomplishing her goal applied linguistics needs to deconstruct received notions of SLA: *target languages* as well as *proficiency* and the identities (native speaker/non-native speaker) it attaches to. I suggest that, in particular, it needs to pay close attention to the sociohistorical circumstances in which SLA takes place. SLA should focus on the historically contextualized learner and teacher.

Applied to the question of the development of World English, this approach yields a crucial starting point to understanding its future course. It highlights the active historical role of non-mother tongue English speakers, both teachers and learners, in the development of World English. The present work suggests that speakers of other languages have both spread and changed English, transforming it into World English.

Appendices

Appendix A Number of "Vernacular Schools" versus "English Schools" in Ceylon, 1889–1927

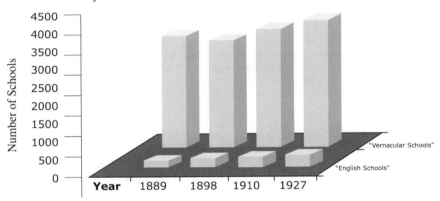

Source: Colonial Office, 1892, 1899; Ormsby-Gore, 1928.

Note: The few dozen or so 'Anglo-Vernacular Schools' or bilingual schools are classed with "English Schools" for years 1889, 1898, 1910 and with "Vernacular Schools" in 1928.

Appendix B Number of government supported "Vernacular Schools" versus government-supported "English Schools" in Ceylon, 1889–1927.

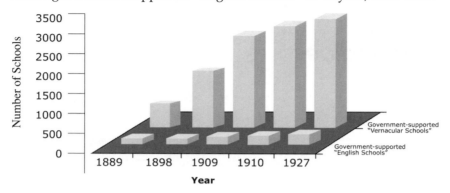

Source: Colonial Office, 1892, 1899, 1910, 1920; Ceylon, Commission on Elementary Education, 1906.

Note: The few dozen or so 'Anglo-Vernacular Schools' or bilingual schools are classed with "English Schools" for years 1889, 1909 and, 1919; for the year 1927 they are classed with "Vernacular Schools." They are not included in the data for 1898.

Appendix C Number of "Vernacular Schools" versus "English Schools" in the Federated Malay States, 1900–1936.

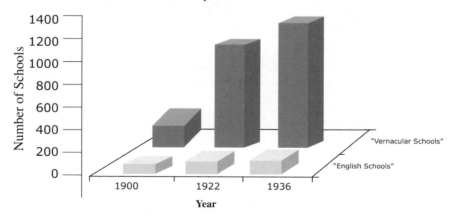

Appendix D Number of "English Schools" versus "Vernacular Schools" in the Unfederated Malay States, 1927–8.

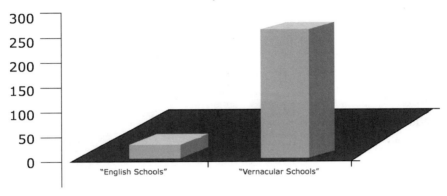

Appendix E Number of students in "Vernacular Schools" versus "English" and "Anglo-Vernacular Schools" as percentage of total number of students in Ceylon, 1889–1939.

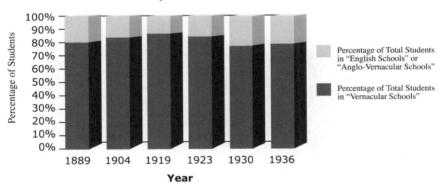

Source: Colonial Office, 1892, 1920, 1925, 1932, 1938; Ceylon, Commission on Elementary Education, 1906.

Appendix F Percentage of total number of students enrolled in "Vernacular Schools" versus "English Schools" in the Federated Malay States, 1900–36.

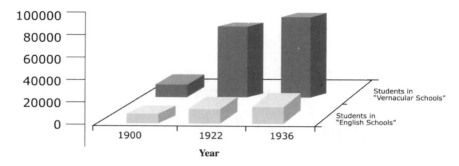

Source: Colonial Office, 1892, 1920, 1925, 1932, 1938; Ceylon, Commission on Elementary Education, 1906.

Appendix G Number of students in "English Schools" versus "Vernacular Schools" in the Federated Malay States, 1900–36.

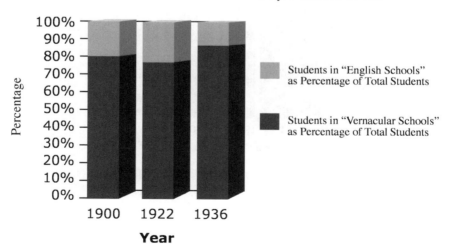

Appendix H Percentage of children of main ethnic groups receiving "Vernacular" or "English" education, in the Federated Malay States, 1928.

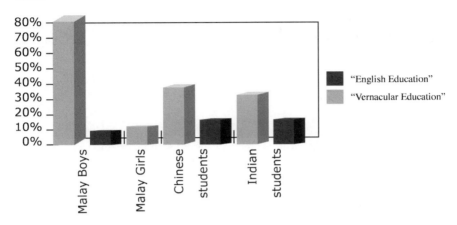

References

Achebe, Ch. (1994) The African writer and the English language. In P. Williams and L. Chrisman (eds) *Colonial Discourse and Post-Colonial Theory: A Reader* (pp. 428–34). New York: Columbia University Press.

Adegbija, E. (1998, November) *Nigerian Englishes: Towards a Standard Variety*. A Keynote Address presented at the 5th Conference of the International Association of World Englishes. University of Illinois at Urbana-Champaign, IL.

Advisory Committee on Native Education in the British Tropical African Dependencies (1925) *Education Policy in British Tropical Africa* (Memorandum submitted to the Secretary of State for the Colonies by the Advisory Committee on Native Education in the British Tropical African Dependencies). London: HMSO.

The Africanist (1977) Forward to 1958! In T. Karis and G. Carter (eds) *From Protest to Challenge: A Documentary History of African Politics in South Africa, 1882–1964. Volume 3, Challenge and Violence, 1953–1964* (pp. 498–500). Stanford, CA: Hoover Institution Press, Stanford University.

Aguirre, A. Jr. (1977) Acceptability judgment of grammatical and ungrammatical forms of intrasential code alternation. Stanford, CA: PhD thesis, Stanford University.

Alatis, J. and Straehle, C.A. (1997) The universe of English: Imperialism, chauvinism, and paranoia. In L.E. Smith and M.L. Forman (eds) *World Englishes 2000* (pp. 1–20). Honolulu: University of Hawaii.

ANC (1977) The ANC spearheads revolution. In T. Karis and G. Carter (eds) *From Protest to Challenge: A Documentary History of African Politics in South Africa, 1882–1964. Volume 3. Challenge and Violence, 1953–1964* (pp. 754–58). Stanford, CA: Hoover Institution Press, Stanford University.

Anderson, B. (1983) *Imagined Communities. Reflections on the Origin and Spread of Nationalism*. London: Verso.

Anderson, R.W. and Shirai, Y. (1996) The primacy of Aspect in first and second language acquisition: The pidgin-creole connection. In W.C. Ritchie and T.K. Bhatia (eds) *Handbook of Second Language Acquisition* (pp. 527–62). San Diego: Academic Press.

Angogo, R. and Hancock, I. (1980) English in Africa: Emerging standards or diverging regionalism? *English World-Wide: A Journal of Varieties of English* 1(1), 67–96.

Annual Report of Governor General of Philippine Islands (1926) Washington: G.P.O.

Asante, M.F. (1993) *The Afrocentric Idea*. Philadelphia: Temple University Press.

Bailey, C.-J.N. (1986) Remarks on standardization, English, and possibilities in developed and developing countries. In G. Nickel and J.C. Stalker (eds) *Problems of Standardization and Linguistic Variation in Present-Day English* (pp. 80–3). Heidelburg: Julius Groos Verlag.

Bailey, R.W. (1991) *Images of English: A Cultural History of the Language*. Ann Arbor: The University of Michigan Press.

Baker, C. (1985) *Aspects of Bilingualism in Wales*. Clevedon: Multilingual Matters.

Baker, C. (1996) *Foundations of Bilingual Education and Bilingualism* (2nd edn). Clevedon: Mulitilingual Matters.

Baker, C. and Prys Jones, S. (1998) *Encyclopedia of Bilingualism and Bilingual Education*. Clevedon: Multilingual Matters.

Bamgbose, A. (1982) Standard Nigerian English: Issues of identification. In B.B. Kachru (ed.) *The Other Tongue* (pp. 99–111). Urbana, IL: University of Illinois Press.

Bamiro, E.O. (2000) *The English Language and the Construction of Cultural and Social Identity in Zimbabwean and Trinbagonian Literatures*. New York: Peter Lang.

Baugh A.C. and Cable, T. (1993) *A History of the English Language* (4th edn). Englewood Cliffs, NJ: Prentice Hall.

Beebe, L. (1980) Sociolinguistic variation and style shifting in second language acquisition. *Language Learning* 30, 433–48.

Berman, E.H. (1982) Educational colonialism in Africa: The role of American foundations, 1910–1945. In R.F. Arnove (ed.) *Philantropy and Cultural Imperialism: The Foundations at Home and Abroad* (pp. 179–202). Bloomington: Indiana University Press.

Bhatt, R. (1995) Prescriptivism, creativity and world Englishes. *World Englishes* 14(2), 247–59.

Bisong, J. (1995) Language choice and cultural imperialism: A Nigerian perspective. *ELT Journal* 49(2), 122–32.

Blassingame, J. (1979) *The Slave Community: Plantation Life in the Antebellum South*. New York: Oxford.

Bodine, A. (1998) Androcentrism in prescriptive grammar: Singular "They," sex-indefinite "He," and "He or She." In D. Cameron (ed.) *The Feminist Critique of Language: A Reader* (pp. 124–38). New York: Routledge.

Bokamba, E.G. (1992) The Africanization of English. In B.B. Kachru (ed.) *The Other Tongue: English Across Cultures* (2nd edn) (pp. 125–47). Urbana: University of Illinois Press.

Branford, B. (1996) English in South African society: A preliminary overview. In V. De Klerk (ed.) *Focus on South Africa* (pp. 35–51). Philadelphia: John Benjamins.

Bright, W. (1968) Toward a cultural grammar. *Indian Linguistics* 29, 20–9.

Brosnahan, L.F. (1963) *The English Language in the World*. Wellington, N.Z.

Brosnahan, L.F. (1973) Some historical cases of language imposition. In R.W. Bailey and J.L. Robinson (eds) *Varieties of Present-Day English* (pp. 40–55). New York: Macmillan.

Brutt-Griffler, J. (1998) Conceptual questions in English as a world language: Taking up an issue. *World Englishes* 17(3), 381–92.

Brutt-Griffler, J. and Samimy, K.K. (1999) Revisiting the colonial in the Post-colonial: Critical praxis for nonnative English-speaking teachers in a TESOL program. *TESOL Quarterly* 33(3), 413–31.

Brutt-Griffler, J. and Samimy, K.K. (2001) Transcending the nativeness paradigm. *World Englishes* 20(1), 99–106.

Buell, R.L. (1928) *The Native Problem in Africa* (Vol. 1). New York: Macmillan.

Burrows, S.M. (1905) Industrial schools and school gardens in Ceylon. In *Board of Education Special Reports on Educational Subjects*, Vol. 1. London: HMSO.

Calcutta University Commission (1917) *Report.* Calcutta.

Cameron, C.H. (1853) *An Address to Parliament on the Duties of Great Britain to India in Respect of the Education of the Natives and their Official Employment.* London: Longman, Brown, Green and Longmans.

Cameron, D. (1990) Demythologizing sociolinguistics: Why language does not reflect society. In J.E. Joseph and T.J. Taylor (eds) *Ideologies of Language* (pp. 79–93). New York: Routledge.

Cameron, D. (1997) Demythologizing sociolinguistics. In N. Coupland and A. Jaworski (eds) *Sociolinguistics. A Reader* (pp. 55–67). New York: St. Martin's Press.

Cameron, D. (1998) Feminist linguistic theories. In S. Jackson and J. Jones (eds) *Contemporary Feminist Theories* (pp. 147–61). New York: New York University Press.

Canagarajah, A.S. (1999) *Resisting Linguistic Imperialism in English Teaching.* New York: Oxford University Press.

Canagarajah, A.S. (2000) Negotiating ideologies through English: Strategies from the periphery. In T. Ricento (ed.) *Ideology, Politics and Language Policies: Focus on English* (pp. 121–32). Philadelphia: John Benjamins.

Carr, H. (1905) The system of education in Lagos. In *Board of Education Special Reports on Educational Subjects*, Vol. 13, 31–72. London: HMSO.

Casartelli, L.C. (1905) Industrial education in Catholic missions. In *Board of Education Special Reports on Educational Subjects*, Vol. 14. London: HMSO.

Census of the British Empire, 1901 (1906). London: HMSO.

Central Statistics Office (1996) *Irish Language* (Census 91). Dublin: Stationery Office.

Ceylon, Commission on Elementary Education (1906) *Correspondence Relating to Elementary Education in Ceylon.* London: HMSO.

Chambers, J.K. (1995) *Sociolinguistic Theory: Linguistic Variation and its Social Significance.* Oxford: Blackwell.

Chick, J.K. and Wade, R. (1997) Restandardisation in the direction of a new English: Implications for access and equity. *Journal of Multilingual and Multicultural Development* 18(4), 271–84.

Chinebuah, I.K. (1976) Grammatical deviance and first language interferance. *West African Journal of Modern Languages* 1, 67–78.

Chirol, V. (1910) *Indian Unrest.* London: Macmillan.

Chirol, V. (1921) *The Egyptian Problem.* London: Macmillan.

Chisanga, T. and Kamwangamalu, N.M. (1997) Owing the other tongue: The English language in Southern Africa. *Journal of Multilingual and Multicultural Development* 18(2), 89–99.

Chishimba, M. (1981) African varieties of English: Text in context. Urbana-Champaign: PhD thesis, University of Illinois.

Chomsky, N. (1965) *Aspects of the Theory of Syntax.* Cambridge, MA: MIT Press.

Clarke, M.J. (1905) The education of natives in South Africa. In *Board of Education Special Reports on Educational Subjects*, Vol. 13. London: HMSO.

Clatworthy, F.J. (1971) The formulation of British colonial education policy, 1923–48. PhD thesis, University of Michigan, Ann Arbor.

CO, Basutoland (1896) *Annual Report on Basutoland, 1894–1895*. London: HMSO.

CO, Basutoland (1898) *Annual Report on Basutoland, 1896–1897*. London: HMSO.

CO, Basutoland (1899) *Annual Report on Basutoland, 1897–1898*. London: HMSO.

CO, Basutoland (1901) *Annual Report on Basutoland, 1899–1900*. London: HMSO.

CO, Basutoland (1903) *Annual Report on Basutoland, 1902–1903*. London: HMSO.

CO, Basutoland (1905) *Annual Report on Basutoland, 1903–1904*. London: HMSO.

CO, Basutoland (1909) *Annual Report on Basutoland, 1907–1908*. London: HMSO.

CO, Basutoland (1910) *Annual Report on Basutoland, 1908–1909*. London: HMSO.

CO, Basutoland (1928) *Annual Report on Basutoland, 1927*. London: HMSO.

CO, Basutoland (1931) *Annual Report on Basutoland, 1930*. London: HMSO.

CO, Basutoland (1936) *Annual Report on Basutoland, 1935*. London: HMSO.

CO, Brunei (1929) *Annual Report on Brunei, 1929*. London: HMSO.

CO, Brunei (1938) *Annual Report on Brunei, 1938*. London: HMSO.

CO, Ceylon (1892) *Annual Report on Ceylon, 1889*. London: HMSO.

CO, Ceylon (1899) *Annual Report on Ceylon, 1898*. London: HMSO.

CO, Ceylon (1901) *Annual Report on Ceylon, 1900*. London: HMSO.

CO, Ceylon (1904) *Annual Report on Ceylon, 1903*. London: HMSO.

CO, Ceylon (1907) *Annual Report on Ceylon, 1906*. London: HMSO.

CO, Ceylon (1910) *Annual Report on Ceylon, 1909*. London: HMSO.

CO, Ceylon (1912) *Annual Report on Ceylon, 1910–1911*. London: HMSO.

CO, Ceylon (1920) *Annual Report on Ceylon, 1919*. London: HMSO.

CO, Ceylon (1925) *Annual Report on Ceylon, 1923*. London: HMSO.

CO, Ceylon (1929) *Annual Report on Ceylon, 1928*. London: HMSO.

CO, Ceylon (1932) *Annual Report on Ceylon, 1930*. London: HMSO.

CO, Ceylon (1938) *Annual Report on Ceylon, 1936*. London: HMSO.

CO, Federated Malay States (1934) *Annual Report on the Federated Malay States, 1933*. London: HMSO.

CO, Fiji (1923) *Annual Report on Fiji, 1922*. London: HMSO.

CO, Fiji (1926) *Annual Report on Fiji, 1925*. London: HMSO.

CO, Fiji (1933) *Annual Report on Fiji, 1932*. London: HMSO.

CO, Gold Coast (1896) *Annual Report on Gold Coast, 1894*. London: HMSO.

CO, Gold Coast (1897a) *Annual Report on Gold Coast, 1895*. London: HMSO.

CO, Gold Coast (1897b) *Annual Report on Gold Coast, 1896*. London: HMSO.

CO, Gold Coast (1899) *Annual Report on Gold Coast, 1898*. London: HMSO.

CO, Gold Coast (1907) *Annual Report on Gold Coast, 1906*. London: HMSO.

CO, Gold Coast (1921) *Annual Report on Gold Coast, 1919*. London: HMSO.

CO, Gold Coast (1948) *Report of the Commission of Enquiry into Disturbances in the Gold Coast, 1948*. London: HMSO.

CO, Kenya (1912) *Annual Report on Kenya, 1910–1911*. London: HMSO.

CO, Kenya (1913) *Annual Report on Kenya, 1911–1912*. London: HMSO.

CO, Kenya (1925) *Annual Report on Kenya, 1924*. London: HMSO.

CO, Northern Nigeria (1914) *Annual Report on Northern Nigeria, 1912*. London: HMSO.

CO, Nyasaland (1906) *Annual Report on Nyasaland, 1904–1905*. London: HMSO.

CO, Nyasaland (1921) *Annual Report on Nyasaland, 1919–1920*. London: HMSO.

CO, Nyasaland (1928) *Annual Report on Nyasaland, 1927.* London: HMSO.
CO, Nyasaland (1932) *Annual Report on Nyasaland, 1931.* London: HMSO.
CO, Nyasaland (1934) *Annual Report on Nyasaland, 1933.* London: HMSO.
CO, Nyasaland (1937) *Annual Report on Nyasaland, 1936.* London: HMSO.
CO, Papua New Guinea. (1896) *Annual Report on Papua New Guinea, 1895–1896.* London: HMSO.
CO, Sierra Leone (1911) *Annual Report on Sierra Leone, 1910.* London: HMSO.
CO, Sierra Leone (1929) *Annual Report on Sierra Leone, 1928.* London: HMSO.
CO, Solomon Islands (1930) *Annual Report on Solomon Islands, 1929.* London: HMSO.
CO, Solomon Islands (1932) *Annual Report on Solomon Islands, 1931.* London: HMSO.
CO, Southern Nigeria (1909) *Annual Report on Southern Nigeria, 1908.* London: HMSO.
CO, Straits Settlements (1922) *Annual Report on Straits Settlements, 1921.* London: HMSO.
CO, Straits Settlements (1923) *Annual Report on Straits Settlements, 1922.* London: HMSO.
CO, Straits Settlements (1933) *Annual Report on Straits Settlements, 1932.* London: HMSO.
CO, Tongan Islands Protectorate (1916) *Annual Report on the Tongan Islands Protectorate, 1915.* London: HMSO.
CO, Tongan Islands Protectorate (1926) *Annual Report on the Tongan Islands Protectorate, 1925.* London: HMSO.
CO, Uganda (1905) *Annual Report on Uganda, 1904–1905.* London: HMSO.
CO, Uganda (1909) *Annual Report on Uganda, 1907–1908.* London: HMSO.
CO, Uganda (1910) *Annual Report on Uganda, 1908–1909.* London: HMSO.
CO, Uganda (1930) *Annual Report on Uganda, 1929.* London: HMSO.
CO, Uganda (1932) *Annual Report on Uganda, 1931.* London: HMSO.
CO, Unfederated Malay States, Kedah (1937) *Annual Report on the Unfederated Malay States, Kedah, 1929.* London: HMSO.
CO, Unfederated Malay States, Kelantan (1929) *Annual Report on the Unfederated Malay States, Kelantan, 1928.* London: HMSO.
CO, Unfederated Malay States, Johore (1928) *Annual Report on the Unfederated Malay States, Johore, 1927.* London: HMSO.
CO, Unfederated Malay States, Johore (1930) *Annual Report on the Unfederated Malay States, Johore, 1929.* London: HMSO.
CO, Unfederated Malay States, Kedah (1929) *Annual Report on the Unfederated Malay States, Kedah, 1927–1928.* London: HMSO.
CO, Unfederated Malay States, Johore (1939) *Annual Report on the Unfederated Malay States, Jahore, 1939.* London: HMSO.
CO, Unfederated Malay States, Kelantan (1932) *Annual Report on the Unfederated Malay States, Kelantan, 1931.* London: HMSO.
CO, Unfederated Malay States, Kelantan (1929) *Annual Report on the Unfederated Malay States, Kelantan, 1928.* London: HMSO.
CO, Unfederated Malay States, Perlis (1928) *Annual Report on the Unfederated Malay States, Perlis, 1927.* London: HMSO.
CO, Unfederated Malay States, Trengganu (1928) *Annual Report on the Unfederated Malay States, Trengganu, 1927.* London: HMSO.

CO, Unfederated Malay States, Trengganu (1932) *Annual Report on the Unfederated Malay States, Trengganu, 1931.* London: HMSO.

CO, Unfederated Malay States, Kedah (1936) *Annual Report on the Unfederated Malay States, Kedah, 1934–1935.* London: HMSO.

CO, Unfederated Malay States, Kedah (1937) *Annual Report on the Unfederated Malay States, Kedah, 1935–1936.* London: HMSO.

CO, Zanzibar (1914) *Annual Report on Zanzibar, 1913.* London: HMSO.

CO, Zanzibar (1927) *Annual Report on Zanzibar, 1926.* London: HMSO.

CO, Zanzibar (1932) *Annual Report on Zanzibar, 1931.* London: HMSO.

CO, Zanzibar (1937) *Annual Report on Zanzibar, 1936.* London: HMSO.

Cook, V. (1993) *Linguistics and Second Language Acquisition.* London: Macmillan.

Cook, V. (1999) Going beyond the native speaker in language teaching. *TESOL Quarterly* 33(2), 185–209.

Cooper, R.L. (1982) *Language Spread. Studies in Diffusion and Social Change.* Bloomington: Indiana University Press.

Cooper, R.L. (1989) *Language Planning and Social Change.* Cambridge: Cambridge University Press.

Coupland, N. and Jaworski, A. (eds.) (1997) *Sociolinguistics. A Reader.* New York. St. Martin's Press.

Cromer, E. (1909) *Modern Egypt.* New York: Macmillan.

Crush, J., Jeeves, A. and Yudelman, D. (1991) *South Africa's Labor Empire: A History of Black Migrancy to the Gold Mines.* Oxford: Westview Press.

Crystal, D. (1997) *English as a Global Language.* Cambridge: Cambridge University Press.

Cull, J.B. (1901) The system of education in Ceylon. In *Board of Education Special Reports on Educational Subjects,* Vol. 5. London: HMSO.

Das, K. (1997) An introduction. In E. deSouza (ed.) *Nine Indian Women Poets: An Anthology* (p. 10). Delhi: Oxford University Press.

Davies, A. (1989) Is International English an Interlanguage? *TESOL Quarterly* 23(3), 447–67.

Davies, A. (1991) *The Native Speaker in Applied Linguistics.* Edinburgh: Edinburgh University Press.

Davies, A. (1996a) Proficiency or the native speaker: What are we trying to achieve in ELT? In G. Cook and B. Seidlhofer (eds) *Principle & Practice in Applied Linguistics: Studies in Honour of H.G. Widdowson* (2nd edn) (pp. 145–57). New York: Oxford University Press.

Davies, A. (1996b) Review article: Ironising the myth of linguicism. *Journal of Multilingual and Multicultural Development* 17(6), 485–96.

DeGraff, M. (ed.) (1999) *Language Creation and Language Change: Creolization, Diachrony, and Development.* Cambridge, MA: MIT Press.

De Klerk, V. (ed.) (1996) *Focus on South Africa.* Philadelphia: John Benjamins Publishing Company.

De Silva, C.R. (1987) *Sri Lanka: A History.* New Delhi: Vikas Publishing House.

De Silva, K.M. (1981) *A History of Sri Lanka.* London: C. Hurst & Co.

Diller, K. (1998, April) *Rethinking Generativity and Chomsky's Position that Language is an Individual Phenomenon: Language as Artificial Life.* The University of New Hampshire Linguistics Colloquium Series. Durham, USA. http://www.unh.edu/linguistics/events/diller.html.

D'souza, J. (1988) Interactional strategies in South Asian languages: Their implications for teaching English internationally. *World Englishes* 7(2), 159–71.

Eleum, J.B. (1905) The system of education in the Straits Settlements. In *Board of Education Special Reports on Educational Subjects*, Vol. 13, 133–70. London: HMSO.

Ellis, R. (1994) *Second Language Acquisition*. Oxford: Oxford University Press.

Fairclough, N. (1989) *Language and Power*. London: Longman.

Fanon, F. (1967) *Toward African Revolution*. New York: Grove Press.

Federal Education Office, Federated Malay States (1905) The system of education in the Federated Malay States. In *Board of Education Special Reports on Educational Subjects*, Vol. 13, 1–60. London: HMSO.

Ferguson, C.A. (1981) Foreword to the First Edition. In B.B. Kachru (ed.) *The Other Tongue: English Across Cultures* (2nd edn, pp. xii–xvii). Urbana: University of Illinois Press.

Ferguson, C.A. (1991) Currents between second language acquisition and linguistic theory. In T. Huebner and C. A. Ferguson (eds) (1991) *Crosscurrents in Second Language Acquisition and Linguistic Theories* (pp. 425–35). Philadelphia: John Benjamins.

Fishman, J.A. (1972) *Language and Nationalism: Two Integrative Essays*. Rowley, Mass.: Newbury House Publishers.

Fishman, J.A. (1977) *The Spread of English: The Sociology of English as an Additional Language*. Rowley, MA: Newbury House Publishers.

Fishman, J.A. (1993) Review of *Linguistic Imperialism*. *Modern Language Journal* 77, 399–400.

Fishman, J.A., Conrad, A. and Rubal-Lopez, A. (eds) (1996) *Post-Imperial English: Status Change in Former British and American Colonies, 1940–1990*. Berlin: Mouton de Gruyter.

Frank, A.G. and Gills, B. (1993) *The World System: Five Hundred Years or Five Thousand?* London: Routledge.

Fredrickson, G.M. (1995) *Black Liberation: A Comparative History of Black Ideologies in the United States and South Africa*. New York: Oxford University Press.

Gee, J.P. (1996) *Social Linguistics and Literacies: Ideologies in Discourses* (2nd edn). London: Taylor & Francis.

Gee, J.P. (1999) *An Introduction to Discourse Analysis: Theory and Method*. New York: Routledge.

Gill, S.J. (1993) *A Short History of Lesotho*. Morija, Lesootho: Morija Museum and Archives.

Gomez, M.A. (1998) *Exchanging our Country Marks: The Transformation of African Identities in the Colonial and Antebellum South*. Chapel Hill, NC: The University of North Carolina Press.

Gonzalez, A. (1987) Poetic imperialism or indigenous creativity?: Philippine literature in English. In L.E. Smith (ed.) *Discourse Across Cultures: Strategies in World Englishes* (pp. 141–56). New York: Prentice Hall.

Gordon, C.J.M. (1905) The system of education in Southern Nigeria. In *Board of Education Special Reports on Educational Subjects*, Vol. 13, 113–22. London: HMSO.

Görlach, M. (1991) *Englishes: Studies in Varieties of English, 1984–1988*. Philadelphia: John Benjamins.

Gough, D. (1996) Black English in South Africa. In V. De Klerk (ed.) *Focus on South Africa* (pp. 53–77). Philadelphia: John Benjamins.

Graddol, D. (1997) *The Future of English?* London: The British Council.

Graddol, D. (2001) English in the future. In A. Burns and C. Coffin (eds) *Analysing English in a Global Context: A Reader* (pp. 26–37). New York: Routledge.

Graddol, D., Leith, D. and Swann, J. (1996) *English: History, Diversity and Change.* London: Routledge.

Greenbaum, S. (1986) English language studies and ESL teaching. In G. Nickel, J.C. and Stalker (eds) *Problems of Standardization and Linguistic Variation in Present-Day English* (pp. 25–35). Heidelberg: Julius Groos Verlag.

Gumperz, J.J. (1971) *Language in Social Groups.* Stanford: Stanford University Press.

Halliday, M. (1970) Language structure and language function. In J. Lyons (ed.) *New Horizons in Linguistics.* Harmondsworth: Penguin.

Halliday, M. (1997) Language in a social perspective. In N. Coupland and A. Jaworski (eds) *Sociolinguistics. A Reader* (pp. 31–8). New York: St. Martin's Press.

Hammond, H.E.D. (1905) The system of education in Southern Rhodesia (1890–1901): Its origin and development. In *Board of Education Special Reports on Educational Subjects*, Vol. 13, 145–80. London: HMSO.

Hardin, G.G. (1979) English as a language of international communication: A few implications from a national point of view. *ELT* 34(1), 1–4.

Harries, P. (1994) *Work, Culture, and Identity: Migrant Laborers in Mozambique and South Africa, c.1860–1910.* London: James Currey.

Henderson, W. (1997) Language and society: Reflections on South African English. *African Affairs*, 113–20.

Hilferding, R. (1981) *Finance Capital: A Study of the Latest Phase of Capitalist Development.* Edited with an introduction by Tom Bottomore; from translations by Morris Watnick and Sam Gordon. Boston: Routledge & Kegan Paul.

Hindley, R. (1990) *The Death of the Irish Language: A Qualified Obituary.* New York: Routledge.

Hirson, B. (1979) *Year of Fire, Year of Ash. The Soweto Revolt: Roots of a Revolution?* London: Zed Press.

Hobson, J.A. (1902) *Imperialism: A Study.* New York: J. Pott & Company.

Holliday, A. (1994) *Appropriate Methodology and Social Context.* New York: Cambridge University Press.

Honey, J. (1997) *Language is Power: The Story of Standard English and its Enemies.* London: Faber.

Hornberger, N.H. (1994) Literacy and language planning. *Language and Education* 8(1,2), 75–86.

Hornberger, N.H. (ed.) (1997) *Indigenous Literacies in the Americas: Language Planning from the Bottom Up.* New York: Mouton de Gruyter.

Huebner, T. and Ferguson, C.A. (eds) (1991) *Crosscurrents in Second Language Acquisition and Linguistic Theories.* Philadelphia: John Benjamins.

Hymes, D.H. (1962) The ethnography of speaking. In T. Gladwin and W.C. Sturtevant (eds) *Anthropology and Human Behaviour.* Washington, DC: Anthropological Society of Washington.

Hymes, D.H. (1964) *Language in Culture and Society: A Reader in Linguistics and Anthropology.* New York: Harper & Row.

Hymes, D.H. (1974) *Foundations in Sociolinguistics: An Ethnographic Approach.* Philadelphia: University of Pennsylvania Press.

Hymes, D.H. (1996) *Ethnography, Linguistics, Narrative Inequality: Toward an Understanding of Voice*. Bristol, PA: Taylor & Francis.

Indian Statutory Commission (Vols 1–17) (1930). London: HMSO.

International Labour Office (1936) *Annual Review, 1935–36*. Geneva: ILO.

Irving, E. (1905) The system of education in Hong Kong. In *Board of Education Special Reports on Educational Subjects*, Vol. 14. London: HMSO.

Johnston, H.H. (1904) Negro labour in the South African Mines. *Journal of the Royal African Society* 3, 228–38.

Jones, T.J. (1921) *Education in Africa: A Study of West, South, and Equatorial Africa by the African Education Commission, under the Auspices of the Phelps-Stokes Fund and Foreign Mission Societies of North America and Europe*. New York: Phelps-Stokes Fund.

Junod, H.A. (1905) The native language and native education. *Journal of the African Society* 17, 1–14.

Kabaka (of Buganda) (1929) Memorandum on the use of the Kiswahili language as the official native language in Buganda. In *Colonial Office Pamphlets about Africa*, microfilm collection, Reel 2. London: The Colonial Office.

Kachru, B.B. (1965) The *Indianness* in Indian English. *Word* 21, 391–410.

Kachru, B.B. (1981) The pragmatics of non-native varieties of English. In L.E. Smith (ed.) *English for Cross-Cultural Communication* (pp. 15–39). New York: St. Martin's Press.

Kachru, B.B. (1983) *The Indianization of English: The English Language in India*. Oxford: Oxford University Press.

Kachru, B.B. (1985) Standards, codifications, and sociolinguistic realism: The English language in the outer circle. In R. Quirk and H.G. Widdowson (eds) *English in the World: Teaching and Learning the Language and Literatures* (pp. 11–30). Cambridge: Cambridge University Press.

Kachru, B.B. (1986) ESP and non-native varieties of English: Toward a shift in paradigm. *Studies in the Linguistic Sciences* 16 (1), 13–34.

Kachru, B.B. (1990) *The Alchemy of English: The Spread, Functions, and Models of Non-Native Englishes*. Urbana: University of Illinois Press.

Kachru, B.B. (ed.) (1992) *The Other Tongue: English Across Cultures* (2nd edn.). Urbana: University of Illinois Press.

Kachru, B.B. (1996) The paradigms of marginality. *World Englishes* 15(3), 241–55.

Kachru, B.B. (1997) English as an Asian language. In M.L.S. Bautista (ed.) *English is an Asian Language: The Philippine Context*. Manila: Macquerie Library Pty Ltd.

Kachru, B.B. and Nelson, C. L. (1996) World Englishes. In S.L. McKay and N.H. Hornberger (eds) *Sociolinguistics and Language Teaching* (pp. 71–102). Cambridge: Cambridge University Press.

Kachru, Y. (1987) Cross-cultural texts, discourse strategies, and discourse interpretation. In L.E. Smith (ed.) *Discourse Across Cultures: Strategies in World Englishes* (pp. 87–100). New York: Prentice Hall.

Kachru, Y. (1993) Interlanguage and language acquisition research. [Review of the book *Rediscovering Interlanguage*]. *World Englishes* 12(2), 265–68.

Kachru, Y. (1999) Culture, context, and writing. In E. Hinkel (ed.) *Culture in Second Language Teaching and Learning* (pp. 75–89). New York: Cambridge University Press.

Karis, T. and Carter, G.M. (eds) (1973) *From Protest to Challenge: A Documentary History of African Politics in South Africa, 1882–1964. Vol. 2: Hope and Challenge, 1935–1952.* Stanford, CA: Hoover Institution Press, Stanford University.

Karis, T. and Carter, G.M. (eds) (1977) *From Protest to Challenge: A Documentary History of African Politics in South Africa, 1882–1964. Vol. 3: Challenge and Violence, 1953–1964.* Stanford, CA: Hoover Institution Press, Stanford University.

Khubchandani, L.M. (1983) *Plural Languages, Plural Cultures: Communication, Identity, and Sociopolitical Change in Contemporary India.* Honolulu: University of Hawaii, for East–West Center.

Kibbee, D.A. (1993) Symposium on *Linguistic Imperialism.* Perspective 2. *World Englishes* 12 (3), 342–47.

Kieswetter, A. (1995) Code-switching amongst African high school pupils. *Occasional Papers in African Linguistics.* Johannesburg: University of the Witwatersrand Press.

King, K.J. (1971) *Pan-Africanism and Education: A Study of Race Philanthropy and Education in the Southern States of America and East Africa.* Oxford: Clarendon.

Kirk-Green, A. (1971) The influence of West African languages on English. In J. Spencer (ed.) *The English Language in West Africa* (pp. 123–44). London: Longman.

Kontra, M., Phillipson, R., Skutnabb-Kangas, T. and Varady, T. (eds) (1999) *Language: A Right and a Resource. Approaching Linguistic Human Rights.* New York: Central European University Press.

Labov, W. (1972) *Sociolinguistic Patterns.* Philadelphia: University of Pennsylvania Press.

Labov, W. (1994) *Principles of Linguistic Change: Internal Factors.* Cambridge, MA: Blackwell.

Labov, W. (1997) Linguistics and sociolinguistics. In N. Coupland and A. Jaworski (eds) *Sociolinguistics. A Reader* (pp. 23–4). New York: St. Martin's Press.

Lambert, W.E. (1974) Culture and language as factors in learning and education. In F.E. Aboud and R.D. Meade (eds) *Cultural Factors in Learning and Education.* Bellingham, Washington: 5th Western Washington Symposium on Learning.

Lanham, L. (1996) A history of English in South Africa. In V. De Klerk (ed.) *Focus on South Africa* (pp. 19–34). Philadelphia: John Benjamins.

Larson-Freeman, D. and Long, M.H. (1991) *An Introduction to Second Language Acquistition Research.* New York: Longman.

Lass, R. (1997) *Historical Linguistics and Language Change.* New York: Cambridge University Press.

League of Nations (1921) *Permanent Mandates Commission, Minutes of the First Session.* Geneva: League of Nations Publications.

League of Nations (1923) *Permanent Mandates Commission, Minutes of the Third Session.* Geneva: League of Nations Publications.

League of Nations (1924a) *Permanent Mandates Commission, Minutes of the Fourth Session.* Geneva: League of Nations Publications.

League of Nations (1924b) *Permanent Mandates Commission, Minutes of the Fifth Session.* Geneva: League of Nations Publications.

League of Nations (1925a) *Permanent Mandates Commission, Minutes of the Sixth Session.* Geneva: League of Nations Publications.

League of Nations (1925b) *Permanent Mandates Commission, Minutes of the Seventh Session.* Geneva: League of Nations Publications.

Lester, R. (1978) *ELT Documents. English as an International Language*. London: British Council.

Lloyd, Lord (1933) *Egypt Since Cromer*, Vol. 1. London: Macmillan Co.

Lodge, T. (1993) *Black Politics in South Africa Since 1945*. New York: Longman.

Lowenberg, P. (1986) Sociolinguistic context and second-language acqusition: Acculturation and creativity in Malaysian English. *World Englishes* 5(1), 71–83.

Lugard, F.D. (1911) Memorandum on "the best methods of training character and inculcating a high moral standard in universities founded primarily for non-Christian races without the compulsory teaching of the Christian religion." In *Report of the Imperial Education Conference, 1911* (pp. 237–43). London: HMSO.

Lugard, F.D. (1923) *The Dual Mandate in British Tropical Africa*. London: Frank Cass.

Lugard, F.D. (1933) Education and race relations. *Journal of the African Society* 32, 1–11.

Luthuli, A.J. (1977) Presidential address by Chief A.J. Lutuli. In T. Karis and G. Carter (eds) *From Protest to Challenge: A Documentary History of African Politics in South Africa, 1882–1964. Volume 3: Challenge and Violence, 1953–1964* (pp. 115–25). Stanford, CA: Hoover Institution Press, Stanford University.

Maconachie, R. (1905) On the education of native races. In *Board of Education Special Reports on Educational Subjects*, Vol. 14. London: HMSO.

Maffi, L. (1999) Linguistic diversity. In D.A. Posey (ed.) *Cultural and Spiritual Values of Biodiversity: United Nations Environment Programme* (pp. 21–45). London: Intermediate Technology Publications.

Magubane, B.M. (1990) *The Political Economy of Race and Class in South Africa*. New York: Monthly Review Press.

Malinowski, B. (1923) The problem of meaning in primitive languages. In Ogden and Richards (eds) (1946) *The Meaning of Meaning* (8th edn) (pp. 296–336). London: Routledge and Kegan Paul.

Mandela, N.R. (1977) "No Easy Walk to Freedom," Presidential address by Nelson R. Mandela. In T. Karis, and G. Carter (eds) *From Protest to Challenge: A Documentary History of African Politics in South Africa, 1882–1964. Volume 3: Challenge and Violence, 1953–1964* (pp. 106–15). Stanford, CA: Hoover Institution Press, Stanford University.

Martinet, A. (1974) Preface. In U. Weinreich (1974) *Languages in Contact* (8th edn) (pp. vii–ix). The Hague: Mouton.

Mason, R.J. (1959) *British Education in Africa*. London: Oxford University Press.

Mayhew, A. (1926) *The Education of India: A Study of British Educational Policy in India, 1835–1920, and of its Bearing on National Life and Problems in India Today*. London: Faber and Gwyer.

Mazrui, A.A. (1973) The English language and the origins of African nationalism. In R.W. Bailey and J. L. Robinson (eds) *Varieties of Present-Day English* (pp. 56–76). New York: Macmillan.

Mazrui, A.A. (1975) *The Political Sociology of the English Language: An African Perspective*. The Hague: Mouton.

Mazrui, A.A. and Mazrui, A.M. (1998) *The Power of Babel: Language & Governance in the African Experience*. Chicago: University of Chicago Press.

McArthur, T. (1998) *The English Languages*. New York: Cambridge University Press.

McKay, S.L. (1996) Literacy and literacies. In S.L. McKay and N.H. Hornberger (eds) *Sociolinguistics and Language Teaching* (pp. 421–46). New York: Cambridge University Press.

McKay, S.L. and Hornberger, N.H. (eds) (1996) *Sociolinguistics and Language Teaching*. New York: Cambridge University Press.

McMahon, A.M.S. (1994) *Understanding Language Change*. New York: Cambridge University Press.

Medgyes, P. (1994) *The Non-Native Teacher*. London: Macmillan.

Mesthrie, R., Swann, J., Deumert, A. and Leap, W.L. (2000) *Introducing Sociolinguisitcs*. Philadelphia: John Benjamins.

Montgomery, W. (1919) Education in parts of the British Empire. In *U.S. Bureau of Education Bulletin*, 49. Washington: GPO.

Mufwene, S.S. (1993a) Introduction. In S.S. Mufwene (ed.) *Africanisms in Afro-American Language Varieties* (pp. 1–31). Athens: The University of Georgia Press.

Mufwene, S.S. (1993b) African substratum: Possibility and evidence. A discussion of Alleyne's and Hancock's papers. In S.S. Mufwene (ed.) *Africanisms in Afro-American Language Varieties* (pp. 192–208). Athens: The University of Georgia Press.

Mufwene, S.S. (1994) New Englishes and criteria for naming them. *World Englishes* 13(1), 21–31.

Mufwene, S.S. (1997) The legitimate and illegitimate offspring of English. In L.E. Smith and M.L. Forman (eds) *World Englishes 2000* (pp. 183–203). Honolulu: University of Hawaii and the East–West Center.

Mühlhäusler, P. (1989) *Pidgin and Creole Linguistics*. Oxford: Basil Blackwell.

Mühlhäusler, P. (1996) *Linguistic Ecology: Language Change and Linguistic Imperialism in the Pacific Region*. New York: Routledge.

Muir, G.B. (1901) The history and present state of education in Cape Colony. In *Board of Education Special Reports on Educational Subjects*, 5. London: HMSO.

Nagy, N. (1999) "Do multiple forms mean multiple grammars?" 2nd International Symposium on Bilingualism, Newcastle, UK.

Nemser, W. (1971) Approximative systems of foreign language learners. *International Review of Applied Linguistics* 9, 115–23.

Niedzielski, H.Z. (1992) The Hawaiian model for the revitalization of native minority cultures and languages. In W.F.K. Jaspaert and S. Kroon (eds) *Maintenance and Loss of Minority Languages* (pp. 269–384). Philadelphia: John Benjamins.

Odlin, T. (1989) *Language Transfer: Cross-Linguistic Influence in Language Learning*. Cambridge: Cambridge University Press.

O'Riagain, P. (1997) *Language Policy and Social Reproduction: Ireland, 1893–1993*. New York: Oxford University Press.

Ormsby Gore, W.G.A. (1928) *Report by the Right Honourable W.G.A. Ormsby Gore, M.P. (Parliamentary Under-Secretary of State for the Colonies) on his Visit to Malaya, Ceylon, and Java During the Year 1928*. London: HMSO.

Orr, C. (1905) *The Making of Northern Nigeria*. London: Frank Cass & Co.

Oxford English Dictionary (1989) Oxford: Clarendon Press.

Papers relating to Legislation Affecting Natives in the Transvaal (1902) London: HMSO.

Pattanayak, D.P. (1981) *Multilingualism and Mother Tongue Education*. Delhi: Oxford University Press.

Pennycook, A. (1994) *The Cultural Politics of English as an International Language*. New York: Longman.

Pennycook, A. (1998) *English and the Discourses of Colonialism*. New York: Routledge.

Pennycook, A (2000) English, politics, ideology: From colonial celebration to post-colonial performativity. In T. Ricento (ed.) *Ideology, Politics and Language Policies: Focus on English* (pp. 107–19). Philadelphia: John Benjamins.

Pennycook, A. (2001) Role of Standard English in ESL/EFL classrooms world-wide. *TESOL 2001*. St. Louis: USA.

Phelps-Stokes, A. (1921) Introduction. In T.J. Jones *Education in Africa: A Study of West, South, and Equatorial Africa by the African Education Commission, under the Auspices of the Phelps-Stokes Fund and Foreign Mission Societies of North America and Europe* (pp. xii–xxviii). New York: Phelps-Stokes Fund.

Phillipson, R. (1992) *Linguistic Imperialism*. Oxford: Oxford University Press.

Phillipson, R. (1993) Symposium on *Linguistic Imperialism*: Reply. *World Englishes* 12(3), 365–73.

Phillipson, R. (1999) International languages and international human rights. In M. Kontra, R. Phillipson, T. Skutnabb-Kangas and T. Varady (eds) *Language: A Right and a Resource. Approaching Linguistic Human Rights* (pp. 25–46). New York: Central European University Press.

Phillipson, R. (2000) English in the new world order. In T. Ricento (ed.) *Ideology, Politics and Language Policies: Focus on English* (pp. 87–106). Philadelphia: John Benjamins.

Phillipson, R. and Skutnabb-Kangas, T. (1996) English only worldwide or language ecology? *TESOL Quarterly* 30 (3), 429–52.

Platt, J. and Weber, H. (1980) *English in Singapore and Malaysia – Status: Features: Functions*. Kuala Lumpur: Oxford University Press.

Platt, J., Weber, H. and Ho, L. (1984) *The New Englishes*. Boston: Routledge and Kegal Paul.

Poplack, S. (ed.) (2000) *The English History of African American English*. Malden, MA: Blackwell.

Prator, C. (1968) The British heresy in TESL. In J. A. Fishman, C. A. Ferguson and J. Das Gupta (eds) *Language Problems in Developing Nations* (pp. 459–76). New York: John Wiley.

Pride, J.B. (1982) Communicative needs in the learning and use of English. In J. Anderson (ed.) *Language Form and Linguistic Variation: Papers Dedicated to Angus McIntosh* (pp. 321–77). Amsterdam: John Benjamins.

Pride, J.B. (ed.) (1982) *New Englishes*. Rowley, MA: Newbury House.

Quinn, N. and Holland, D. (1987) Culture and congnition. In D. Holland and N. Quinn (eds) *Cultural Models in Language and Thought* (pp. 3–40). Cambridge: Cambridge University Press.

Quirk, R. (1981) International communication and the concept of nuclear English. In L. Smith (ed.) *English for Cross-Cultural Communication* (pp. 151–65). New York: Macmillan Press.

Quirk, R. (1985) The English language in a global context. In R. Quirk and H. Widdowson (eds) *English in the World: Teaching and Learning the Language and Literatures* (pp. 1–6). Cambridge: Cambridge University Press.

Quirk, R. (1988) The question of standards in the international use of English. In P.H. Lowenberg (ed.) *Language Spread and Language Policy: Issues, Implications and Case Studies* (GURT 1987) (pp. 229–41). Washington, DC: Georgetown University Press.

Quirk, R. (1990) Language varieties and standard language. *English Today* 21, 3–10.

Quirk, R. (1995) *Grammatical and Lexical Variance in English.* London: Longman.

Rampton, M.B.H. (1990) Displacing the "native speaker": Expertise, affiliation, and inheritance. *ELT Journal* 44, 97–101.

Rao, R. (1938) *Kanthapura.* London: Allen and Unwin.

Report of the Deputation sent by the American Board of Commissioners for Foreign Missions to India and Ceylon in 1901 (1905) In *Board of Education Special Reports on Educational Subjects,* Vol. 14, 328–29. London: HMSO.

Report of Governor General of Philippine Islands, 1918 (1919) Washington.

Report of the Governor General of the Phillipine Islands, 1924 (1926) Washington.

Report of the Governor General of the Philippine Islands, 1925 (1927) Washington.

Report of the Imperial Education Conference (1911) London: HMSO.

Report of the Philippine Commission (Vol. 1). (1900) Washington.

Report of the Philippine Commission, 1904 (Part 3). (1905) Washington.

Reports of the Taft Philippine Commission (1901) Washington.

Ricento, T.K. and Hornberger, N.H. (1996) Unpeeling the onion: Language planning and policy and the ELT professional. *TESOL Quarterly,* 30(3), 401–27.

Ritchie, W.C. and Bhatia, T.K. (eds) (1996) *Handbook of Second Language Acquisition.* San Diego: Academic Press.

Romaine, S. (1986) The syntax and semantics of the code-mixed compound verb in Panjabi/English bilingual discourse. In D. Tannen and J.E. Alatis (eds) *Languages and Linguistics: The Interdependence of Theory, Data and Application* (pp. 35–50). Washington, DC: Georgetown University Press.

Romaine, S. (1995) *Bilingualism* (2nd edn). Cambridge, MA: Blackwell.

Romaine, S. (1996) Bilingualism. In W. C. Ritchie and T. K. Bhatia (eds) *Handbook of Second Language Acquisition* (pp. 571–601). San Diego: Academic Press.

Russell, J. (1887) *The Schools of Greater Britain. Sketches of the Educational Systems of the Colonies and India.* London: William Collins and Sons.

Russell, R. (1901) The system of education in Natal. In Board of Education Special Reports on Educational Subjects, Vol. 5. London: HMSO.

Said, E.W. (1993) *Culture and Imperialism.* New York: Alfred A. Knopf.

Sargant, E.B. (1905) Education in South Africa. In *The Empire and the Century: A Series of Essays on Imperial Problems and Possibilities.* London: John Murray.

Sargant, E.B. (1908) *Report on Native Education in South Africa, Part III – Education in the Protectorates.* London: HMSO.

Saussure, F. de. (1922) *Cours de Linguistique Generale* (2nd edn). Paris: Payot.

Saville-Troike, M. (1996) The ethnography of communication. In S.L. McKay and N.H. Hornberger (eds) *Sociolinguistics and Language Teaching* (pp. 351–82). New York: Cambridge University Press.

Schilling, D.G. (1972) British policy for African education in Kenya, 1895–1939. PhD thesis. University of Wisconsin.

Seidlhofer, B. (1999) Double standards: teacher education in the expanding circle. *World Englishes* 18(2), 233–45.

Selinker, L. (1972) Interlanguage. *International Review of Applied Linguistics* 10, 209–31.

Selinker, L. (1992) *Rediscovering Interlanguage.* London: Longman.

Sey, L.A. (1973) *Ghanaian English: An Exploratory Survey.* London: Macmillan.

Shelvankar, K.S. (1940) *The Problem of India*. New York: Penguin Books.

Silva-Corvalan, C. (1998) On borrowing as a mechanism of syntactic change. In A. Schwegler, B. Tranel and M. Uribe-Etxebarria (eds) *Romance Linguistics: Theoretical Perspectives* (pp. 225–46). Philadelphia: John Benjamins Publishing Company.

Singh, R.P. (1979) *Education in an Imperial Colony*. New Delhi: National.

Singh, R. (1996) *Lectures Against Sociolinguistics*. New York: P. Lang.

Skutnabb-Kangas, T. (1981) *Bilingualism or Not: The Education of Minorities*. Clevedon: Multilingual Matters.

Skutnabb-Kangas, T. and Phillipson, R. (1990) *Wanted! Linguistic Rights*. Roskilde: Roskilde Universits-center.

Skutnabb-Kangas, T. and Phillipson, R. (eds) (1994) *Linguistic Human Rights. Overcoming Linguistic Discrimination*. New York: Mouton de Gruyter.

Sloley, H.C. (1905) The system of education in Basutoland. In *Board of Education Special Reports on Educational Subjects*, Vol. 13, 123–44. London: HMSO.

Smith, L. (1976) English as an international auxiliary language. *RELC Journal* 7(2).

Smith, L. (1983a) Preface. In L. Smith (ed.) *Readings in English as an International Language* (pp. v–vi). Oxford: Pergamon Press.

Smith, L. (1983b) English as an international language: No room for linguistic chauvinism. In L. Smith (ed.) *Readings in English as an International Language* (pp. 7–11). Oxford: Pergamon Press.

Smith, L. (1987) *Discourse Across Cultures: Strategies in World Englishes*. New York: Prentice Hall.

Southern Rhodesia (1929) *Report of the Director of Native Development for the Year 1929*. Salisbury, Southern Rhodesia: Government Printing House.

Soyinka, W. (1993) *Language as Boundary. Act, Dialogue and Outrage: Essays on Literature and Culture*. New York: Pantheon Books.

Sridhar, S.N. (1994) A reality check for SLA theories. *TESOL Quarterly* 28(4), 800–5.

Sridhar, K.K. and Sridhar, S.N. (1992) Bridging the paradigm gap: Second-language acquisition theory and indigenized varieties of English. In B.B. Kachru (ed.) *The Other Tongue: English Across Cultures* (2nd edn). Urbana: University of Illinois Press.

Sridhar, S.N. and Sridhar, K.K. (1994) Indigenized Englishes as second languages: Toward a functional theory of second language in multilingual contexts. In R.K. Agnihotri and A.L. Khanna (eds) *Second Language Acquisition: Sociocultural and Linguistic Aspects of English in India* (pp. 41–63). London: Sage Publications.

Stewart, J. (1905) On native education – South Africa. In *Board of Education Special Reports on Educational Subjects*, Vol. 13. London: HMSO.

Strevens, P. (1978) English as an international language. When is a local form of English a suitable target for ELT purposes? *ELT Documents. English as an International Language*. London: British Council.

Third Annual Report of the Philippine Commision (1903). Washington: G.P.O.

Thomason, S.G. (1986) Contact-induced change: possibilities and probabilities. In W. Enninger and T. Stolz (eds) *Akten des 2. Essener Kolloquiums zu Kreolsprachen und Sprachkontakten*. Bochum: Studienverlag Dr N. Brockmeyer.

Thomason, S.G. and Kaufman, T. (1988) *Language Contact, Creolization, and Genetic Linguistics*. Berkeley: University of California Press.

Thorburn, S.S. (1907–08) Education and good citizenship in India. *Royal Colonial Institute* 39, 34–163.

Tollefson, J. (1991) *Planning Language, Planning Inequality: Language Policy in the Community*. London: Longman.

Toribio, J. (1999) Spanglish?! Bite your tongue! Spanish-English code-switching among Latinos. *Reflexiones*, 5–22.

Transvaal (1902) Papers relating to legislation affecting natives in the Transvaal. London: HMSO.

Trudgill, P. and Hannah, J. (1985) *International English: A Guide to Varieties of Standard English* (2nd edn). London: Edward Arnold.

Trudgill, P. and Hannah, J. (1994) *International English. A Guide to the Varieties of Standard English*. London: Edward Arnold.

Tsuda, Y. (1997) Hegemony of English vs ecology of language: Building equality in international communication. In L.E. Smith and M.L. Forman (eds) *World Englishes 2000* (pp. 21–31). Honolulu: University of Hawaii.

Valdes-Fallis, G. (1976) Social interaction and code-switching patterns. In G.D. Keller, R.V. Teschner and S. Viera (eds.) *Bilingualism in the Bicentennial and Beyond* (pp. 52–85). Jamaica, NY: Bilingual Press.

Valdes, G. (1981) Code-switching as a deliberate verbal strategy: A microanalysis of direct and indirect requests among Chicano bilingual speakers. In R. Duran (ed.) *Latino Language and Communicative Behavior* (pp. 95–108). Norwood, NJ: Ablex Press.

Wakelin, M. (1975) *Language and History in Cornwall*. Leicester: Leicester University Press.

Wallerstein, I. (1980) *The Modern World System II: Mercantilism and the Consolidation of the European World-Economy, 1600–1750*. New York: Academic Press.

Wardhaugh, R. (1998) *An Introduction to Sociolinguistics* (3rd edn). Malden, MA: Blackwell.

Weedon, C. (1997) *Feminist Practice and Poststructuralist Theory*. Cambridge, MA: Blackwell Publishers.

Weinreich, U. (1974) *Languages in Contact* (8th edn). The Hague: Mouton.

Welldon, J.E.C. (1895) The imperial aspects of education. *Royal Colonial Institute* 26, 330–44.

Widdowson, H.G. (1994) The ownership of English. *TESOL Quarterly* 28(2), 377–81.

Widdowson, H.G. (1996) Authenticity and autonomy in ELT. *ELT Journal* 50(1), 67–8.

Widdowson, H.G. (1997) EIL, ESL, EFL: Global issues and local interests. *World Englishes* 16 (3), 135–46.

Widdowson, H.G. (1998) EIL: Squaring the circles. A reply. *World Englishes* 17(3), pp. 397–401.

Wiley, T.G. (1996) Language planning and policy. In S.L. McKay and N.H. Hornberger (eds) *Sociolinguistics and Language Teaching* (pp. 103–47). New York: Cambridge University Press.

Wiley, T.G. (2000) Continuity and change in the function of language ideologies in the United States. In T. Ricento (ed.) *Ideology, Politics and Language Policies: Focus on English* (pp. 67–85). Philadelphia: John Benjamins.

Williams, C.H. (1997) "English-Welsh." In H. Goebl, P.H. Nelde and Z.S.W. Wolck (eds) *Contact Linguistics: an International Handbook of Contemporary Research* (Vol. 2). Berlin: Walter de Gruyter.

Willinsky, J. (1998) *Learning to Divide the World: Education at Empire's End*. Minneapolis: University of Minnesota Press.

Wissing, R.J. (1987) Language contact and interference in the acquisition of English proficiency by Bantu-speaking students. Unpublished Masters thesis. University of South Africa.

Wood, P. (1974) *Black Majority: Negroes in Colonial South Carolina from 1670 Through the Stono Rebellion*. New York: Knopf.

World Englishes (1998) Professional notes. *World Englishes* 17(3), 419.

Index